Responses to
101 Questions
on the Dead Sea Scrolls

Joseph A. Fitzmyer, S.J.

PAULIST PRESS
New York/Mahwah
1992

Library of Congress Cataloging-in-Publication Data

Fitzmyer, Joseph A.
    Responses to 101 questions on the Dead Sea scrolls / Joseph A. Fitzmyer.
        p. cm.
    Includes bibliographical references and index.
    ISBN 0-8091-3348-2
    1. Dead Sea scrolls—Introductions.   2. Dead Sea scrolls—Relation to the New Testament.   I. Title.
BM487.F55   1992
296.1'55—dc20   92-21584
                                                                      CIP

Published by Paulist Press
997 Macarthur Boulevard
Mahwah, N.J. 07430

Printed and bound in the United States of America

CONTENTS

iii

PREFACE

Interest has been renewed in the Dead Sea Scrolls after a long interval. When they were first discovered, the Dead Sea Scrolls were headline news. Interest in them continued for about a decade or so; then one heard practically nothing more. Now after almost 45 years since the discovery of the first cave interest has been renewed, because it has been realized that the vast majority of the fragmentary texts from one cave still lie unpublished. Those to whom they were entrusted for publication have not come through, and as a result of recent developments they are being taken away from such persons and entrusted to others who are expected to publish them within the next few years. As a result all sorts of questions about the scrolls are being asked, because the present public is no longer aware of the circumstances of their finding or of the way things developed since their discovery. I was involved in some of the early developments, and people are constantly asking me about the details of this or that event or scroll. Hence my attempt to answer 101 questions about the Dead Sea Scrolls.

I write this book on the basis of much personal knowledge of the DSS. I began my graduate studies (1953–56) at the Johns Hopkins University in Baltimore, MD, under Prof. William F. Albright, who was one of the experts consulted about the authenticity and date of the first scrolls discovered, and at a time when the discovery was just beginning to make an impact. Though the scrolls were first discovered in 1947, it was 1950 before any of the texts were published. Later, I was added to the international team piecing together the fragments from Cave 4. My task was to begin a concordance of nonbiblical texts, on which I worked in the scrollery of the Palestine Archaeological

Museum during the year 1957–58, just before I began to teach New
Testament at Woodstock College in Woodstock, MD. Though I have
been a professor of New Testament studies, my chief interest has
always been in the Semitic background of these Christian writings,
and that has meant the study of the influence of the Aramaic language
and of the impact of the Dead Sea Scrolls on them. I have tried to
keep abreast of all the developments about the scrolls over the years
since and have published a number of books and articles on them.

What has been published of the scrolls has appeared in many
diverse places, and it is not easy to keep track of such publications.
Years ago I began to put together a list of such publications, and that
list has recently been published in its third edition, *The Dead Sea
Scrolls: Major Publications and Tools for Study: Revised Edition* (SBL
Resources for Biblical Study 20; Atlanta, GA: Scholars Press, 1990).
It is already in need of further revision, in light of so many recent
developments. That is a book, however, that is mainly bibliographical,
an aid to students. It does not answer the questions that people ask
about the scrolls today. But it will be of help to those who want to
look up a certain text, learn about its contents, and see what has been
the result of the study of it. In contrast to that book, this book hopes
to answer at least some of the questions that arise about the scrolls
and give some explanation of their discovery, their provenience, their
contents, and of some of the modern developments that have sur-
rounded the publication and study of them.

The 101 questions and answers that form the bulk of this book
fall into four groups: (1) questions about the discovery of the caves
and the content of the scrolls (§ 1–38); (2) questions about the impact
of the scrolls on the study of the OT and ancient Judaism, in particular
the Qumran community (§ 39–67); (3) questions about the impact
of the scrolls on the study of the New Testament and early Christianity (§ 68–84); and (4) questions about recent developments of
headline-news character and charges about suppression of the scrolls
(§ 85–101).

References to other works will be kept at a minimum, but a list
of important books for further reading and study will be supplied
in the Select Bibliography at the end.

Lastly, it is my pleasant duty to thank various persons who have
helped me in the composition and production of this book: Alan C.

Mitchell, S.J., for much good advice and assistance, John Pragasam, S.J., for some scientific assistance, Lawrence E. Boadt, C.S.P., for his helpful cooperation, and the members of the Paulist Press staff for their speedy work on this book.

Joseph A. Fitzmyer, S.J.
Professor Emeritus, Biblical Studies
The Catholic University of America
Resident at the Jesuit Community,
Georgetown University,
Washington, DC 20057

ABBREVIATIONS

1. General

Ant.	Flavius Josephus, *Antiquities*
b.	*Babylonian Talmud,* followed by the name of the tractate
BAGD	W. Bauer, W. F. Arndt, F. W. Gingrich and F. W. Danker, *A Greek-English Lexicon of the New Testament and Other Early Christian Literature* (2d ed.; Chicago/London: University of Chicago, 1979)
BARev	*Biblical Archaeology Review*
BASOR	*Bulletin of the American Schools of Oriental Research*
Bib	*Biblica*
BMAP	E. G. Kraeling, *The Brooklyn Museum Aramaic Papyri: New Documents of the Fifth Century B.C. from the Jewish Colony at Elephantine* (New Haven, CT: Yale University, 1953)
BZ	*Biblische Zeitschrift*
CBQ	*Catholic Biblical Quarterly*
CBQMS	Catholic Biblical Quarterly Monograph Series (Washington, DC: Catholic Biblical Association)
col.	column
DJD	Discoveries in the Judaean Desert (Oxford: Clarendon)
DSS	Dead Sea Scrolls

DSSHU	E. L. Sukenik, *The Dead Sea Scrolls of the Hebrew University* (Jerusalem: Hebrew University and Magnes Press, 1955)
DSSMPTS	J. A. Fitzmyer, *The Dead Sea Scrolls: Major Publications and Tools for Study, Revised Edition* (SBL Resources for Biblical Study 20; Atlanta, GA: Scholars, 1990)
ESBNT	J. A. Fitzmyer, *Essays on the Semitic Background of the New Testament* (London: Chapman, 1971; Missoula, MT: Scholars, 1974)
EstBib	*Estudios Bíblicos*
frg.	fragment
GCS	Griechische christliche Schriftsteller (Leipzig: Hinrichs; Berlin: Akademie)
HSS	Harvard Semitic Studies (Atlanta, GA: Scholars)
IEJ	*Israel Exploration Journal*
J.W.	Flavius Josephus, *Jewish War*
JBL	*Journal of Biblical Literature*
JJS	*Journal of Jewish Studies*
JQR	*Jewish Quarterly Review*
JSOT	JSOT Press (now Academic Press, Sheffield, UK)
JSOTSup	Supplements to the *Journal for the Study of the Old Testament*
Jub.	*Jubilees, The Book of*
KJV	*King James Version* (of the Bible)
LXX	Septuagint (Old Greek translation of the OT)
m.	*Mishnah,* followed by the name of the tractate
ms(s).	manuscript(s)
MT	Masoretic Text (the medieval Hebrew text of the OT)
NAB	*New American Bible*
NIV	*New International Version* (of the Bible)
NRSV	*New Revised Standard Version* (of the Bible)
NT	New Testament
NTTS	New Testament Tools and Studies (Leiden: Brill)
OT	Old Testament
PSBA	*Proceedings of the Society of Biblical Archaeology*

QS	Qumran Scrolls
RB	*Revue Biblique*
RevQ	*Revue de Qumran*
RSV	*Revised Standard Version* (of the Bible)
SBJ	*La Sainte Bible de Jérusalem*
SBT	Studies in Biblical Theology (London: SCM; Naperville, IL: Allenson)
TAG	J. A. Fitzmyer, *To Advance the Gospel: New Testament Studies* (New York: Crossroad, 1981)
( )	parentheses in a translation enclose words added to fill out the meaning in English
[ ]	square brackets denote letters supplied for a lacuna or broken text
‹ ›	angular brackets designate letters or words added by a modern editor
{ }	braces enclose words added to translation to explain preceding word(s)

2. Dead Sea Scrolls

C	Cairo Genizah texts
CD	Cairo (Genizah text of the) Damascus (Document)
D	Damascus Document
gr	Greek text in the DSS
H	*Hôdāyôt,* Thanksgiving Psalms
Ḥev	Naḥal Ḥever texts
M	*Milḥāmāh,* War Scroll
Mas	Masada texts
Mird	Khirbet Mird texts
Mur	Wadi Murabbaʿat texts
p	Pesher (commentary)
paleo	Written in paleo-Hebrew script (like Phoenician script)
pap	papyrus, text written on papyrus, not skin
Q	Qumran

1Q, 2Q, 3Q, etc.	Numbered caves of Qumran, yielding written material, followed by the abbreviation of the biblical or apocryphal book
1QapGen	Genesis Apocryphon of Qumran Cave 1
1QDM	*Dibrê Môšeh,* Words of Moses, from Qumran Cave 1
1QIsa[a,b]	Copy a or b of Isaiah from Cave 1
1QMyst	Mysteries text from Qumran Cave 1
1QpHab	Pesher on Habakkuk from Qumran Cave 1
1QS	*Serek hayyaḥad,* Community Rule (Manual of Discipline) from Qumran Cave 1
1QSa	Appendix A of 1QS (Messianic Rule of the Congregation)
1QSb	Appendix B of 1QS (Collection of Blessings)
3Q15	Copper Plaque from Qumran Cave 3
4QCatena[a]	Copy a of Catena (String) of OT texts from Qumran Cave 4 (4Q177)
4QAgesCreat	Ages of Creation text from Qumran Cave 4 (4Q180)
4QD[a-h]	Copies a to h of the Damascus Document from Qumran Cave 4
4QDibHam[a-c]	Copies a to c of *Dibrê hammĕ'ôrôt,* Words of the Luminaries, from Qumran Cave 4
4QEn[a-g]	Copies a to g of Enoch from Qumran Cave 4
4QEnastr[a-d]	Copies a to d of Astronomical Enoch from Qumran Cave 4
4QEnGiants[a-f]	Copies a to f of Enoch Giants from Qumran Cave 4
4QEzra	Ezra text from Qumran Cave 4
4QFlor	Florilegium (or Eschatological Midrashim) from Qumran Cave 4 (4Q174)
4QLXXLev[b]	Copy b of the Septuagint version of Leviticus from Qumran Cave 4
4QMišm	*Mišmĕrôt hakkôhānîm,* Courses of the Priests, text from Qumran Cave 4
4QMMT	*Miqṣāt ma'ăśê hattôrāh,* Collection of Deeds of the Law from Qumran Cave 4
4QPBless	Patriarchal Blessings from Qumran Cave 4

4QpNah	Pesher on Nahum from Qumran Cave 4
4QPrNab	Prayer of Nabonidus from Qumran Cave 4
4QŠirŠabb	*Šîrôt ('ôlat) haššabbāt,* Songs of the Sabbath Sacrifice, from Qumran Cave 4
4QTanḥ	*Tanḥûmîm,* Consolation, from Qumran Cave 4 (4Q176)
4QTestim	Testimonia-list from Qumran Cave 4 (4Q175)
4QTLevi	Testament of Levi from Qumran Cave 4
4QTQehat	Testament of Qehat from Qumran Cave 4
11QMelch	Melchizedek text from Qumran Cave 11
11QpaleoLev	Leviticus text written in paleo-Hebrew script from Qumran Cave 11
11QPsᵃ	Copy a of Psalms Scroll from Qumran Cave 11
11QTemple	Temple Scroll from Qumran Cave 11
11QtgJob	Targum of Job from Qumran Cave 11
S	*Serek hayyaḥad,* Rule of the Community (Manual of Discipline)
Ṣe	Naḥal Ṣe'elim texts
ŠirŠabb	*Šîrôt ('ôlat) haššabbāt,* Songs of the Sabbath Sacrifice
XII	Twelve Minor Prophets

In the abbreviations used for the DSS sometimes a siglum is used to designate the material on which the text is written (pap = papyrus, cu = copper); if the text is written on skin, nothing is used. Then comes a siglum for the provenience of the text (1Q = Cave 1 of Qumran, Mas = Masada). Then comes the title of the work (Gen = Genesis, pHab = pesher of Habakkuk). Then a superscript letter designates the copy of the text (4QDᵇ = second copy of the Damascus Document from Qumran Cave 4). Finally, the language of the text may be indicated (aram = Aramaic; gr = Greek). Qumran texts that appear in the DJD series also have a boldface number; thus 4QFlor is also 4Q174. Arabic numbers are used for caves, columns, and lines; the latter are usually separated by a colon (European writers often use a period or a comma instead). In fragmentary texts, when there are several fragments and they must be numbered separately within a work, the columns are then designated by lower-case roman numerals. Thus

1Q27 1 ii 25, which means text 27 from Qumran Cave 1, fragment 1, column ii, line 25 (in such cases, colons, periods, and commas are not used). Similarly, 4QpIsa^c 4–7 ii 2–4, which means the third copy (copy c) of the pesher on Isaiah from Qumran Cave 4, joined fragments 4–7, column ii, lines 2–4.

THE 101 QUESTIONS AND RESPONSES

1. What are the Dead Sea Scrolls?

The term "Dead Sea Scrolls" is used today in two senses, one generic and one specific.

In the generic sense, "Dead Sea Scrolls" refers to texts, not retrieved from the Dead Sea, but discovered in caves along the northwest shore of that Sea between the years 1947 and 1956. These "scrolls" are sometimes complete, but the vast majority of them are fragmentary texts or documents of various sorts that date roughly from the end of the third century B.C. to the seventh or eighth century A.D. They are not all related to one another, but have been found in caves or holes in seven different localities on the northwest shore of the Dead Sea. In this generic sense they include even some discovered at the end of the last century in a genizah ("hideaway" used for the deposit of old or worn-out Jewish scrolls and books) of the Synagogue of Ezra in Old Cairo in the last decade of the nineteenth century. The sites along the Dead Sea include Qumran, Masada, Wadi Murabba'at, Naḥal Ḥever, Naḥal Ṣe'elim, Naḥal Mishmar, and Khirbet Mird. Some people at times include in this generic sense even texts found at Wadi ed-Daliyeh, a site in Transjordan to the northeast of the Dead Sea. But it is questionable whether they should be included under the designation "Dead Sea Scrolls" even in the wide sense, because they are totally unrelated and come from a different area and from a much earlier period in history.

In the specific sense, "Dead Sea Scrolls" is used of the scrolls and fragments found in eleven caves in the area of Qumran. DSS is thus used of the Qumran Scrolls because of the great number of the texts

1

from these caves and because of the nature and importance of the documents that have come from them. Though about 273 holes and caves in the cliffs along the northwest shore of the Dead Sea, from Hajar el-'Aṣbaḥ (=Hebrew 'Eben habbohen, or "the stone of Bohan," Josh 15:6) to Ras Feshkha, a stretch of about eight kilometers, were scoured by archaeologists (10–29 March 1952), artifacts showing habitation of the caves were found in only 39 of them; of these, 25 caves had artifacts and pottery similar to that found in Cave 1 and at the community center. But only eleven caves in the vicinity of Qumran yielded written material, and today these are the numbered caves, Cave 1 to Cave 11. From these eleven caves came the DSS, which have been hailed as "the greatest manuscript discovery of modern times" (W. F. Albright).

2. What is Qumran and what relation do the Dead Sea Scrolls have to it?

Qumran is the modern Arabic name used for Khirbet Qumran and the Wadi Qumran. Arabic *khirbeh* means a "stone ruin," and Arabic *wâdī*, a "(dried up) torrent-bed"; the latter is the equivalent of Hebrew *naḥal*. Close by and slightly to the north of the Wadi Qumran and on the top of a marly plateau at the base of cliffs that sit a little more than a kilometer back from the shore of the Dead Sea there is Khirbet Qumran. The plateau is bounded on the south by the wadi, and on the west and north by ravines. Khirbet Qumran was a site known to explorers and regarded since the end of the nineteenth century as the remains of a Roman fort. It had never been excavated.

When Cave 1 was discovered in 1947 in a cleft high up in the cliffs a little over a kilometer to the north of Khirbet Qumran, it was eventually suspected that Khirbet Qumran, which lay to the south, might be related to it. So it was excavated under the direction of Roland de Vaux, O.P., director of the Ecole Biblique et Archéologique Française of Jerusalem, between 1951–56. The excavations of Khirbet Qumran revealed three main things: (a) traces of an aqueduct, which brought water from the Wadi Qumran to the community center; (b) a community center on the western part of the plateau, a complex of a tower and many rooms used for communal purposes and for crafts; and (c) a cemetery, which occupied the eastern half of the plateau and was separated from the community center by a long wall. Related to Khirbet Qumran were the 25 caves, which seem to have been where members of the community lived. Also related to it were two farm areas, one about a kilometer and a quarter south of Khirbet Qumran, near 'Ain Feshkha (a spring of brackish water), and another above the cliffs in the Buqei'a. Of the numbered caves, wherein written material was found, caves 4–10 were situated near or along the south edge of the plateau, whereas caves 1–3 and 11 were more remote, over a kilometer or more to the north of the community center.

A preliminary report of the excavations of Khirbet Qumran and of the agricultural dependency near 'Ain Feshkha has been written by de Vaux in *L'Archéologie et les manuscrits de la Mer Morte* (The Schweich Lectures of the British Academy 1959; London: Oxford University Press, 1961); in a revised English translation, *Archaeology and the Dead Sea Scrolls* (see Select Bibliography). Consult also his chapter, "Archéologie," in M. Baillet, J. T. Milik, and R. de Vaux, *Les 'petites grottes' de Qumrân* (DJD 3; Oxford: Clarendon Press, 1962) 1–36. Further archaeological information can be found in E.-M. Laperrousaz, *Qoumrân* (see Select Bibliography).

3. How did the scrolls come to be deposited in the caves?

It is not known for sure how the scrolls came to be in the Qumran caves. In Cave 1 the scrolls were wrapped in linen and stored in jars. There was no evidence of habitation in that cave. Hence one concludes that it served as a storage cave; the same seems to have been true of Cave 3. In Caves 2, 5–11, however, artifacts, signs of habitation, were found. Hence the scrolls discovered in these caves may have been the remains of the private library of the persons who lived in them. As for Cave 4, at the south end of the plateau, the cave from which no complete scroll has come, "at least 15,000 fragments" (according to the official report) were gathered from the debris that had accumulated there over a meter high during the centuries. In this case, the scrolls had not been wrapped in linen or stored in jars, and it looked like a place in which the sectarians had simply dumped the scrolls of their community library at the time (A.D. 68) when the center was about to be destroyed by the Romans who were en route to the siege of Jerusalem. It seems that they were deposited there in haste, perhaps with the hope that they would eventually be found intact by members who might some day return. There they lay until 1952.

4. Who discovered the QS?

The scrolls of what is called today Cave 1 are said to have been discovered by a Bedouin shepherd boy who was driving his flock of sheep and goats to water them at the spring, 'Ain Feshkha. He was Muhammad edh-Dhib (Muhammad the Wolf), a member of the Ta'amireh Bedouins. Details about the discovery are a matter of hearsay, but it seems that, when one of the animals went astray, he went in search of it, and seeing a hole in the cliff a little over a kilometer to the north of Khirbet Qumran, he tossed a stone into it. Hearing it make a peculiar sound, he decided to investigate. The next day he returned with a companion and clambered into the cave and discovered large terracotta jars with lids in which scrolls wrapped in linen had been stored. Eventually, it was revealed that seven major scrolls were recovered from this cave. Subsequently, archaeologists visited the cave and recovered some 70 fragmentary texts, some of which were related to the seven major scrolls and thus guaranteed that these had indeed come from that cave.

By now the Ta'amireh Bedouins were alerted to the possibility of discovering other such documents in caves. Members of that tribe of Bedouins discovered Cave 2 in 1952. Archaeologists from the Palestine Archaeological Museum, the Ecole Biblique, and the American School of Oriental Research, who explored the cliffs, discovered Cave 3. The Bedouins again discovered Cave 4, being led to it by a story recounted by a Bedouin elder, who had seen a wounded partridge fly into a hole at the south edge of the marly plateau on which Khirbet Qumran was situated. They opened the hole, discovered the cave, and began to clean it out until they were stopped by authorities of the Jordanian Department of Antiquities. It was eventually excavated by a joint group from the Department, the Ecole Biblique, and the Palestine Archaeological Museum. These archaeologists also discovered the nearby Cave 5, and in particular J. T. Milik recovered the fragments, which he subsequently published. The small Cave 6 was found by Bedouins, as was Cave 11. In the latter case, the Bedouins noticed a bat fly into a crevice of the cliffs a little south of Cave 3, which they then opened and proceeded to clean out completely, recovering many valuable texts from the guano-filled cave. Archaeologists, however, did eventually retrieve a few fragments from Cave 11, which served again to verify the texts subsequently bought from the Bedouins as actually derived from that cave. Caves 7–10 were discovered by the archaeologists during the excavation of Khirbet Qumran.

In this regard it is important to note that fragments of QS were indeed found by the archaeologists, since this has been denied or at least queried at times. Thus, E. R. Lacheman wrote in 1954, "The fact still remains that not a single document has been found by an archaeologist" (*JQR* 44 [1953–54] 290). This was said at a time when the claims of the Bedouin discoverers were not being trusted. Apropos of the Cave 1 texts S. Zeitlin once wrote, "Were they indeed discovered by Bedouin, or were they planted in the cave to be discovered later, and hence the entire discovery is a hoax?" (*JQR* 47 [1956–57] 267).

5. When were the QS discovered?

The seven major scrolls of Cave 1 were discovered early in 1947, prior to the Arab-Jewish War of 1948–49. It was only after the war, in 1949, that the cave was identified by Capt. Philippe Lippens, a Belgian member of the United Nations Truce Supervision Organization, and a British officer of the Jordanian Arab Legion; it was then visited and excavated by archaeologists of the Jordanian Department of Antiquities, the Ecole Biblique, and the Palestine Archaeological Museum. During that excavation 72 fragments were recovered. Cave 2 was discovered by Bedouins in February 1952. During the exploration of the cliffs by the joint-team of archaeologists in March 1952, Cave 3 was found by them. Caves 4 and 6 were discovered by the Bedouins in September 1952. Caves 5, 7-10 were found by the excavators of Khirbet Qumran in February and March of 1955.

Cave 11, which had been missed by the archaeological exploration team of 1952, was found by Bedouins in 1956.

6. In what country were the QS discovered?

The scrolls of Qumran Cave 1, discovered in 1947, were found in the territory of the British Mandate of Palestine, which included the entire area from the western shore of the Dead Sea area to the Mediterranean. At that time the State of Israel did not exist. It came into being on 14 May 1948, when Israel declared its independence. The First Arab-Jewish War broke out immediately afterwards (15 May) and lasted until the ceasefire and truce of 7 January 1949. The area in which the rest of QS, i.e. of Caves 2–11, were subsequently to be discovered became part of the so-called West Bank, which after that truce was occupied by Jordan, and in 1950 the Hashemite Kingdom of Jordan declared its sovereignty over the West Bank and Gaza, which lasted until the Six-Day War of 1967, when Israel occupied that territory. The rights of Jordan to the West Bank had been recognized officially only by Great Britain and Pakistan.

The texts recovered from the Wadi Murabba'at caves and at Khirbet Mird in 1952 were also found in the territory of the Jordanian controlled West Bank. However, the texts that Bedouins found at other sites (Naḥal Ḥever, Naḥal Mishmar, and Naḥal Ṣe'elim) actually came from across the border, from the part of the Judean Desert that had come to belong to the State of Israel.

7. Where are the QS today?

The seven major scrolls of Cave 1 are housed today in the Shrine of the Book, part of the Israel Museum, in Jerusalem, Israel. The Copper Plaque from Cave 3 and a few fragments of Cave 1, published in DJD 1, are in the Museum of the Department of Antiquities, Amman, Jordan. Some of the fragmentary texts of Cave 1 are in the Palestine Archaeological Museum of East Jerusalem, now called the Rockefeller Museum, and those that came into the possession of the Ecole Biblique have been acquired by the Bibliothèque Nationale of Paris. The thousands of fragments from Cave 4 are still in the "scrollery," the name given to the records room of the Palestine Archaeological Museum, where the texts of Cave 11 are also kept.

8. Who owns the QS?

The seven major scrolls of Cave 1 are the property of the State of Israel. Apart from these scrolls, it is not easy to say who owns the rest. According to a "distribution list" in DJD 1 (p. xi), some of the 72 fragments of Cave 1 were destined for the Department of Antiquities of Jordan in Amman, some for the Palestine Archaeological Museum in East Jerusalem, and some for the Ecole Biblique. An appended note says that all the fragments of the latter institution were subsequently acquired by the Bibliothèque Nationale, Paris.

Because the material from Caves 2–11 was found in the West Bank between 1952–56, Jordan laid claim to it. In May 1961 it nationalized the fragments in East Jerusalem and banned the exhibition of them in any other country but Jordan (*New York Times,* 2 May 1961, p. 5; *London Times,* 3 May 1961, p. 10; cf. DJD 6. 4).

But the matter is complicated. When the thousands of fragments from Cave 4 were brought to the scrollery of the Palestine Archaeological Museum, many of them had to be bought from the Bedouins, who had originally discovered the cave and had begun to clean it out. An effort was thus made by the Jordanian Department of Antiquities to buy all the fragments from the Bedouins because it was realized that only so would it be possible to work on the giant jigsaw puzzle that those fragments would create. For this reason the fragments had to be kept in Jerusalem. Otherwise, the Bedouins might have sold them to foreigners as archaeological treasures, and the fragments would have been dispersed without any hope of ever joining them to reconstitute texts. Yet neither the Museum nor the Department of Antiquities had sufficient funds for such a purchase. The British director of the Department, G. Lankester Harding, with the approval of the Jordanian government, appealed to foreign institutions for help (see § 10). Later, when Jordan decided to nationalize the QS, they became the property of that country, the government of which was to reimburse the foreign institutions (DJD 6. 5). It is not known whether that reimbursement ever took place.

At the time of the Six-Day War (1967), the Palestine Archaeo-logical Museum, which itself had been nationalized by Jordan in 1966, came under the jurisdiction of Israel, which occupied East Jerusalem and the West Bank. But this was "jurisdiction" by occupation, a con-tested authority, and so the answer to the question is involved in the political situation of the Middle East. It constitutes a ticklish ques-tion of international law. So it is not easy to say who really owns the QS that were still in the Museum as of 1967. This has also complicated many issues connected with the publication of the QS. See § 85 below.

9. How did Israel acquire the seven major scrolls of Cave 1?

When Cave 1 was discovered by Muhammad edh-Dhib early in 1947, he brought the seven scrolls eventually to a Syrian cobbler of Bethlehem, Khalil Iskander Shahin (popularly known as Kando), who also sold antiquities. Along with another Syrian Christian, George Isaiah, Kando brought four of the scrolls to their Metropolitan (Arch-bishop), Mar Athanasius Yeshue Samuel, superior of St. Mark's Monastery in Jerusalem and head of Jacobite Syrian Christians there. The Metropolitan bought the four scrolls from Kando (reportedly for £24). Thus the Isaiah Scroll A (1QIsaᵃ), the Manual of Discipline (1QS), the Pesher on Habakkuk (1QpHab), and the Genesis Apocry-phon (1QapGen) came into the possession of the Metropolitan. The other three scrolls, Isaiah Scroll B (1QIsaᵇ), the War Scroll (1QM), and the Thanksgiving Psalms (1QH), were eventually sold to Prof. Eleazar Lipa Sukenik of the Hebrew University of West Jerusalem.

Just prior to the First Arab-Israeli War, in February 1948, the Metropolitan brought his four scrolls to what was then called the American School of Oriental Research (now the W. F. Albright Institute of Archaeological Research) in East Jerusalem, where three of them (1QIsaᵃ, 1QS, 1QpHab) were photographed by John C. Trevor. The fourth, the Genesis Apocryphon, could not be unrolled, being badly stuck together. Once the Arab-Jewish War broke out, the Metropolitan took the four scrolls to Homs in Syria and then to Beirut. In January 1949 he brought them to the United States, where they were deposited in a New York bank safe-deposit box for several years. The Genesis Apocryphon was still unrolled.

On 1 June 1954 an advertisement appeared in the *Wall Street Journal* (p. 14): "'The Four Dead Sea Scrolls' Biblical manuscripts, dating back to at least 200 BC, are for sale. This would be an ideal gift to an educational or religious institution by an individual or group. Box F 206." Yigael Yadin, the son of Prof. Sukenik, a former officer in the Israeli Army during the Arab-Jewish War and subsequently the Deputy Prime Minister of Israel, was in the United States at that time, and learned about the advertisement. Through a New York banker as a middleman, he bought the four scrolls from the Metropolitan for $250,000 on 1 July 1954. On 2 July the scrolls were taken to the Israeli Consulate in New York and eventually were sent, one by one, to Jerusalem. Thus the four scrolls became the property of the State of Israel and joined the three that Sukenik had earlier acquired from Kando. All seven are today in the Shrine of the Book, part of the Israel Museum in Jerusalem. The Genesis Apocryphon was then unrolled, and part of it was published by Israeli scholars in 1956.

10. How did various foreign institutions get involved in the Cave 4 publication project?

When the Bedouins discovered Cave 4 and brought the initial batches of fragments to the Ecole Biblique and the Palestine Archaeological Museum on 20 September 1952, the Jordanian government, on the advice of G. Lankester Harding, offered to buy up these batches (and other fragments that the Bedouins still had), allotting 15,000 Jordanian dinars (pegged at the pound sterling, which was then worth $5.60) for the acquisition of such material. This amount hardly sufficed, and again on the advice of Lankester Harding the Jordanian government authorized the invitation to foreign institutions to help to pay for some of the fragments. This was done with the understanding that the fragments would remain in the scrollery of the Palestine Archaeological Museum until they were definitively published, when they would be equitably divided up among the various contributing foreign institutions along with the Department of Antiquities of Jordan, the Palestine Archaeological Museum, and the Ecole Biblique, which had also provided funds.

The following foreign institutions offered financial aid (in the order of their support): $15,000 from McGill University of Montreal (Canada); £700, and later several thousand more, from the Vatican Library; £1000 from a friend of University of Manchester (England), which then doubled this amount; £4,500 from the governments of Bonn and Baden-Württemberg on behalf of the University of Heidelberg (Germany), and a sizeable amount from the McCormick Theological Seminary (Chicago, IL, USA).

These institutions were eventually to become proprietors of certain Cave 4 fragmentary texts. During the year that I worked in the scrollery (1957–58) most of the plates of glass, under which the fragments were preserved, were labelled for one or other of these institutions. In July 1958 further funds came from McCormick Theological Seminary, the All Souls Unitarian Church of New York, and the University of Oxford for the purchase of the "last" nine fragments of Cave 4. According to John M. Allegro (*The Dead Sea Scrolls,* 50), the Jordanian Government "began to have wise second thoughts on the desirability of dispersing the fragments around the world. They asked the 1952 [sic!] donors to accept the return of their money rather than the pieces."

11. Did any Cave 4 fragments fail to end up in the scrollery of the Palestine Archaeological Museum?

During the year that I worked in the scrollery we constantly heard rumors that fragments, supposedly from Cave 4, had been sold by antiquities dealers in East Jerusalem to tourists who were often anxious to acquire a fragment of the DSS. In fact, one such fragment had been bought by an American, who had enough sense to send it back to the Museum. When the curator brought the fragment to the scrollery, J. T. Milik looked at it and recognized immediately that it belonged to one of his texts. He went to the plate where other fragments of the text were preserved, and it fitted in exactly, making a perfect join with about five or six other fragments.

Again, D. N. Freedman and K. A. Mathews report that a Prof. Georges Roux of France acquired frg. L of 11QpaleoLev, which was later photographed and is published in appendix A of their edition of *The Paleo-Hebrew Leviticus Scroll (11QpaleoLev)* (Philadelphia, PA: American Schools of Oriental Research, 1985) 83–85 (+pl. 5).

Rumors still circulate in Jerusalem today about "two more scrolls," apparently from Cave 11, which are in some unknown person's possession (see Allegro, *The Dead Sea Scrolls*, 48).

12. Could the QS lack any connection with the Qumran community?

No one will deny that some of the QS, either biblical or non-biblical, may have been composed elsewhere, or even copied elsewhere. Such texts would have been brought to the Qumran area by those who came to live there. But that the bulk of the QS discovered in the caves have nothing to do with the community whose center has been discovered and excavated at Khirbet Qumran is highly unlikely. Some scholars have maintained such ideas: that the scrolls were brought from Jerusalem or that they really represent the library of the Jerusalem Temple, having been deposited in the caves for safekeeping because of the advance of the Romans against Jerusalem. So, with varying nuances, K.-H. Rengstorf, E. Y. Kutscher, and more recently N. Golb of the University of Chicago.

But the proximity of the caves to the center, as well as the similarity of artifacts, pottery, and other archaeological evidence found in the caves and Khirbet Qumran suggest otherwise (see R. de Vaux, *Archaeology*, 53–57; DJD 6. 15–22; confirmed by the investigations of E.-M. Laperrousaz, *Qoumrân*, 155–75). Hence, it is hardly likely that the QS lack all connection with the Qumran community.

Moreover, the Israeli scholar E. Tov has shown in a number of convincing articles that a distinction has to be made between "imported texts," i.e. those which were copied elsewhere and brought to Qumran and texts written in what he calls "the Qumran system," i.e. scrolls copied "on the spot, possibly in the so-called *scriptorium*," "the product of a scribal school recognizable by several features": distinctive orthography, scribal marks, the use of initial or medial forms of letters in a final position, and distinctive ways of writing the divine names. These features are characteristic of 1QIsa[a], 1QH, 1QM, 1QS, 1QpHab, 11QTemple, 1QDM, 1QpZeph, 4QFlor, 4QTanh, 4QCatena[a], 4QpHos[a], 4QpPs[a], 4QpIsa[c], 4QDibHam[a]. (See "Hebrew Biblical

Manuscripts from the Judaean Desert: Their Contribution to Textual Criticism," *JJS* 39 [1988] 5–37; "The Orthography and Language of the Hebrew Scrolls Found at Qumran and the Origin of These Scrolls," *Textus* 13 [1986] 31–57). Such evidence argues strongly for the relation of the QS to the community that lived at Khirbet Qumran.

If the QS represented the library of the Jerusalem Temple, one would have to explain why so much of it has to do with concerns of a clearly sectarian group of Jews. One would also have to ask why the Jerusalem authorities would have carted the Temple library to a spot so distant and so inaccessible merely to hide them for safekeeping from the Romans; surely other places close by could have been found. No one seems to have come from Jerusalem to retrieve the scrolls so deposited after the war of A.D. 66–70. Hence such considerations make it likely that the scrolls found in the various Qumran caves were indeed the property of the sect whose communal center was Khirbet Qumran.

13. What QS have been definitively published?

All the seven major scrolls of Cave 1 have been published by either American or Israeli scholars. The 72 fragmentary texts have also been published by French or Polish scholars in DJD 1 (volume 1 of the series, Discoveries in the Judaean Desert). One text of Cave 1, the Genesis Apocryphon, has recently been subjected to new photographic techniques, and some badly preserved columns of the text (12–17) have now been better read; these columns are to be published shortly by Israeli scholars. The total number of Cave 1 texts is 79.

All the texts of Caves 2–3, 5–10 have also been definitively published in DJD 3. From Cave 2 there are 33 fragmentary texts, and from Cave 3, 15 texts. From Cave 5, 25 fragmentary texts were recovered; from Cave 6, 31 texts; from Cave 7, 19 fragments; from Cave 8, 5 fragmentary texts; from Cave 9, 1 papyrus fragment; and from Cave 10, one ostracon with two Hebrew letters on it. In all, from these minor caves 130 fragmentary texts have been published.

Most of the texts of Cave 11 have been published by American, Dutch, or Israeli scholars in independent publications. All told, they apparently number about 25 texts; a few of the smaller fragments still await publication, which is reported to be imminent.

Details about where these scrolls or fragments have been published can be found in my book, *DSSMPTS*.

The problem has been the scandalous delay in the publication of the many fragmentary texts from Cave 4. Texts **128–186** and **482–520** have been definitively published in the DJD 5, 6, 7, i.e. a mere 98 texts. In addition to these 98 definitively published, about 20 other texts (biblical and nonbiblical) have been published in preliminary form by graduate students at Harvard University. Some of the editors, to whom the texts were entrusted, have at times published parts of still other texts. These fragmentary texts vary in size, from one fragment to many joined fragments, or many identified as belonging to the same text.

According to the last report (1991), work on the jigsaw puzzle has now yielded 584 fragmentary texts from Cave 4. That means that roughly 80 percent of the Cave 4 fragmentary texts still await publication.

From all the eleven caves, of the 818 known Qumran texts, about 350 of them have been definitively published, i.e. roughly 40 percent.

14. Are the QS all texts of the OT?

No. Though many of the scrolls and fragments do contain books of or passages from the OT, the majority of the texts are nonbiblical Jewish literature. Of the 584 fragmentary texts of Cave 4 only 127 are biblical. The nonbiblical writings are part of what is often called Intertestamental Jewish Literature, a misnomer, because that term really means "between the two testaments" and would therefore be a Christian name for such literature of the Jewish people. A better term would be Parabiblical Jewish Literature, designating a body of Jewish literature that grew up alongside of the Hebrew Bible. But there are also sectarian texts, which would not be part of such parabiblical literature, even though such sectarian writings often quote the Hebrew Scriptures.

As for the biblical texts themselves, fragments of every book of the Hebrew canon have turned up in the eleven caves save for Esther and Nehemiah. In the case of the latter, it must be recalled that Ezra and Nehemiah at that time would have formed one book, which is represented by 4QEzra (still to be published). The absence of Esther from the Qumran biblical texts may be sheer chance, for it is reported that there is a text from Cave 4 that quotes from this book. Moreover, a number of fragments of deuterocanonical OT texts have turned up: Sirach, Tobit, Epistle of Jeremiah. These books are part of the OT in the Greek translation of the Septuagint and find place in the canon of the OT used by Roman Catholics today. Part of the problem here is to determine what books would have been considered sacred or canonical writings by the Qumran community, i.e. books that "render the hands unclean" (*m. Yadaim* 3:2), to use the later Jewish and rabbinic terminology for what Christians have called "canonical." There is no way of being sure what texts the Qumran community would have so regarded.

15. Of what sort are the nonbiblical writings of Qumran?

The nonbiblical writings are quite varied. On the one hand, there are some that are closely related to the OT itself: targums, i.e. translations of the OT into Aramaic; translations of a few biblical texts into Greek, as in the Septuagint; paraphrases of many OT writings, which embellish the text (like the Aramaic Genesis Apocryphon from Cave 1 or the Hebrew book of *Jubilees* from Cave 4); other paraphrases, which expand the pentateuchal regulations (like the Temple Scroll from Cave 11); writings that imitate OT compositions (like the Thanksgiving Psalms of Cave 1). There are also commentaries on OT texts, the pesharim from various caves.

On the other hand, there are nonbiblical texts that have nothing to do directly with the OT. Such writings are sectarian compositions: rule books (like the Manual of Discipline of Caves 1 and 4; the Damascus Document of the Cairo Genizah and Cave 4); the War Scroll, which prescribes conduct for the sect's holy war; the Thanksgiving Psalms, which record many tenets and beliefs of the Qumran community. There are many sectarian hymnic compositions, benedictions, liturgical texts, sapiential writings. The pesharim, which have been mentioned above as related to the OT, are clearly sectarian compositions.

As examples of otherwise known parabiblical Jewish literature, one would have to mention *1 Enoch* (now partly preserved in its original Aramaic form) and the *Testaments of the Twelve Patriarchs* (now partly preserved in Hebrew or Aramaic, depending on the Testament).

Whether all these nonbiblical writings are to be regarded as "sectarian" is problematic. In some cases, they contain nothing that is specifically characteristic of the Qumran community's tenets. Such writings may have been used by the members of the community, but there is little reason to think that the sect's members would have composed them.

There is, moreover, the interesting writing 4QMMT (*miqṣāt ma'ăśê hattôrāh*), which exists in multiple copies from Cave 4 and seems to be a letter written by a leader of the community to some other Jews (possibly Pharisees), setting forth what the leader and his community considered to be "the deeds of the law," i.e. important things prescribed by the Mosaic law that were neglected by these other Jews. The leader of the community seeks to draw such matters to the attention of these Jews.

16. In what languages have the QS been written?

The vast majority of the Qumran texts are written in Hebrew, but a sizeable number of them has been preserved in Aramaic, a sister language of Hebrew. This was the language used by most of the Jews of Palestine in the last two centuries B.C. and the first centuries A.D. There are also a few texts in Greek, i.e. texts of the Greek OT, found in Caves 4 and 7.

The Hebrew texts are not only biblical, i.e. scrolls and fragments of the Hebrew Scripture, but also many nonbiblical writings: texts of parabiblical literature known previously only in Greek, Ethiopic, or Latin translations; and texts of sectarian writings that have come to light for the first time.

Similarly, there are biblical texts in Aramaic, Daniel and Tobit, and also three fragmentary targums (Aramaic translations of passages of Leviticus and Job). In addition, a number of previously unknown Aramaic writings, among which the most important are the Genesis Apocryphon of Cave 1 and the fragments of Enoch of Cave 4.

17. Are there any NT texts among the QS?

None that are certainly so identified. In 1972 José O'Callaghan startled the scholarly world when he published an article, "¿Papiros neotestamentarios en la cueva 7 de Qumrān?" *Bib* 53 (1972) 91–100 (which can be found in an English translation in the supplement to *JBL* 91/2 [1972] 1–14). In this article and in several others subsequently published he claimed to have identified a number of fragments of Qumran Cave 7 with passages in the Greek NT. Of the 19 Greek fragments discovered in Cave 7, O'Callaghan regarded 7Q4 as part of 1 Tim 3:16; 4:1, 3; 7Q5 as part of Mark 6:52–53; 7Q6 1 as Mark 4:28; 7Q6 2 as Acts 28:38; 7Q7 as Mark 12:17; 7Q8 as Jas 1:23–24; 7Q9 as Rom 5:11–12; 7Q10 as 2 Pet 1:15; and 7Q15 as Mark 6:48. Most other scholars, however, have been extremely skeptical about his claim, thinking that they are rather fragments of a Greek translation of the OT, which have not yet been rightly identified. The problem with these Cave 7 fragments is that they are so small and contain so few letters that they almost defy certain identification. A Spanish colleague of O'Callaghan at the Biblical Institute, the OT professor L. Alonso Schökel, and a German scholar, Carsten P. Thiede, have tried to support O'Callaghan's contention. The latter has published a booklet, *Die älteste Evangelien-Handschrift? Das Markus-Fragment von Qumran und die Anfänge der schriftlichen Überlieferung des Neuen Testaments* (Wuppertal: Brockhaus, 1986; 2d ed., 1990), in English, *The Earliest Gospel Manuscript? The Qumran Papyrus 7Q5 and Its Significance for New Testament Studies* (Exeter, UK: Paternoster, 1992). But this publication has not gone without protest and criticism; see H.-U. Rosenbaum, "Cave 7Q5! Gegen die erneute Inanspruchnahme des Qumran-Fragments 7Q5 als Bruckstück der ältesten Evangelien-Handschrift," *BZ* 31 (1987) 1898–2005. It is reported that there have recently been a symposium in Germany and another in Italy that have tried to lend support to O'Callaghan, but little has been heard about it.

18. How are the QS dated?

Though archaeological data, such as pottery and coins that have at times been found in the caves along with the fragments, have been used, the dating is done mostly by palaeography, i.e. the comparative study of forms of ancient handwriting.

Scholars such as W. F. Albright, N. Avigad, S. A. Birnbaum, F. M. Cross, R. S. Hanson, and J. T. Milik have done most of this palaeographic work. Initially, the texts, as they came to light, were compared with other known ancient texts, such as the Nash Papyrus of the late Maccabean period (see S. A. Cook, "A Pre-Massoretic Biblical Papyrus," *PSBA* 25 [1903] 34–56 + pls. I–III) and ancient inscriptions from the Roman period (see W. F. Albright, *BASOR* 115 [1949] 10–19). In time, these scholars were able to put the handwriting of the QS into four main palaeographic categories (though the terminology differs from scholar to scholar):

(a) Archaic: from about 250 B.C. (or the end of the third century) to 150 B.C.

(b) Hasmonean: 150–30 B.C.

(c) Herodian: 30 B.C.–A.D. 70

(d) Post-Herodian or Ornamental: A.D. 70–135.

Within these categories scholars at times further distinguish formal and cursive handwriting. After many years of study, this palaeographic method has been judged to be fairly accurate, within a margin of ± 50 years.

In addition to palaeography, radiocarbon dating has also been used. Carbon-14, a radioactive isotope of carbon, breaks down at a precisely measurable rate, independently of its environment. Cosmic rays from outer space, bombarding the earth with apparent constancy, change nitrogen in the earth's atmosphere into Carbon-14. When the latter reacts with oxygen in the air, it makes carbon dioxide. Plants derive most of their carbon from carbon dioxide in the air and water. Animals feed on plants, and so all living things end up with carbon-14 in their system. When such a living thing dies, it dies with a certain amount of carbon and carbon-14. The latter continues to radiate, but no further carbon-14 is taken in. In fact, the residue carbon-14 begins to break down and return to nitrogen. The breakdown goes on at a constant rate, and its "half-life" is measurable, i.e. the time during which one half of the radiant energy will degenerate. This half-life was at first reckoned as 5568 years. In order to test ancient organic material, it is necessary to burn a bit of it. Initially, scholars were reluctant to submit such valuable documents to this testing. Moreover, given the margin of error (± 200 years, or even ± 80 years), the palaeographers felt that they could come up with better datings than such results.

In 1951 W. F. Libby, a scientist at the Institute for Nuclear Studies of the University of Chicago, tested some of the linen wrappings that were used to encase the scrolls in the jars found in Cave 1. The resultant radiocarbon dating was 1917 ± 200 years, or A.D. 33, ± 200 years, i.e. between A.D. 233 and 168 B.C. (see O. R. Sellers, *BASOR* 123 [1951] 24–26). In 1956 some palm wood from Khirbet Qumran was similarly tested at the Laboratory of the Royal Institution in London, which turned out to be 1940 ± 80 years old, thus yielding a date of A.D. 16, ± 80 years.

In 1961 it was announced at the National Bureau of Standards, Washington, DC that the technique of radiocarbon dating had been refined, making it necessary to use only a very small bit of the material and correcting the half-life from 5568 to 5730, ± 40 years. This resulted in a correction of the date for the linen to 20 B.C. See R. Stuckenrath, "On the Care and Feeding of Radiocarbon Dates," *Archaeology* 18 (1965) 277–81; H. Godwin, "Half-life of Radiocarbon," *Nature* 195 (#4845, 8 September 1962) 984; E.-M. Laperrousaz and G. Odent, "La datation d'objets provenant de Qoumrân, en particulier par la méthode utilisant les propriétés du carbone 14," *Semitica* 27 (1977) 83–98.

Recently, a number of fragments and scrolls have again been tested by radiocarbon dating, this time by a refined method of it, called Accelerator Mass Spectroscopy. Reports on these tests have been published in articles by G. Bonani et al., "Radiocarbon Dating of the Dead Sea Scrolls," *Atiqot* 20 (July 1991) 27–32; and "Radiocarbon Dating of Fourteen Dead Sea Scrolls," *Radiocarbon* (forthcoming, 1992). This testing was done in Zurich, Switzerland at the Institut für Mittelenergiephysik, and 14 samples were used. Of these one was from Wadi ed-Daliyeh, eight were from Qumran, two from Masada, and one each from Wadi Ṣe'elim, Wadi Murabba'at, and Khirbet Mird. Those from Daliyeh, Ṣe'elim, Murabba'at, and Mird bore internal absolute dates. Neither these absolute dates nor the palaeographic dating of the other ten had been disclosed to the scientists in Zurich, who thus worked independently. By and large, the carbon-14 datings confirm the palaeographic datings. For the documents with internal dates, the carbon-14 dating coincided in three out of four cases, and in the fourth there was a difference of only 10 years. For eight out of the other ten dated palaeographically, the radiocarbon dating confirmed the palaeographic dates; in one case there was a difference of 50 years (the limit of the margin of error set by palaeographers), and in another (4QTQehat) the radiocarbon dating was registered about 200 years earlier than the Hasmonean date given by palaeographers (300 B.C. rather than 100 B.C.).

Some of the Qumran fragments have been dated according to the measurement of the shrinkage temperature of fibres of skin or leather. Animal skins contain a fibrous component called collagen that degenerates. The degenerate changes are reflected in the lowering of the shrinkage temperature of the skin. Parchment fragments, subjected to progressive heat, begin to shrink, and the older the parchment the lower the temperature at which this occurs. This method of measurement was developed at the Department of Leather of the University of Leeds in Leeds, England. A group of fragments, some from Qumran, and others with known dates, were measured by this method and yielded a relative chronology. The scientists used this method on (a) English parchments from A.D. 1193 to 1955; (b) Murabba'at skins (from A.D. 132-35); (c) fragments from Cave 4 of Qumran; (d) fragments from Egyptian Aramaic letters written on skin (from the fifth century B.C.); and (e) a rawhide axe-hafting from Egypt (from 1300 B.C.). The result of the testing was that the Qumran Cave 4 fragments were more closely related to those of (b), (d), and (e) than to (a), being slightly older than those of (b). In other words, the Qumran fragments were not as old as the fifth-century Egyptian Aramaic letters, but older than the skins of Murabba'at (see D. Burton, J. B. Poole and R. Reed, "A New Approach to the Dating of the Dead Sea Scrolls," *Nature* 184 [#4685, 15 August 1959] 533-34).

Lastly, there are some indications in some of the scrolls that might be used as an internal date. For instance, there is reference to a historical figure [*Dmy*]*trws,* who is almost certainly Demetrius III Eucerus, one of the Seleucid rulers in the second century B.C. (4QpNah 3-4 i 2). There is also a calendaric fragment, as yet unpublished, which mentions *Šĕlāmṣiyôn,* the Hebrew name of Queen Alexandra, the successor to Alexander Janneus, Hyrcanus, and the massacres of '*Emilyôs,* Aemilius Scaurus, the first Roman governor of Syria (ca.

63 B.C.). Such internal references help to locate in a general way the existence of the Qumran community and its literature in the last two pre-Christian centuries. They help then in excluding the identification of the Qumran community with a Christian movement and establish its roots in Judaism of the last centuries B.C.

19. What sort of texts were discovered in Cave 1?

The seven major scrolls of Cave 1 are the following: (a) *1QIsa*ª: This text, dated palaeographically to 125–100 B.C. and now by radiocarbon to 202–107 B.C., contains all 66 chapters of the book of Isaiah, save for a few words broken off the bottom of a few columns. It is written on 54 columns of varying width, on 17 pieces of sheepskin sewed together to form a scroll, measuring 24.5 ft. in length and 10.5 in. in height. This scroll bears singular testimony to the fidelity with which the book of Isaiah was copied throughout the centuries by Jewish scribes, since the oldest Hebrew text of Isaiah that was known prior to the discovery of the QS was the Cairo Codex of the Former and Latter Prophets dated to A.D. 895 (in its colophon). Though there are spelling differences, which might have been expected, the remarkable thing about the text is that only 13 variant readings that it contained were considered important enough to be used in the 1952 edition of the *RSV.* Moreover, this scroll displays no awareness of the distinction of First, Second, and Third Isaiah, since chaps. 39–40 are copied on the same piece of skin, and the same is true of chaps. 55–56. See M. Burrows, *The Dead Sea Scrolls* (New York: Viking, 1955) 305–15. Apart from those 13 variant readings, the text of 1QIsaª is textually insignificant. Together with 1QIsaᵇ and at least 15 other fragmentary texts of Isaiah from Qumran, it reveals that the text of Isaiah was relatively stabilized as early as the second century B.C.

(b) *1QIsa*ᵇ: This text of Isaiah, dated palaeographically to the end of the first century B.C. or the first part of the first Christian century, is fragmentary. It contains parts of chaps. 7–8, 10, 12, 13, 15, 16, 19, 20, 22, 23, 24, 25, 29, 30, 35, 37–41, 43–51, being fairly well preserved from chap. 41 on. It is usually judged to be closer to the Masoretic tradition than 1QIsaª, i.e. closer to the medieval Hebrew text-tradition of the OT. Its spelling differences are less striking than those of 1QIsaa.

(c) *1QS*: The *serek hayyahad*, "Rule of the Community," more commonly called "The Manual of Discipline." This is a copy of a community rule-book written in Hasmonean script, dated ca. 100–75 B.C. It contains eleven columns of a Hebrew sectarian writing; for a description of its contents, see § 28 below. Ten or eleven further fragmentary copies of the same text were discovered in Cave 4, which are as yet unpublished; one fragment of Cave 5 (5Q11) is related to this text; another fragment (5Q13) may be related.

(d) *1QM* : The *milhāmāh*, "War," or "The War Scroll." The text, written in Herodian script, contains a set of instructions for the conduct of an eschatological war to be waged by the "sons of light" (= the Qumran community) against the "sons of darkness" (= the forces of evil). It gives expression to the dualistic and eschatological beliefs of the community; for a description of its contents, see § 30 below. Further copies of the same text are represented by 4QMa-g.

(e) *1QH*: The *hôdāyôt*, "the Thanksgiving Psalms," so called because many of the hymns begin with the words *'ôdĕkā 'ādônāy*, "I thank you, O Lord." This copy is written in Herodian script, dated palaeographically to 50 B.C.–A.D. 68 and now by radiocarbon to 21 B.C.–A.D. 61. It may have been originally two different compositions that have been joined. It is a collection of at least 25 psalms or hymns, which resemble the canonical psalms and are imitative of them. See further §31 below.

(f) *1QpHab*: The *pēšer Ḥăbaqqûq*, "Commentary on Habakkuk." It contains 13 fragmentary columns and quotes the text of the prophet Habakkuk verse by verse (1:1–2:20), and then comments on the meaning of each verse, relating the prophet's words to the history or theology of the Qumran sect.

(g) *1QapGen*: The Genesis Apocryphon is an Aramaic document, dated palaeographically to the end of the first century B.C. or the beginning of the first century A.D., and now by radiocarbon to 73 B.C.–A.D. 14. Its text begins with a recasting of the story of the Nephilim or Watchers (Genesis 6), recounts the birth of an extraordinary child (Noah) to his parents Lamech and Bitenosh (Gen 5:28–29), tells of Noah's partitioning of the land after the flood among his sons (Gen 10:18–28), and part of the story of Abram (Gen 12:8–15:4), embellishing the latter with a description of Sarai's beauty and of Abram's exploration of the promised land. The fragment 1Q20 is now known to be part of what has to be called column 0 of 1QapGen. To col. 1 belongs the so-called Trevor fragment, soon to be published. See further § 33 below.

In addition to these major texts of Cave 1 there are 72 other fragmentary texts, of which 15 are biblical. The most important of the nonbiblical fragments are three pesharim (on Micah, Zephaniah, and the Psalms) and two appendices to the Manual of Discipline (1QSa, "The Messianic Rule of the Congregation," and 1QSb, a "Collection of Blessings").

20. What sort of texts were discovered in Cave 2?

From Cave 2 were recovered 18 fragmentary texts of the OT, one (2Q5) of Lev 11:22–29 written in paleo-Hebrew writing, which resembles the ancient Phoenician script. Another (2Q18), dated paleographically to the second half of the first century B.C., includes two important fragmentary columns of deuterocanonical Sirach in Hebrew (=Sir 6:14–15, 20–31). This is a very early copy of the Hebrew text of Sirach, which was first discovered only at the end of the last century in the Cairo Genizah, dating from the 10th–12th centuries A.D., and preserved today in the Library of the University of Cambridge in England. Previous to the discovery of that Hebrew text, the deuterocanonical book of Sirach was known only in Greek and Latin translations. Now these fragmentary columns in Hebrew from Cave 2 provide another partial copy of that important deuterocanonical book.

In addition, there were 15 fragmentary nonbiblical texts found in Cave 2, among which are two copies of the Hebrew text of *Jubilees* (2Q19, 2Q20) and an Aramaic description of the New Jerusalem (2Q24).

21. What sort of texts were discovered in Cave 3?

In Cave 3 the archaeologists found 14 fragmentary texts, three biblical (Ezek 16:31–33; Ps 2:6–7; Lam 1:10–12; 3:53–62) and eleven nonbiblical, one being a pesher (commentary) on Isaiah 1:1 (3Q4).

In addition, there was also the famous Copper Plaque (3Q15). On it were inscribed 12 columns of a text, containing a list of places where treasure (money, gold, silver, and precious objects) had been buried. The amounts of hidden treasure are fantastically great (e.g. 4600 talents of silver and gold). No one knows for certain how to interpret the text. See further § 34.

22. What sort of texts were discovered in Cave 4?

Cave 4 has turned out to be the most important cave of all. No complete scroll was found there. The largest single piece is the five-column pesher (commentary) on Nahum (4QpNah), which measures about 56 cms. But the Bedouins and the archaeologists recovered from this cave "at least 15,000 fragments" according to the official report (DJD 6. 8), which is undoubtedly a very conservative figure. These fragmentary texts constituted a huge jigsaw puzzle, which began in late 1952 and lasted until about 1960. It is now known that these fragmentary texts number about 584. Of these 127 are biblical, the rest are nonbiblical texts. Among the latter, the phylacteries, mezuzot, and targums (4Q128–157) have been published in DJD 6, and the pesharim and other texts related to the OT, biblical paraphrases, catenae of OT texts, etc. (4Q158–186) were published in DJD 5. Among the nonbiblical texts there are various copies of *1 Enoch* in Aramaic, most of which J. T. Milik published in 1976. There are ten or eleven copies of the Manual of Discipline, known from Cave 1, eight copies of the Damascus Document, which was originally discovered in two manuscripts in the Cairo Genizah in 1896, the Semitic originals of some of the *Testaments of the Twelve Patriarchs* (extant until now only in Greek), and fragments of the original Hebrew text of *Jubilees*. In addition, there are fragmentary copies of the book of Tobit (four in Aramaic, one in Hebrew — of a deuterocanonical book, previously extant only in Greek and Latin translations), fragmentary copies of the Thanksgiving Psalms, known from Cave 1, and many sapiential works previously unknown. There is also the famous "Son of God" text (4Q246), not yet fully published, a collection of Beatitudes (4Q525), recently published, and the long-awaited 4QMMT, *miqṣāt ma'áśê hattôrāh*, "collection of deeds of the law." The texts of this

Cave are extremely important for the text-critical study of the OT and for the study of the Palestinian background of many NT ideas.

23. What sort of texts were discovered in Caves 5 and 6?

In Cave 5 there were recovered protocanonical biblical texts, numbering eight (Deut 7:15–24; 8:5–9:2; 1 Kgs 1:1, 16–17, 27–37; Isa 40:16, 18–19; Amos 1:3–5; Ps 119:113–20, 138–42; Lam 4:5–8, 11–15, 16, 18–19, 20–22; 5:1–3, 4–12, 13, 16–17; Lam 4:17–20, and a phylactery too difficult to open), and nonbiblical texts, numbering 17. Among the latter were a copy of the Manual of Discipline (5Q11), with part of 1QS 2:4–7,12–14, a copy of the Damascus Document (5Q12), with part of CD 9:7–10, and an important copy of an Aramaic description of the New Jerusalem (5Q15). By contrast, little of importance was recovered from Cave 6. There are seven biblical texts, two of them written in paleo-Hebrew script (6Q1 [Gen 6:13–21] and 6Q2 [Lev 8:12–13]); also (but in square characters) 1 Kgs 3:12–14; 12:28–31; 22:28–31; 2 Kgs 5:26; 6:32; 7:8–10; 7:20–8:5; 9:1–2, 19–21; Ps 78:36–37; Cant 1:1–6, 6–7; Dan 8:20–21; 10:8–16; 11:33–36,38. There are also 24 nonbiblical texts, insignificant narrative, prophetic, juridical, liturgical, and hymnic writings.

24. What texts were found in Cave 7?

This was the cave of surprises. Of the 19 tiny fragments recovered from Cave 7 all of them are written in Greek. Two of them have been identified as OT texts: 7Q1 as Exod 28:4–7, and 7Q2 as Epistle of Jeremiah 43–44 (=Bar 6:43–44). The rest has almost defied accurate decipherment because the fragments are so tiny and contain so few letters. For an attempt to decipher some of them, see § 17 above.

25. What texts were discovered in Caves 8, 9, 10?

Cave 8 yielded only four biblical texts, one of which is a phylactery and another a mezuzah; also Gen 17:12–19; 18:20–25 and Ps 17:5–9, 14; 18:6–9, 10–13. There is also one nonbiblical hymnic text.

From Cave 9 came only one small papyrus fragment with six Hebrew characters on it; and from Cave 10 an ostracon with two Hebrew letters.

26. What texts were discovered in Cave 11?

Cave 11, like Caves 1 and 4, was important. It yielded a text of Leviticus in paleo-Hebrew script (11QpaleoLev), a Psalms Scroll (11QPsa), the Targum of Job (11QtgJob), the almost complete Temple Scroll (11QTemplea), and a number of other nonbiblical texts.

The Psalms Scroll (11QPsa) seems to be a community prayer-book, in which canonical psalms are copied in a noncanonical ordering together with other psalms previously known from the Greek and Syriac tradition and with prose inserts. See § 36 below.

The Targum of Job (11QTgJob) is an Aramaic translation of part of the Hebrew book of Job, which shows how the Jews in pre-Christian times understood this difficult book of the OT. See § 37 below.

The Temple Scroll (11QTemple) is a Hebrew text longer than the book of Isaiah, preserved in 66 columns. Written in Herodian script, this copy is dated palaeographically to the end of the first century B.C. or the beginning of the first century A.D., and now by radiocarbon to 97 B.C.–A.D. 1. But a fragmentary copy of a small part of the text from Cave 4 is dated palaeographically ca. 135 B.C. So the document was probably composed in the second century B.C. It purports to be the community's Second Torah. See § 35 below.

27. Are any of the QS related to the texts discovered at Masada or Khirbet Mird or in the caves of Murabba'at, Nahal Hever, Se'elim, and Mishmar?

At Masada, the former Herodian fortress and palace where the Jews of Judea made their last stand against the Romans after the destruction of Jerusalem, were found a number of fragmentary texts that seem to have been written by some of the same scribes who copied texts found in the Qumran caves. Among these there were small biblical fragments of Genesis, Leviticus, Deuteronomy, Ezekiel, and the Psalms; more important still was the fragmentary copy of Sirach in Hebrew, which has been published by Y. Yadin, *The Ben Sira Scroll from Masada: With Introduction, Emendations and Commentary* (Jerusalem: Israel Exploration Society, 1965). It contains another early form of the Hebrew text of Sir 39:27–44:17c (see § 20 above). Among the nonbiblical texts found there were fragments of *Jubilees* and the Songs of the Sabbath Sacrifice (MasŠirŠabb). Both of these are related to fragments discovered in Qumran Cave 4. Thus both biblical and nonbiblical fragments of Masada are related to similar texts from the Qumran caves. This suggests that some of the members of the Qumran community joined the Zealots who made their last stand at Masada against the Roman troops, who finally encircled the fortress and captured it. Josephus has described the last stand in *J.W.* 7.8.1 § 252–7.9.2 § 406.

There is little connection, however, between the QS and the texts that have been recovered from the caves of Murabba'at, Ḥever, Ṣe'elim, and Mishmar, since most of these caves have yielded documents that were carried to them by refugees who fled from the Romans. Some of them are letters, others legal documents. They are written in Aramaic, Greek, and Hebrew and in some cases are dated from the years between the two Jewish revolts against the Romans. Some of them have to do especially with the Bar Cochba revolt of A.D. 132-35. The texts of Murabba'at have been published by P. Benoit, J. T. Milik, and R. de Vaux, *Les grottes de Murabba'at* (DJD 2; 2 vols.; Oxford: Clarendon, 1961). Some of those of Naḥal Ḥever have been published by E. Tov (in collaboration with R. A. Kraft), *The Greek Minor Prophets Scroll from Naḥal Ḥever (8ḤevXIIgr)* (DJD 8; The Seiyâl Collection I; Oxford: Clarendon, 1990). Of these texts the two most important are MurXII (Mur 88), which contains a fragmentary copy of the Hebrew text of ten of the Minor Prophets (Joel to Zechariah), and 8ḤevXIIgr, which has preserved in fragmentary form a Greek translation of six of the Minor Prophets (Jonah, Micah, Nahum, Habakkuk, Zephaniah, and Zechariah). Some of the Ḥever Aramaic texts are to be published shortly. The overall importance of the texts from these caves is the testimony that they bear to the trilingualism that prevailed at this time in Judea, showing that Aramaic, Greek, and Hebrew were all being used by the people who took refuge in these caves from the Romans.

As for the texts from Khirbet Mird, there is no connection at all with the QS. In a sense they should not be considered part of the DSS, since Khirbet Mird is situated in the Judean Desert between Qumran and Jerusalem and the texts found there come from the remains of a Christian monastery and date from the sixth to the eighth centuries A.D. The site was discovered more or less about the same time as the Qumran caves and in the popular mind was (wrongly) associated with the DSS. Khirbet Mird has yielded some Christian Palestinian Aramaic texts, a few fragments of Greek literature, and about a hundred Arabic texts. So the documents retrieved from Khirbet Mird really have nothing to do with the Qumran community or the QS.

28. What is the Manual of Discipline?

This is the modern name given to a text, the ancient title of which seems to have been *Serek hayyaḥad,* "The Rule of the Community," which came to light for the first time in Cave 1 (1QS). Ten or eleven fragmentary copies of it were also recovered from Cave 4 (4QSa-j/k), as well as a fragment of it from Cave 5 (5Q11, =1QS 2:4–7, 12–14); and another fragment (5Q13) may be related. 1QS is a rather well-preserved eleven-column rule book of the Qumran community. The modern title was given to it by Millar Burrows, who first published its text (*The Dead Sea Scrolls of St. Mark's Monastery, Volume II, Fascicle 2: Plates and Transcription of the Manual of Discipline* [New Haven, CT: American Schools of Oriental Research, 1951]). Burrows was a Methodist, and this text reminded him of a similarly named book of the Methodist Church tradition.

The Manual of Discipline has an introduction, which states the aim and purpose of the community (1:1–15). It then describes the rite for entrance into the Covenant of the community (1:16–3:12), the theological tenets of the community, e.g. its doctrine about the two spirits, the spirit of truth and the spirit of iniquity, which God has created to govern human life (3:13–4:26); again the purpose of the community and its rules for communal life, for the assembly of members, and for the admission of candidates (5:1–6:23). It gives the penal code of the community (6:24–7:25), a description of the model, pioneer community (8:1–9:26), and the text of a hymn, in which the community praises the Creator, sings of God's righteousness, and gives thanks to him for his goodness (10:1–11:22).

1QS is a copy dated palaeographically ca. 100–75 B.C., but the text is clearly composite and underwent revision at various times; its levels of composition have to be sorted out. (In 4QS[e], which seems to be an older copy of the rule book, the text of 1QS 9:2 is copied directly after 8:15.) It is clearly an important text, revealing much about the Qumran community and its life. It agrees remarkably with many details, but not all, of what Josephus tells us about the Essenes (*J.W.* 2.8.2–13 § 119–61). It seems to envisage a community which was only male, the members of which formed the New Covenant (see Jer 31:31; 32:37–41).

Among the fragments recovered from Cave 1 (see DJD 1), there are two appendixes of this Manual. 1QSa (1Q28a), an independent rule book, often called "The Rule of the Congregation" or "The Messianic Rule of the Congregation," is a two-column text with further regulations about members and gatherings "at the end of days": (1) 1:1–3, the rule for the whole congregation of Israel at the end-time; (2) 1:4–5, regulations for new arrivals (including women and children); (3) 1:5–18, regulations for troops and members of various ages; (4) 1:19–25, special cases (old men, mental cases, Levites); (5) 1:26–2:11a, rules for the meeting of the whole community; (6) 2:11b–22, the order of the messianic assembly and banquet. This rule may reflect the Qumran community at a different stage of its development, since it mentions women and children, who are not mentioned in 1QS proper.

1QSb (1Q28b) is a Collection of Blessings: (1) 1:1–28, a blessing of God-fearers; (2) 2:1–3:21, blessing of the high priest (possibly = the Messiah of Aaron of 1QS 9:11); (3) 3:22–5:19, blessing of the priests; (4) 5:20–29, blessing of the prince of the congregation (*nĕśî' hā'ēdāh,* known from CD 7:20).

29. What is the Damascus Document?

The ancient title of this document is unknown. Commonly called "The Damascus Document" (CD [=Cairo Damascus]), it is sometimes referred to as the "Zadokite Documents." It is represented by two texts discovered in the genizah of the Ezra Synagogue of Old Cairo in 1896 by Solomon Schechter. He published them as the first part of *Documents of Jewish Sectaries* (2 vols.; Cambridge, UK: University Press, 1910; repr. with a prolegomenon by J. A. Fitzmyer, New York: Ktav, 1970). Volume 1 of this publication contains "Fragments of a Zadokite Work, Edited from Hebrew Manuscripts in the Cairo Genizah Collection now in the Possession of the University Library, Cambridge." (The second volume contains "Fragments of the Book of the Commandments by Anan," i.e. Anan ben David, the founder of Qaraite Judaism in early medieval times.)

The text of CD published by Schechter is double: Text A, a copy dated to the 10th century A.D., containing 16 cols. (actually written on both sides of eight parchment leaves [text A1 containing cols. 1–8, and text A2, cols. 9–16]); and Text B, a copy dated to the twelfth century A.D., containing two cols., numbered 19 and 20 (actually written on two sides of one long parchment leaf). Column 19:1ff. agrees somewhat with A1, 7:5ff., but from 19:33–20:34 Text B has no parallel in Text A; this is a supplementary exhortation.

Though found in Cairo, CD is related to the QS, since it is a fuller copy of a text, fragments of which have turned up in Qumran Cave 4 (4QD^{a-h}, as yet officially unpublished, but "bootlegged" in *A Preliminary Edition,* mentioned in § 92 below), Cave 5 (5QD [5Q12], published in DJD 3. 181), and Cave 6 (6QD [6Q15], published in DJD 3. 128-31). Four of the five fragments from Cave 6 correspond to CD A1: (1) CD 4:19–21; (2) CD 5:13–14; (3) CD 5:18–6:2; (4) CD 6:20–7:1; but frg. 5 corresponds to nothing in CD. This is not surprising because the text of this rule book was often revised, as Texts A and B of CD itself manifest, and there is no guarantee that all the copies belong to the same recension of it. 5QD corresponds to CD 9:7–10. Of the 4Q fragments it is known that copy b is dated between 75–50 B.C. and that copy e has cols. 15–16 of CD between cols. 8 and 9. For the way all these fragments are related to the text of CD, see *DSSMPTS,* 132–33.

The text of CD contains two main parts: (I) *An Exhortation* (1:1–8:21 [+19:1–20:34]), which includes (a) a meditation on the lessons of the history of Israel (1:1–2:1); (b) on the predestination of the righteous and the wicked (2:2–13); (c) a second meditation on the lessons of history (2:14–4:12a); (d) the three nets of Belial in which Israel is ensnared (4:12b–6:1); (e) the community of the New Covenant (6:2–7:6); and (f) the diverse fates of those faithful to the Covenant and of apostates (7:9–8:17 [+19:5–20:34]). (II) *Constitution: Life in the New Covenant* (15:1–16:20; 9:1–14:22), which includes (a) rules for entrance into the Covenant and for oaths (15:1–16:16); (b) regulations within the community (9:1–10:10a); (c) rites to be observed in the community (10:10b–12:18); (d) organization of the community (12:19–14:19); (e) a penal code (14:20–22).

This is a subsidiary rule book, but it is not known just how it is to be related to the Manual of Discipline of Cave 1. It contains references to "camps," but no one knows to what this term refers. Moreover, it mentions "Damascus" (6:5,19; 7:15,19; 8:21; 19:34; 20:12), which may be a covert or cryptic name for Babylon, whence the community may have come. If so, then the regulations of CD may represent the rule that governed their life there, in camps in the land of exile. But the exhortation in the first part of CD seems to refer rather to the situation in Judea itself.

The fact, moreover, that multiple fragmentary copies of CD were found in Cave 4 along with multiple copies of the Manual makes it clear that the two rule books were somehow related to the same group of Jews in Judea.

30. What is the War Scroll?

The War Scroll of Cave 1 was published by E. L. Sukenik, *The Dead Sea Scrolls of the Hebrew University* (Jerusalem: Hebrew University and Magnes Press, 1955), pls. 16–34, 47 (lower), transcription, 1–19. Belonging to it are fragments of the same scroll (1Q33) and also fragmentary copies of the text from Cave 4 (4QM^{a-g} [4Q491–497], published in DJD 7).

The War Scroll is a book of instructions for an eschatological war of forty years that the Qumran community, called "the sons of light," was expecting to wage along with God and his angels against its enemies, "the sons of darkness," at the end of time. It describes the military equipment, army formations, plans for battle, and the prayers and exhortations to be uttered by the high priest and other priests or levites. It is thus a vademecum for the community's holy war, describing in detail its marshalling for the great and final battle.

The text of 1QM is fragmentary, consisting of the tops of 19 cols. It begins with a generic description of the war to come, the final carnage, and the destruction of the sons of darkness (col. 1). In more detail, it describes the preparation for the final war (1:?–2:14), gives rules about trumpets, standards, and shields to be used in the struggle (2:15–5:2), and describes the infantry battle-array and its weapons (5:3–6:6), then the array of the cavalry (6:8–17). It gives details about recruitment and the required age of soldiers (6:?–7:7), about the role of priests and levites in the camp (7:9–9:9). It supplies a rule for a change in battle-array in the case of an attack (9:10–18). Then comes the high priest's exhortation in the battle-liturgy (9:?–12:18), and a blessing uttered by all the leaders in the community at the time of victory (12:?–14:1). There follows a ceremony for thanksgiving (14:2–18), and a description of the last battle against the Kittim (= the Romans, 14:?–19:13). The troops and the camps of the sons of light are organized according to the instructions of Num 2:1–5:4; they are led by the angels Michael, Raphael, and Sariel and oppose the sons of darkness, led by Belial. This text does not mention a Davidic Messiah, and the main role in the community so organized for holy war is played by the high priest.

1QM and its fragments (1Q33) are written in Herodian script, and the Cave 4 fragments are said to date from the first century A.D. From internal evidence, the composition of 1QM is dated to the second half of the first century B.C. This date, established by Y. Yadin, is based on details of army organization and armor, which seem to show dependence on a Herodian Hebrew army manual, modelled on Roman treatises *De re militari*. The organization of the eschatological army is similar to what is known of Herod's army. For instance, the soldier's *kîdôn*, "sword" (1QM 5:12–13) was attached to his belt by two straps of "five palms" and not to the belt directly, revealing pre-Augustan Roman army customs, which were instituted under Julius Caesar. Again, the troop-movements are described as *kĕnāpîm*, "wings" (1QM 9:11), which are quite similar to Roman *alae*. Similarly, the *battê šôqayim*, "greaves," used for the cavalry and not for the infantry (1QM 6:15), recalls Roman usage. However, other scholars date the composition to at least a century earlier.

Though the literary genre of the text differs from that of the book of Revelation, it contains many details that shed light on that NT writing: the same motif of the holy war against enemies of God's people, a similar use of OT texts (especially of the book of Daniel), of symbolic names for adversaries, and of the role of angels.

31. What are the Thanksgiving Psalms?

The Thanksgiving Psalms of Cave 1 were also published by Sukenik in *DSSHU,* pls. 35–47 (upper), 48–58, transcription, 1–18, frgs. 1–66. Along with many related fragments of Cave 4 (as yet unpublished), this text is a sort of prayer book of the Qumran community. 1QH (H = *Hôdāyôt,* "thanks," a modern Hebrew title for the scroll; its ancient name was *Hôdôt*) was written in Herodian script and contains 18 cols. and 66 frgs.; also related to it is 1Q35. It seems that it was originally copied in two scrolls or two pieces eventually sewn together.

1QH contains at least 25 hymns, which in general resemble the canonical psalms. It not only echoes the phraseology of the latter, but is said to contain about 673 implicit citations of or allusions to OT passages, many from the canonical psalter and the Servant Songs of Isaiah. They retain some of the parallelism of the canonical psalms, but in general that feature has begun to break down and disappear. These hymns are rather wordy, prolix, and repetitious. At times they develop in an allegorical way some OT images: e.g. pangs of childbirth (3:7–12; 5:30–31), the fortress (3:7, 13; 6:25–35), or the ship (3:6, 13–18; 6:22–24; 7:4–5). Some of the hymns seem to refer to the experience of an abandoned teacher; those which are couched in the first person singular are often thought to refer to the experience of the Teacher of Righteousness, but that identification is not certain and is, in fact, contested by some interpreters. The *Hôdāyôt* give expression to many of the theological tenets of the Qumran community, praising God for his greatness, uprightness, and bounty and thanking him for deliverance from opposition, persecution, and personal tribulation. They also describe the human condition and its tendency to sin and misconduct. In their mode of composition they are not unlike the hymns in the Lucan infancy narrative (Benedictus, Magnificat, Gloria, Nunc Dimittis).

These psalms may be examples of what Philo wrote about the Therapeutae in Egypt, who were, according to him, related to the Palestinian Essenes: "They not only practice contemplation, but also compose songs and hymns to God in all sorts of meters and melodies (*De vita contemp.* 3 § 29; cf. 10 § 80, 83, 84).

32. What are the pesharim?

Pēšer is a special word that is best translated as "commentary." Basically, it means "interpretation," and the word occurs frequently in this type of writing, especially to introduce comments on verses of the OT text that are quoted. It designates a kind of Jewish writing that came to light for the first time when the QS were discovered. Related in general to the term *midrāš*, it designates a specifically Qumran kind of midrash. Such pesher-commentaries have been composed on various prophetic writings of the OT and on the Psalms, but none are extant on the Pentateuch or the historical writings of the OT. There are, for instance, pesharim on Isaiah, Habakkuk, Micah, Zephaniah, Hosea, Nahum, and the Psalter.

As a literary form, the pesher quotes the OT text verse by verse and then comments on it, by actualizing the words of the prophet, i.e. modernizing the text by relating it to the history or theological tenets of the Qumran community. It is thus a very definite sectarian composition, which would not be current even in Jewish circles outside of this community. The commentary is composed with the conviction that what the prophet or psalmist of old wrote had pertinence not only to his own times, but also to the life of this community. At times the commentator finds hidden meaning in the words by departing from the grammar or wording of the original. The peculiar exegesis given to the words of the prophet or psalm is often introduced by the phrases, *pišrô ʿal,* "the interpretation of it (is) about," *pišrô ʾăšer,* "the interpretation of it (is) what . . . ," or *pēšer haddābār ʾăšer,* "the interpretation of the word/matter (is) what. . . ." Such an interpretation of the prophet's words is said to have been made known by God to the Teacher of Righteousness concerning "all the secrets of the words of his servants, the prophets" (1QpHab 7:4–5). There is no certainty that the pesharim were all composed by one author, but whoever the authors were, they employed a common mode of interpretation that may be derived from the Teacher. This kind of interpretation, which is apocalyptic and supplies a hidden meaning to an OT writing, provides an interesting parallel to the use of *mystērion,* "secret," and the preposition *eis,* "unto, concerning," in Eph 5:32.

Such a literary form was unknown prior to the discovery of the QS and differs considerably from the rabbinic writings of the Mishnah or Talmud, or even of the rabbinic midrashim. It differs because it is a specific form of *exegesis* of the OT text, related to the history of the Qumran sect, whereas the rabbinic writings were the eventual distillation and codification of an oral tradition (the *tôrāh še-bĕ-'al peh*) that had grown up alongside of the written word of God, the Hebrew Scriptures (the *tôrāh še-biktāb*).

See M. P. Horgan, *Pesharim: Qumran Interpretations of Biblical Books* (CBQMS 8; Washington, DC: Catholic Biblical Association, 1979).

33. What is the Genesis Apocryphon?

Part of the Genesis Apocryphon from Cave 1 was published by N. Avigad and Y. Yadin in *A Genesis Apocryphon: A Scroll from the Wilderness of Judaea. Descriptions and Contents of the Scroll, Facsimiles, Transcription and Translation of Columns II, XIX–XXII* (Jerusalem: Magnes Press of the Hebrew University and Heikhal Hasefer, 1956). Recently with new photographic techniques it has been possible to read more of the badly preserved intervening cols. 12–17.

The Genesis Apocryphon is a form of parabiblical literature, which retells the story of parts of Genesis in Aramaic, embellishing it, and adding haggadic details. It should probably be called more properly *Kĕtāb 'ăbāhātā',* "Book of the Patriarchs," because it recounts in embellished form the stories of Noah and Abraham. It is related to the kind of literature one finds in *Jubilees.* There is no indication in this text of any specifically sectarian doctrines or traits; hence it is probably not a sectarian composition. Like *Jubilees,* it probably stems from a wider circle of Jews, but was used by the members of the Qumran community. Only one copy of it has been found.

Among the embellishments of the Genesis story is an elaborate description of Sarai's beauty and of the journey that Abram makes to explore the promised land. The former describes Sarai's hair, color of her face, the slenderness of her arms and hands, the comeliness of her legs. The latter depicts Abram travelling from the delta in Egypt up the coast to the Taurus Mountains, then across the desert to the Tigris, down along the river to the Red Sea (the ancient name for the Persian Gulf), around the Arabian peninsula, up to the Reed Sea, and back to his starting point in the Delta of the Nile.

34. What is the Copper Plaque?

The Copper Plaque was published by J. T. Milik in DJD 3, 199–302 (+ pls. XLVIII–LXXI). A bootlegged edition of it was also published by J. M. Allegro, *The Treasure of the Copper Scroll: The Opening and Decipherment of the Most Mysterious of the Dead Sea Scrolls, A Unique Inventory of Buried Treasure* (Garden City, NY: Doubleday, 1960).

Though often called the "Copper Scroll," it is not really a scroll at all. It was actually a plaque made of copper, which had been rolled up in two pieces so that at first sight it looked like two scrolls. But it must have been hung on a wall somewhere. It was clear that the copper plaque contained an inscription because some of the letters of the inscribed text showed on the reverse, and, indeed, a German scholar, Karl Georg Kuhn, had managed to determine the nature of the inscribed text. The copper on which the text had been written had become oxidized and quite brittle so that the plaque could not be unrolled. It had to be cut between the columns, which were discernible on the reverse, by a saw used to split pen nibs. When finally opened, the twelve columns of inscribed text listed sixty-four places where treasures were buried.

The text immediately created a problem: Did it record places where real treasure was buried? Was it the treasure of the Qumran community? Was it the treasure of the Jerusalem Temple, stored away by Zealots for safekeeping in view of the possible destruction of the Temple by the Romans? Was it the treasure for the Third Temple to be, which Bar Cochba would build, if his revolt were to succeed? Or was it merely a fiction about "buried treasure"? If so, why would one want to inscribe it on a plaque of copper? Yet there are other inscribed ancient examples of imaginary buried treasure troves.

Whatever its purpose or record, the text inscribed on this plaque is important for the study of the Hebrew language, since it has been written in a form of Hebrew intermediate between late postexilic biblical Hebrew (and even Qumran Hebrew) and the Hebrew of the Mishnah. The form of spelling and handwriting relates it to about A.D. 100. J. T. Milik, the official editor of the text, has dated it between A.D. 30–130. Though it was found in what is called today Cave 3, it is far from certain that it is related to the rest of the Qumran texts and fragments or had anything to do with the Qumran community. It contains no sectarian terminology and does not mention anyone or anything connected with that community. J. M. Allegro, believing that the list told of real buried treasure, mounted an expedition in December 1960 and January 1961 to dig in some of the desert spots easily identified in the text, but found nothing. If the text did indeed record real buried treasure, it has apparently all disappeared over the centuries.

35. What is the Temple Scroll?

The Temple Scroll of Cave 11 (11QTemple[a]) was published by Y. Yadin in a modern Hebrew edition, *Mgylt hmqdš: Hhdyr wṣyrp mbw' wpyrwš* (3 vols. with a supplement; Jerusalem: Israel Exploration Society, Archaeological Institute of the Hebrew University, Shrine of the Book, 1977); also in an English edition, *The Temple Scroll* (3 vols. with a supplement; Jerusalem [as above], 1983). There are also some frgs. of another copy of the text from Cave 11 (11QTemple[b]) as well as from Cave 4 (4QTemple[a]).

The Temple Scroll purports to be the community's Second Torah: perhaps the sealed book of the Law hidden until Zadok came (CD 5:2–5; 4Q177 1–4:14). It not only quotes many pentateuchal regulations, but often sharpens them and reformulates them in such wise as to make them more stringent and rigorous. Its demands for cultic purity, in particular, are very strict. The scroll frequently omits the name of Moses, where it appears in the MT, and casts the regulations into utterances of God himself, who speaks in the first person singular. For instance, Deut 21:5 prescribes, "The priests, the sons of Levi, shall come forward, since the Lord your God has chosen them to minister to him and to bless in the name of the Lord." In 11QTemple 63:3 this prescription becomes, "The priests, the sons of Levi, shall come forward, since I have chosen them to minister before me and to bless in my name."

Mainly because of this Yadin was led to think that the community regarded this scroll as Scripture. For other scholars 11QTemple is a supplement to Deuteronomy, as Deuteronomy itself was to the rest of the Pentateuch. Recently Michael O. Wise has concluded that this scroll was intended to replace Deuteronomy 12–26, the biblical "law of the land," emphasizing not "the place," but the role that the *miqdāš*, "the sanctuary" or "the Temple," was to play in the eschaton.

The way in which the Temple is to be reconstructed (see 1 Chr 28:19) is given great attention, whence the title given to the text. It was to be built in three square concentric courts with three gates in each wall, each bearing the name of a tribe of Israel. There were also to be booths in the outer walls for the levitical priests who would be on duty in their courses. But there is also a section that lays down strict regulations for the king, who is forbidden both polygamy and divorce. Yet what is laid down for the king is also prescribed for the commoner.

It seems that the Temple Scroll is a composite of four source-documents: a Deuteronomy source, i.e. an independent writing based on the canonical book of Deuteronomy; a Temple source, which gives the details about how the Temple was to be constructed, a text related to the Aramaic descriptions of the New Jerusalem, known from several Qumran caves; a Midrash to Deuteronomy source, i.e. an interpretation of parts of the book of Deuteronomy that reads like a political treatise; and the Feast Day Calendar source, i.e. a listing of feast days and details for their celebration, perhaps meant to replace Deuteronomy 16 and adding some new festivals. The four sources have been carefully combined into a redactional unity and thus make the whole document a law for the community.

It seems to have been composed ca. 150 B.C. and may reveal that the Teacher of Righteousness, known from other QS, had been one of the priestly elite attached to the Temple and involved in the regulations about periodic three-day pilgrimages made to Jerusalem (see 1 Macc 10:34-35). The purpose of the scroll was to be a New Deuteronomy, a law for the remnant of Israel during an earthly eschaton, until God would usher in "the day of creation" (29:9). As Yadin himself insisted, it seems to be a document related to the community described in part of the Damascus Document, especially to ms. B of the Cairo form of the text, cols. 19-20. An important analysis of this scroll has been written by M. O. Wise, *A Critical Study of the Temple Scroll from Qumran Cave 11* (Studies in Ancient Oriental Civilization 49; Chicago, IL: Oriental Institute of the University of Chicago, 1990).

36. What is the Psalms Scroll of Cave 11?

The Psalms Scroll (11QPs^a) was part of the cache retrieved by the Bedouins in 1956 and bought from them (for about £48,000) by the Palestine Archaeological Museum, where it was kept in a safe until 1961, when the American School of Oriental Research through its director, Paul W. Lapp, and its president, Henry A. Detweiler, was able to get funds (£25,000) from the foundation of Kenneth K. and Elizabeth Hay Bechtel to secure the rights from the Jordanian government to publish this text. The American School entrusted it to James A. Sanders for publication: *The Psalms Scroll of Qumrân Cave 11 (11QPs^a)* (DJD 4; Oxford: Clarendon, 1965). He also published another book on it, *The Dead Sea Psalms Scroll* (Ithaca, NY: Cornell University, 1967).

This scroll is a remarkable document, containing the text of a number of canonical psalms along with others that are preserved only in a Greek or Syriac translation. The canonical psalms are given in the following order, along with various added inserts: Ps 101:1-8; 102:1-2, 18-29; 103:1; 109:21-31; 105:25-45; 146:9-10; 148:1-12; 121:1-8; 122:1-9; 123:1-2; 124:7-8; 125:1-5; 126:1-6; 127:1; 128:4-6; 129:1-8; 130:1-8; 131:1; 132:8-18; 119:1-6, 15-28, 37-49, 59-73, 82-96, 105-20, 128-42, 150-64, 171-76; 135:1-9, 17-21; 136:1-16, 26b; 118:1, 15, 16, 8, 9, 29; 145:1-7, 13-21+?; Syriac Ps II; a nonbiblical Plea for Deliverance; Ps 139:8-14; 137:1, 9; 138:1-8; Sir 51:13-20b, 30; a nonbiblical Apostrophe to Zion; Ps 93:1-3; 141:5-10; 133:1-3; 144:1-7, 15;

Syriac Ps III; Ps 142:4-8; 143:1-8; 149:7-9; 150:1-6; a nonbiblical Hymn to the Creator; 2 Sam 23:7; a nonbiblical text listing David's Compositions; Ps 140:1-5; 134:1-3; 151A,B (=Syriac Ps I).

This fragmentary text is written in the late Herodian hand and dated to the first half of the first century A.D. It preserves the Hebrew text of Psalm 151, known from the LXX and also known as Syriac Psalm I, and the Hebrew text of Syriac Psalms II and III. Whether this scroll represents the form of the psalter as known in the Qumran community or is rather a sort of prayer book that has reordered the canonical psalms for some liturgical purpose is difficult to say. The latter is more likely.

The important prose insert about David's Compositions (27:2-11) tells of his having composed "3,600 psalms, and songs to sing before the altar at the whole-burnt *tamid* offering every day, for all the days of the year, 364; for the *qorban* of the sabbaths, 52 songs; for the *qorban* of the New Moons, for all the Feast Days, and for the Day of Atonement, 30 songs. All the songs that he uttered were 446, and songs for making music over the stricken, 4. The total was 4,050." In 1 Kgs 5:12 it is recorded that Solomon uttered 3000 proverbs, and his songs numbered 1005. So, according to this text, David surpassed Solomon in the number of songs and hymns that he composed. Moreover, the text gives evidence of the special calendar used by the community; see § 60 below.

37. What is the Targum of Job of Cave 11?

The Targum of Job of Cave 11 (11QtgJob) was published by J. P. M. van der Ploeg and A. S. van der Woude, *Le targum de Job de la grotte xi de Qumrân* (Koninklijke Nederlandse Akademie van Wetenschappen; Leiden: Brill, 1971).

This fragmentary text is written in Herodian script and probably dates from the last half of the first century B.C. It contains a targum, an Aramaic translation, of about a sixth of the Hebrew text of the book of Job, roughly from 17:14 to 42:11 with lacunae; the best preserved part corresponds to the Hebrew text of Job 37:10-42:11. The Aramaic in which it is written seems to be older than that of the Genesis Apocryphon of Cave 1 and closer to that of Daniel. It is a good example of an early pre-Christian targum, which shows that written targums did exist in this period despite the prohibition of them recorded in rabbinic writings of a later date (*m. Yadaim* 4:5; *b. Shabbat* 115a). Moreover, this targum is a quite literal rendering of the Hebrew of Job and differs considerably from the later Targum of Job, which was known before the discovery of the QS (see P. de Lagarde, *Hagiographa chaldaice* [Leipzig: Teubner, 1873; repr. Osnabrück: Zeller, 1967] 85–118). This early Aramaic translation of Job may be the version to which a note in the Greek appendix of the LXX of Job (42:17b) refers, when it records, "This is translated from the Syriac book" (*ek tēs Syriakēs biblou*).

38. How have the QS aided the study of the text of the OT?

Before the discovery of the DSS the oldest Hebrew copy of the whole OT was the so-called Ben Asher text found in Codex B 19A of the Public Library of Leningrad and dated to A.D. 1008, which was used by P. Kahle in the third edition of Kittel's *Biblia Hebraica* of 1937, and often reprinted. Since the Qumran biblical documents yield a form of the Hebrew OT at least a thousand years older than such a codex, their testimony to the text of the OT is precious. Here we must also include the biblical texts retrieved from Wadi Murabba'at, Naḥal Ḥever, and Masada. All together, these documents date from the middle of the third century B.C. to the beginning of the second century A.D. and reveal how the OT texts were being copied in the Palestine of those centuries. For the biblical texts copied specifically at Qumran, their dates would be roughly 150 B.C. to A.D. 68, dates that are confirmed by pottery and other artifacts found in the caves related to Khirbet Qumran. The *terminus ad quem* for the Masada texts would be A.D. 74; for Naḥal Ḥever and Murabba'at, A.D. 132–35 (the Bar-Cochba revolt).

On the one hand, these biblical texts have often merely confirmed the readings of the medieval Masoretic Text, the commonly used Hebrew text of modern critical editions of the OT. There are, of course, many spelling differences. *Scriptio plena,* "full writing" (i.e. with an abundant use of consonants as vowel letters) outstrips the *scriptio defectiva,* "defective writing," especially in the QS, but this is really insignificant. On the other hand, the Qumran biblical texts have presented forms of some OT books that differ from the MT. In such cases, they may agree with the differences found either in the Samaritan Pentateuch or in the Greek OT, the Septuagint. This is especially important in the latter case, since such Qumran texts now reveal that the LXX was not a careless translation of the Hebrew or a deliberate changing of it, as some once thought, but actually a careful translation of a different Hebrew form or recension of certain books. This is particularly important for the book of Jeremiah, which in its LXX form is roughly one eighth shorter than the MT; and a short Hebrew form related to the LXX is now attested in 4QJer[b]. A form of the Hebrew text of 1–2 Samuel related to that of the LXX has also been found in 4QSam[a] and 4QSam[b].

Most of the Qumran biblical texts were written in the scripts of the customary square characters, sometimes called the "Assyrian script" or the "Aramaic script," but Caves 1, 2, 4, 6, and 11 have yielded OT texts copied in the paleo-Hebrew script, a script that imitated ancient Phoenician writing. Most were copied on skin, but papyrus biblical texts were retrieved from caves 1, 4, 6, and 9 (if 9Q1 is indeed a fragment of a biblical text). In one case (4QNum[b]) certain verses have been written in red ink (20:22–23; 22:21; 23:13; 23:27; 31:25,28,48; 32:25; 33:1); the significance of this has not yet been determined.

Textual critics debate among themselves how best to characterize the differing text-traditions represented by the Qumran biblical documents. The American scholars, W. F. Albright and F. M. Cross, have distinguished local texts: the proto-Masoretic type of text stemming from Babylon, the Septuagintal type stemming from Egypt, and the proto-Samaritan type stemming from Palestine. But Israeli scholar, S. Talmon, rejects the geographical designations and relates the types to varying religio-sociological backgrounds. Still others, like the Israeli E. Tov, prefer not to speak of text-types or recensions, but only of independent unaffiliated texts.

In any case, the most important Qumran OT texts are the copies of Isaiah from Cave 1 and those from Cave 4 of the following books: Exodus, Samuel, Jeremiah, and Daniel. These texts from Cave 4 are the books that manifest the most striking and important textual variants.

39. What do the QS contribute to our understanding of apocalyptic literature?

The Qumran sect has often been called "an apocalyptic community" (F. M. Cross, *Ancient Library of Qumran,* 78). This term is explained by Cross as "a *Heilsgemeinschaft* [community seeking salvation], imitating the ancient desert sojourn of Mosaic times in anticipation of the dawning Kingdom of God. They are priestly apocalyptists, not true ascetics" (ibid.). But, though the explanation offered characterizes well the Qumran community, it may be queried whether the appellation "apocalyptic" is correct. Other scholars such as H. Stegemann and J. Carmignac have protested against such a use of the term. Part of the problem stems from the way the adjective "apocalyptic" is used.

Apocalyptic literature is a peculiarly Jewish form of writing. Examples of it are already found in the OT itself, especially in post-exilic writings, e.g. Isaiah 24–27, 34–35, 56–66; Joel; Zechariah 9–14; Daniel 7–12. It is a literary form that emerged from OT prophecy, and it is often said that, when prophecy died out, apocalyptic took over.

Derived from Greek *apokalypsis,* "revelation, disclosure," the name "apocalyptic" denotes a type of literature that arose in the time of Israel's struggles with occupying powers. It is thus a form of persecution literature, which sought to assure its readers that God was still in control of human history and that despite the setbacks experienced by his people his dominion would win out in the end.

It is literature concerned with the eschaton. "Eschatological," however, does not designate the same thing as apocalyptic, for it describes rather the details of the end-time; it denotes content, a teaching that affirms end-time realities, whereas "apocalyptic" denotes rather the form in which that eschatological teaching can be cast. Mixed in with this Jewish apocalyptic tradition are elements derived from Greek mythology and Iranian dualism. So even though it is a peculiarly Jewish form of writing and thinking, it has borrowed foreign motifs.

Apocalyptic writing is highly symbolic, making use of distinctive stage-props such as visions of the end-time, ecstasies and dreams, mythic struggles or cosmic battles, stars and other heavenly bodies, angelic warriors and interpreters, demons and chimaeric beasts, numbers, colors, strange animals, cryptic names, pseudonymous and dualistic expressions. It often alludes to contemporary historical events, but describes them in predictive form so that the account reads like what is going to happen. The present age is wicked and under the control of the devil and its demons, but God and his transcendental rule will prevail. The task of apocalyptic writing was intended to reveal God's world-plan and to predict the end of this age and the breaking in of a coming age.

Such full-blown apocalyptic writing is not found in the QS, but some traces of it occur. The dualism expressed in the Manual of Discipline in its teaching about the two spirits may be distinctive of this group of Jews, but there is little in it of the usual apocalyptic stage-props (see § 54). The text that is most apocalyptic is the War Scroll (see § 30 above). Though the author of this scroll has drawn upon contemporary Roman military practices, the holy war, in which God will do battle with his angels on the side of the sons of light (= the Qumran community) actually becomes a description of an eschatological battle that the Qumran community believes it will engage in. They will be the forces of good to wage that war against the forces of evil. The community's banners, trumpets, and shields are inscribed with slogans, mottoes, and prayers, and the whole battle is to be conducted as a semiliturgical act under the guidance of the high priest. The angels, Michael, Raphael, and Sariel lead the forces of the sons of light against Belial and the Kittim (= the Romans). Many of the standard apocalyptic stage-props are used in this text, but it contains none of the apocalyptic visions such as one finds in Daniel 7–12, Zech 9:9–14:21 or *1 Enoch* 1:1–36:6; 83:1–90:42.

Traces of apocalyptic may be found in other Qumran writings, especially in the pesharim, for there the community expresses its belief that it was already living in the end-time; perhaps too in the Manual of Discipline where its belief is expressed in the coming of three figures, a prophet like Moses and the Messiahs of Aaron and Israel (see § 45 below). But this is properly speaking an eschatological conviction, and may not be "apocalyptic" in the true sense. Yet such a conviction enabled the community itself to think apocalyptically and formulate that conviction in the apocalyptic stage-props used in the War Scroll.

In any case, there is no reason to regard the Qumran community as "apocalyptic."

40. What light do the QS shed on ancient forms of the Hebrew or Aramaic languages?

In general, the biblical texts of Qumran merely reflect the ancient Hebrew or Aramaic of the OT itself, despite the fuller form of writing that they display. Some of the biblical texts with their variant readings preserve forms of Hebrew words that are of great interest to the Semitic philologian. But the nonbiblical texts have brought to light forms of both these languages that were previously unknown.

Many of the nonbiblical texts are written in a form of postbiblical Hebrew that mediates between the late postexilic Hebrew writings of the OT and the Hebrew of the Mishnah. Since the latter is a very distinct form of the language, differing considerably from biblical Hebrew, it is good to have Qumran Hebrew texts that date from a period after the last books of the OT were composed and before that of the Mishnah, which was set in writing sometime about the beginning of the third century A.D. The kind of Hebrew in which the Qumran texts are written was not wholly unknown, because there were a few inscriptions on ossuaries and tombs that date from roughly the same period. But now the corpus of such postbiblical Hebrew writings has been greatly increased, so that E. Qimron could devote a small book to the study of it, *The Hebrew of the Dead Sea Scrolls* (HSS 29; Atlanta, GA: Scholars 1986).

The same can be said for Qumran Aramaic texts. By and large, these texts are not sectarian, and there is little reason to think that most of them were composed by members of the Qumran community itself, though one or other may have been. Since Hebrew is used for most of the sectarian writings (the rule books, the War Scroll, the Thanksgiving Psalms, the prayer-books), one has the impression that the Qumran community tried to insist on the use of this traditional and sacred language. By contrast, most of the Aramaic texts seem to have been "imported texts," documents composed elsewhere in Judea and brought to Qumran for reading, study, and meditation. Among these would be the Genesis Apocryphon, the Books of Enoch, the Targum of Job, the Testament of Levi, etc. The number of such Aramaic texts does not surpass that of the Hebrew texts, but it is sufficient to put to rest the famous question once raised whether there was any real creative Aramaic literary composition in Judea between the final redaction of the book of Daniel (about 165 B.C.) and the beginning of the Aramaic texts of the rabbinic tradition, *Měgillat Ta'ănît,* "Scroll of Fasting" (usually dated about A.D. 100).

The Qumran literature in Aramaic now forms a corpus of Palestinian texts along with Nabatean, Palmyrene, Hatran, and the Old Syriac inscriptions. They constitute an important phase in the development of the Aramaic language. This phase is usually called Middle Aramaic (used roughly from 200 B.C. to A.D. 300) and is regarded as a development from the earlier Imperial or Official Aramaic (used from 700 to 200 B.C.), to which the Aramaic parts of the OT belong. Our knowledge of the corpus of ancient Aramaic literature has grown tremendously in the twentieth century; most of what is now known as belonging to it was unknown prior to 1910. Hence the Aramaic QS have made a significant contribution to the study of Middle Aramaic, an important phase of this language.

41. What light do the QS shed on ancient Judaism?

The QS have brought to light a vast amount of detailed information about a form of Judaism that was previously little known. Whether the identification of the Qumran community with the Essenes is correct or not (see § 65–67 below), all sorts of information about a distinctive group of Jewish people in the last two centuries B.C. and the first century A.D. have been retrieved in the QS.

The information garnered from these scrolls describes the way of life of ancient Jews who lived in common, held their fortunes in common, ate in common, prayed in common, and worked in common. We have recovered first-hand documents related to such a mode of life: the rule books, the prayer books, the literature of such ancient Jewish people.

More important, we have learned that Judaism of these early centuries was far from monolithic. Before the DSS were discovered, there was no information about Palestinian Judaism of these centuries apart from what the books of the Maccabees and the writings of Flavius Josephus had passed on. Consequently, there was the tendency to extrapolate from the writings of Philo of Alexandria (in Egypt) and above all from the rabbinical literature of the third and fourth centuries.

The heart of rabbinic literature is the Mishnah, but Jewish tradition itself acknowledges that its source, the oral tradition passed down by the Pharisees, was codified under Rabbi Judah the Prince only about A.D. 200. When it was put in writing is unknown, but it was scarcely earlier than the third century A.D. Even though it quotes earlier rabbis and was the outgrowth of earlier Pharisaism, i.e. of one form of Judaism, there was the tendency to regard it as "normative" even in the first centuries B.C. or A.D. That rabbinic tradition did not stop with the Mishnah. In time, the Gemara was added and the two came to form the Talmud. But the Gemara was of two forms, one Palestinian (usually dated about A.D. 450), the other Babylonian (usually dated about A.D. 500–550). The latter was the more important of the two. Yet both Talmuds were used as the sources for this so-called normative Judaism of the first century.

Josephus had written about three kinds of Jewish "philosophy" in his day (*J.W.* 2.8.2 § 119): about Pharisees, Sadducees, and Essenes. He, in fact, described the last group in greater detail than the others. But since very little was known about any of them from direct sources, the diversity of which Josephus spoke was often forgotten and later rabbinic material was often used and predicated of the first century, usually without proper distinctions. This mode of extrapolation still goes on, unfortunately, even after the discovery of the DSS. A good example of it, produced by modern Jewish scholars, is found in volume 1 of the series Compendia rerum iudaicarum ad Novum Testamentum, entitled *The Jewish People in the First Century: Historical Geography, Political History, Social, Cultural and Religious Life and Institutions* (ed. S. Safrai and M. Stern; Assen: Van Gorcum; Philadelphia, PA: Fortress, 1974). In chap. 1 the "Hebrew and Aramaic sources" for this study of first-century Judaism are given as the Mishnah, Baraita and Tosephta, Talmud, and Midrashim. Moreover, they are explicitly described as "sources" coming "from the period of the Second Temple until the end of the Talmudic period" (p. 1). But there is no excuse for such careless extrapolation today, when the evidence from the QS is abundant, and newer and more accurate studies have now been made of the rabbinic tradition itself. The Qumran tradition, being older, differs at times from the later rabbinic tradition, not in all matters to be sure, but sufficiently to make one hesitate to use the later tradition as evidence for first-century Judaism. So, as a result of the discovery of the DSS, the diversity of pre-70 A.D. Judaism is apparent, and early Pharisaism was not the only kind of Judaism, and scarcely "normative." Indeed, we realize that what we read in the QS is no more "normative" of first-century Judaism than the Pharisaic branch.

42. Were the members of the Qumran community Torah-observant Jews?

They were indeed. The QS speak of the members of the community as *'ôśê hattôrāh,* "doers of the law," i.e. those who observe the Mosaic Law (1QpHab 7:11; 8:1; 12:5). Their purpose was "to separate from the congregation of the men of iniquity in order to become a community in law and in wealth, responsible to the sons of Zadok, the priests who keep the Covenant, and to the majority of the men of the community, who hold fast to the Covenant" (1QS 5:1-3). "Whoever comes to the council of the community shall enter the Covenant of God in the sight of all who have freely pledged themselves; he shall undertake with a binding oath to turn with all his heart and all his soul to the Law of Moses, according to all that He has commanded, and to all that has been revealed by Him to the sons of Zadok, the priests, who keep the Covenant and seek His good pleasure" (1QS 5:7-9). Indeed, the words of Isa 40:3, "prepare in the desert the way of. . . . [four dots instead of the tetragram]" are interpreted, "This is the study of the Law, which He commanded through Moses, that they may act according to all that has been revealed from age to age and as the prophets have revealed through His holy Spirit" (1QS 8:15-16). Indeed, it is prescribed that "wherever there are ten men, there shall not lack one who studies the Law continually, day and night, concerning the conduct of one with another. And the Many shall keep vigil in common for a third of every night in the year, to read the Book, to study the Law, and to bless in common" (1QS 6:6-8). Similarly, the Damascus Document quotes the words of Num 21:18, *"The well that the princes sank, that the nobles of the people dug with a staff,"* and comments on it: "The 'well' is the Law, and 'those who sank it' are the returnees of Israel, who went forth from the land of Judah and sojourned in the land of Damascus. God called them all 'princes,' because they sought him, and their renown was not questioned by anyone" (CD 6:4-7). Again, "They shall indeed take care to act according to the exact interpretation of the Law during the age of wickedness and to separate from the sons of the Pit" (6:14-15).

But the community seemed not to be satisfied with only the Law of Moses, because they had another book, called *sēper hehŏgî,* a name whose translation is not certain, perhaps "the Book of Meditation" (1QSa 1:7; CD 10:6; 13:2). Just what this book was is not certain either, but Y. Yadin, who published the Temple Scroll, has plausibly suggested that it may well have been the book in question. For the Temple Scroll, despite its modern title, was a sort of Second Torah or New Deuteronomy for the community. See § 35 above. So if this text served the community as another form of Scripture, it reveals that this Qumran community was indeed a group of Torah-observant Jews.

43. How do the authors of the QS conceive of God?

The authors who have written the QS are Jews to the hilt; so they express their reverence and respect for "the God of Israel" (1QS 3:24), the God of their ancestors, Yahweh of the OT. In line with the general trend of postexilic Judaism they regarded Yahweh as the exalted and transcendent creator of all. The community sang its praise of God in its prayers and hymns: "Blest are You, my God, who opens the heart of Your servant unto knowledge" (1QS 11:15-16). "Who is like unto You in the he[ave]ns and on earth, O God of Israel, who does such great deeds as You, who possesses such mighty power as Yours?" (1QM 10:8-9). "Who can comprehend your glory?" (1QS 11:20). "As for You, O God of our fathers, we bless Your name for ever!" (1QM 13:7).

In the Psalms Scroll of Cave 11, which was a sort of prayer book of the community, the sectarians sang to God with many of the psalms of the canonical psalter. But it also includes an additional "Hymn to the Creator," which uses some phrases from Jer 10:12-13 and Ps 135:7:

Great and holy is Yahweh,
   the holiest unto every generation.
Majesty goes before Him,
   and following Him the swarm of many waters.
Grace and fidelity surround His presence;
   fidelity, justice, and righteousness are the foundation
      of His throne.
He has separated light from deep darkness;
   He established the dawn with the knowledge
      of His heart.
Then all His angels saw (it) and sang aloud,
   for He has made them see what they did not know:
He crowns mountains with fruit,
   good food for every living being.
Blest be He who makes the earth by His power,
   who establishes the world by His wisdom.
By His understanding He has stretched out
   the heavens,
  and caused the [wind] to go forth from its
   sto[rehouses].
He has made [lightning for the ra]in,
   and caused mist[s] to rise [from] the end
      [of the earth].

                  (11QPs^a 26:9–15)

The Qumran community, like other Jews, considered themselves to be God's chosen people: "Who is like Your people, Israel, which You have chosen for Yourself from all the peoples of the lands, a people of holy ones of the Covenant, schooled in (Your) law and learned in insi[ght   ], who hearken to the voice of the Honored One" (1QM 10:9–10). It repeated the dictum of Deut 14:2, "You are a people holy to your God," as the guide of its conduct (11QTemple 48:7, 10). The opening sentence of its rule book states its purpose: "To seek God with (one's) heart and all (one's) soul, to do what is good and right before him, as he commanded through Moses and all His servants the prophets, to love all that He has chosen and to hate all that He has rejected" (1QS 1:1–4).

But the Qumran community considered that God had made a

special pact with it, in virtue of which it withdrew from contact and intercourse with other Jews, considering them all "sons of darkness." "All who embrace the rule of the community shall enter the Covenant before God to act according to all that He has commanded and not to turn from Him because of any fear, dread, or temptation that may com[e to pa]ss during the dominion of Belial" (1QS 1:16-18). Indeed, they considered themselves those who "entered the New Covenant in the land of Damascus" (CD 6:19; 8:21; 19:34; 20:12; cf. 1QpHab 2:3), thus those who embodied the pact that the prophet Jeremiah foretold (31:31). Accordingly, they interpreted the words of the prophet Habakkuk to be verified in their communal existence, understanding Hab 2:3 to refer to themselves as "men of fidelity, the doers of the Law whose hands do not become slack in the service of the truth . . . , the doers of the Law in the house of Judah, whom God will rescue from the house of judgment because of their striving and their fidelity to the Teacher of Righteousness" (1QpHab 7:10–8:3).

In a special way the authors of the QS manifest their reverence for the God whom they serve by the way they wrote his name. Normally, the archaic name *'El,* "God" (lit. "the Mighty One") is used (1QS 1:2, 7, 8; 1QpHab 1:11; 2:3, 4, 8, 9; 4QTestim [4Q175] 10; 4QpPsa [4Q171] 1,3-4 iii 16), written in paleo-Hebrew script (4QAgesCreat [4Q180] 1:1; 4Q183 1 ii 3; 1QpMic [1Q14] 12:3, even in the midst of a pesher), and even as a form of address, *'Elî,* "my God" (1QS 11:15; 1QH 2:34; 5:11, 14, 18; 11:3, 15). Sometimes *'El* is substituted for the sacred name of the Deity, the tetragram, e.g. in an OT quotation or allusion (CD 3:8, alluding to Ps 106:40). It is combined sometimes with various epithets, such as *'El 'elyôn,* "God Most High" (1QH 4:31; 6:33); *'El 'ēlîm,* "God of gods" (1QM 14:16); *'El Yiśrā'ēl,* "God of Israel" (1QS 3:24), *'El haddē'ôt,* "the God of knowledge" (1QS 3:15; 1QH 1:26; frg. 4:15), or *'El yĕšû'ôt,* "the God of salvific deeds" (1QS 1:19), or *'El qannā'* "a jealous God" (11QTemple 2:12).

The usual OT name *'Elôhîm* is used less frequently (1QS 8:14; 1QM 10:4,7; 4Q158 1-2: 18; 4Q185 1-2 i 14; 1-2 iii 13; 11QTemple 57:8; 64:12); in the form *'Elôhê ṣĕbā'ôt* (1QSb 4:25). But *'Elôhîm* is sometimes substituted for the tetragram in quotations or allusions (1QM 10:7, quoting Num 10:9).

Sometimes *'Elyôn,* "the Most High," is used alone as a substitute for the name of "God" (1QS 4:22; 10:12; 11:15; CD 20:8), or in parallelism with *'El* (4QTestim [4Q175] 10, as in Num 24:16).

Another substitute is *šadday,* "the Almighty" (4QTestim [4Q175] 11, as in Num 24:16).

In the Thanksgiving Psalms, the name most frequently used is *'ădônāy,* "Lord" (1QH 2:20, 31; 3:19, 37; 4:5; 5:5, 20; 7:6, 28, 34; 10:14; 11:33; 14:8, 23; 16:8) and less frequently simply *'ādôn* (1QH 10:8; 1QSb 5:8; 1Q14 14:1). *'Adônāy* also occurs elsewhere (1QM 12:8, 18; 1QSb 2:22; 3:1; 5:23). It is used as a substitute for the tetragram in 1QH 7:28, where Exod 15:11 is imitated, and the two names are often substituted in 1QIsaᵃ (e.g. 3:20–25, equalling Isa 3:15–18).

The tetragram *Yhwh,* which seems to be called "the name of the Glorified One" (1QS 6:27), is used more frequently than one would expect (e.g. 4Q158 1-2:16,18; 4:8; 7-8:3; 4QFlor [4Q174] 1-2 i 3; 21:1; 11QTemple 21:3, 8, 10, 16; 22:14, 16); sometimes it is written in paleo-Hebrew characters, when the text is otherwise in square characters (1QpHab 6:14; 10:7,14; 11:10; 1QpMic [1Q14] 1-5:1, 2; 4QpPsᵃ 1-2 ii 4, 12, 24; 11QPsᵃ 2:2, 4, 6, 11; 3:2, 4, 5, 8, 10, 13, etc.; even in the non-canonical additions, 26:9 [see above]; 19: 4, 6, 7, 11, 13, 16). In a few instances the name is written simply as *Yah* (11QTemple 14:1, 2, thus providing a variant of Ps 135:1-3).

Occasionally, four dots are substituted for the tetragram (1QS 8:14, quoting Isa 40:3); it is even used in the Isaiah Scroll A of Cave 1 (33:7, in a supplement added above the line to Isa 40:7; 4QSamᶜ 1:3, equalling 1 Sam 25:31; 3:7, equalling 2 Sam 15:8; 4QTestim [4Q175] 1, 19, equalling Exod 20:21b [in its Samaritan expansion] and Deut 33:11; and in 4QTanḥ [4Q176] 1-2 i 6, 7, 9, quoting Isa 40:1-5; 1-2 ii 3, quoting Isa 49:14; 8-11:6, 8, 10, quoting Isa 54:5, 6, 8 and adding the tetragram once where it does not exist in the MT).

A peculiar Qumran practice was the writing of the tetragram in square characters, but in red ink, in fragments as yet unpublished from Caves 4 and 11, but reported in *RB* 63 (1956) 56. Also peculiar is the Qumran substitute for the tetragram, *hw'h',* which seems to be a combination of the third personal masculine pronoun *hû'* and the first two letters of *hā'ĕlôhîm* (1QS 8:13).

Other epithets are used for God, such as *qādôš, 'ădônāy ûmelek hakkābôd,* "the Holy One, the Lord and King of Glory" (1QM 12:8; cf. 1QM 19:1).

A Greek text of Leviticus from Cave 4 even has the tetragram represented as *Iaō* (4QLXXLev^b), a form of the name for the God of Israel that is known to the Greek writers Diodorus of Sicily (*Library of History* 1.94.2) and Origen (*Comm. in Ioan.* 1.1.7; GCS 4. 53).

These variant names for God in the Qumran texts not only reveal the reverence for God that the Qumran community had, but also show that the tendency not to read or pronounce the tetragram as *Yahwēh*, but as *'ădônāy* was well under way by the time these texts were copied. This reverence of Palestinian Jews in the last pre-Christian centuries was manifested in the writing of the tetragram in Hebrew script even in Greek translations of the OT, a practice that was gradually abandoned in preference of the Greek translation *Kyrios*. This became in time a Greek title for the God of Israel, but it was borrowed by early Jewish Christians for Jesus, as is evident in the NT. The use of *Kyrios* as a translation of *Yhwh* in manuscripts of the LXX was actually the work of the Christian scribes who were responsible for the great parchment copies of it (Sinaiticus, Vaticanus, Alexandrinus, etc.).

44. What do the QS tell us about how the people who wrote them understood time and history?

The community's view of world history was built on a conviction of God's predestination and a deterministic ordering by him of all things in the world that are moving inexorably toward a fixed end. Such a conviction pervades the Qumran literature. Thus the Damascus Document begins, "Now listen, all you who know righteousness {echoing Isa 51:7}, and scrutinize the deeds of God. For He has a dispute with all flesh and will exercise judgment over all who contemn Him. When they proved faithless and abandoned Him, He hid His face from Israel and from His sanctuary and handed them over to the sword. But when He recalls the Covenant of their forebears, He has left a remnant for Israel and has not handed them over to destruction" (1:1-5).

Again, the Qumran psalmist sings:

You have fashioned every spirit and [established thei]r deeds, and a Law for all their works. You have stretched

out the heavens for Your glory, appoin[ted] all [their hosts]
according to Your good pleasure, and the mighty winds
according to their laws. Before they became Your [holy]
angels and eternal spirits in their dominions: luminaries
for their mysteries, stars in [their] paths, [and all the storm
winds] for their tasks, meteors and lightnings for their service, and the providential treasures for their functions,
[and   ] for their mysteries. You have created the earth
by Your power, the seas and the deep [   ]. You have
established their [   ]by Your wisdom, and all that is in
them You have set up according to Your good pleasure.
[You have given them over to the governance] of the spirit
of man, which You have fashioned in the world for everlasting days and generations to come (1QH 1:8-16).

The first appendix to the Manual of Discipline even has a rule
to govern the doings of the community in the eschaton: "This is the
rule for the congregation of Israel at the end of days, when they are
gathered [together to wal]k according to the regulation of the sons
of Zadok, the priests, and the men of their Covenant, (in) which [they]
have turned [from walking along] the path of the people" (1QSa 1:1-3).

45. Did the Qumran community have a messianic expectation?

Yes, very definitely, for its sectarian writings speak of the awaited
coming of a prophet and Messiahs of Aaron and Israel:

They shall depart from no counsel of the Law to walk in
all the stubbornness of their hearts, but they shall be
governed by the primitive precepts in which the men of
the community were first instructed, until the coming of
a prophet and the Messiahs of Aaron and Israel (1QS 9:11).

Again, "until there arises the Messiah of Aaron and Israel" (CD 12:23);
"[until there arises the Messi]ah of Aaron and Israel, and he will
expiate their iniquity" (CD 14:19); "at the coming of the Messiah of

Aaron and Israel" (CD 19:10); "from the day of the gathering in of [erasures, then] the Teacher of the Community, until there arises a Messiah from Aaron and from Israel" (CD 20:1).

So the Qumran community lived in the expectation of the coming of a prophet, undoubtedly the one promised to Moses, "I shall raise up for them a prophet like you from among their kinsmen and shall put my words into his mouth" (Deut 18:18), and apparently two Messiahs, a priestly Anointed One and a Davidic, political Anointed One. The copy of the Manual of Discipline from Cave 1, dated palaeographically to about 100–75 B.C., clearly attests a pre-Christian messianic belief. Yet what seems to be a reference to two Messiahs sometimes is formulated in the singular as "the Messiah of Aaron and Israel." The latter is often found in the medieval copies of the Damascus Document.

This messianic belief has often been thought to be reflected in another Qumran text written by the same scribe, 4QTestimonia, a one-page text made up of four quotations: Exod 20:21 (in the proto-Samaritan pentateuchal tradition, which there combines Deut 5:28–29 with Deut 18:18–19, the promise of a prophet like Moses), Num 24:15–17 (Balaam's oracle about a star coming from Jacob and a scepter from Israel), Deut 33:8–11 (the blessing of Levi), and Josh 6:26 (with comments taken from the apocryphal "Psalms of Joshua," found in other texts of Cave 4). Thus it mentions a prophet like Moses, a star identified as a priest, the scepter as a Davidic royal Messiah, and a blessing of Levi.

There is also the difficult text of 1QSa 2:12, whose meaning is debated: "when (or if) [God] begets [t]he Messiah among them, [the priest], the head of the whole congregation of Israel, shall enter . . . ." Also 1QSa 2:14, "afterwards the [Mes]siah of Israel shall [take his seat], and then there will sit before him the heads of the Thou[sands of Israel, ea]ch according to his dignity"); 1QSa 2:20 ("afterwar[ds the Messiah of Israel [will ex]tend his hands to the bread"). These lines are all found in the so-called "Messianic Rule of the Congregation" in the end of days, in which the relation of "the priest" to the "Messiah of Israel" is not clear.

In 4QPBless 3 there is again mention of an expected Messiah, "until the coming of the Righteous Messiah, the sprout of David." The "sprout of David" is also mentioned in 4QFlor 1-2 i 11; 4QpIsa^a

8-10:17. In 1Q30 1:2 there is mention of a "[M]essiah of holiness," but the context is lost.

Other Qumran texts refer to a *māšîaḥ*, but the title is then attributed to historical figures or prophets regarded as God's "anointed one(s)." In 1QM 11:7, "through your Anointed Ones, who perceive the testimonies," where the title *māšîaḥ* seems to be used of prophets of old. In CD 2:12 we read, "He instructed them through His [agents] anointed with the Spirit of holiness and those who perceive his truth," probably anointed prophets of old. Similarly, in CD 6:1, "and also through his holy Anointed Ones; but they prophesied falsehood." 6QD (6Q15) 3:4, "[against the commandments of God (given) through Mos]es and also by the holy Anointed Ones," probably prophets of old.

Such texts make it clear that the Qumran community had definite messianic expectations. Moreover, these ideas emerged shortly after or about the same time as the emergence of the messianic expectation in Judaism itself. For though the title *māšîaḥ* was used in the OT of historical personages, its occurrence in the OT is relatively rare when used of a future, expected messiah. It is used of historical figures in the following places: (a) of Saul or generically of some king: 1 Sam 24:7bis, 11; 26:9, 11, 16, 23; 2 Sam 1:14, 16 (cf. 1 Sam 2:10, 35; 12:3, 5; 16:6; Ps 28:8); (b) of David: 2 Sam 19:22; 22:51; 23:1; Ps 2:2; 20:7; 84:10; 89:39, 52; 132:10, 17; 18:51; (c) of Solomon: 2 Chr 6:42; (d) of Zedekiah: Lam 4:20; (e) of the patriarchs: Ps 105:15; 1 Chr 16:22 (disputed reference); (f) of Cyrus, the Persian king: Isa 45:1; (g) of Israel as a whole(?): Hab 3:3; cf. Ps 28:8; (h) of priests: Lev 4:3, 5, 16; 6:15 (*hakkōhēn hammāšîaḥ*); (i) perhaps of the prophets: Ps 105:15; 1 Chr 16:22 (disputed reference).

In passages where *māšîaḥ* is used of David and his dynasty (1 Sam 2:10, 35; Ps 132:7), one begins to detect a future connotation. But here it is still a far cry from a title for a future, expected Messiah. These passages express a guarantee of the future of David's dynasty. In time, however, an expectation is detected in the promise of a future David: Whereas Jer 36:30 speaks of "no descendant of him {Jehoiakim} to sit upon David's throne," Jer 30:9 promises that the people of Israel "will serve the Lord, their God, and David, their king, whom I shall raise up for them" (see also Ezek 34:23; 37:24). In such passages about a future David, one sees the beginning of the messianic expectation being formulated in terms of a person, but that David is not yet called *māšîaḥ*.

The future sense of that title emerges for the first and only time in Dan 9:25-26: *'ad māšîaḥ nāgîd šābū'îm šib'āh,* "seventy weeks until an anointed one, a prince . . ."; and *yikkārēt māšîaḥ,* "(the) anointed one shall be cut off." And this in a book that received its final redaction only about 165 B.C. By now one could translate these two instances as "Messiah" (with a capital M). It is significant, then, that the Qumran community's expectation of (two) Messiahs emerges either along with this or shortly afterwards. In any case, there is nothing in the QS about a unique Messiah who is to play a role in the realization of salvation, such as the NT ascribes to Jesus the Messiah.

46. Who was the Teacher of Righteousness?

Môreh haṣṣedeq, "the Teacher of Righteousness," is identified in the QS as a priest (*hakkôhēn,* 4QpPsª 1,3-4 iii 15; 1QpHab 2:8), presumably a member of the Zadokite line, one whom God raised up to guide the groping community in its early days (CD 1:11). The community regarded him as one whom God endowed with a special understanding of Scripture, especially of "the words of his servants, the prophets" (1QpHab 7:5). Sometimes he is called *môreh hayyaḥad,* "teacher of the community" (CD 20:1), or simply "the Teacher" (CD 20:28; cf. 20:32; cf. 1QpMic [1Q14] 8-10:4). He is never named, but details about him are given in 1QpHab 1:13; 2:2; 5:10; 7:4; 8:3; 9:9-10; 11:5, so that he must have been a historical figure, even though we cannot yet identify him. He is often regarded as the author of those Thanksgiving Psalms of Cave 1 that are formulated in the first singular and refer figuratively to trials and troubles.

According to B. Z. Wacholder, the Teacher of Righteousness was Zadok, a pupil of Antigonus of Socho. This Zadok lived toward the end of the third century B.C. and was a companion of Baytus, who is mentioned with him in later Talmudic and Qaraite sources, especially in the *Abot de-Rabbi Natan.* This Zadok would have composed ca. 200 B.C. the Temple Scroll, which Wacholder calls 11QTorah. Later, Zadok "discovered" this text and its specific teachings, and it became what the Damascus Document refers to as "the sealed book of the

Law" (5:2). It also becomes the text on which all the other sectarian DSS depend, especially CD, 1QS, 1QM, and even *Jubilees,* thus claimed to be of Qumran origin (*Dawn of Qumran,* 96, 119, 141–48). This is an intriguing suggestion, but one encumbered with too many problems to be convincing. I know of no one who agrees with Wacholder's thesis.

47. Did the Qumran community believe that its Teacher of Righteousness was a Messiah?

There is no text that so identifies the Teacher of Righteousness. The QS that mention him tell us that he was persecuted by *hakkôhēn hārāšā',* "the Wicked Priest," who is probably to be identified with Jonathan Maccabee, who reigned ca. 162–142 B.C. and usurped the high priesthood (cf. 1QpHab 8:16; 9:9; 11:12; 12:2, 8).

The title *ṣemaḥ dāwîd,* "Sprout of David," is predicated of a figure called *mĕšîaḥ haṣṣedeq,* "the Messiah of Righteousness," in 4QPBless 3. It is also predicated of some successor on the Davidic throne (according to 2 Sam 7:11–14, paraphrased): "I will be to him a father, and he will be my son. He is the Sprout of David, who is to arise with the Interpreter of the Law who [   ] in Zi[on at the e]nd of days" (4QFlor [4Q174] 1-2 i 11–12). The *dôrēš hattôrāh,* "Interpreter of the Law," is also mentioned cryptically in CD 6:7 and identified with the coming "star" of Balaam's Oracle (Num 24:17) in CD 7:18. In some way, these are allusions to expected future figures, even messianic figures, but there is no text that simply equates the Teacher of Righteousness with any of these personages. So one cannot simply identify either the "Sprout of David" or the "Interpreter of the Law" with the Teacher of Righteousness. The Teacher was a historic figure, not an expected future leader.

48. Did the community think that the Teacher of Righteousness had been put to death?

That is not impossible, for the Wicked Priest "pursued the Teacher of Righteousness to devour him in his venomous wrath, even to the house of his exile and at a time appointed for rest. On the Day of Atonement, he appeared before them to devour them and to make them stumble on the Day of Fasting, their sabbath of repose" (1QpHab 11:5–8). Does the verb "devour" mean that the Wicked Priest "killed" the Teacher of Righteousness? It has been so understood. But then it is also used of the community as a whole in the latter part of the quotation, and so its sense is not clear.

Another reference to the Wicked Priest speaks of him as one "who s[pie]s upon the right[eous one and seeks] to kill him . . . but God will not aban[don him] and will not [do him evil wh]en he is judged" (4QpPs^a 3-10 iv 8–9). Here *ḥṣd[yq]*, lit. "the righteous (one)," could mean the "Teacher of Righteousness," but it does not necessarily mean that, and even Allegro, who published the text, footnoted the term with a reference to CD 1:20, which speaks generically of enemies banding together "against the life of the righteous (one)," which may simply be a collective singular referring to the community as a whole.

Moreover, if such texts mean that the Teacher was indeed put to death, how is one to interpret 4QpPs^a 1-2 ii 17–19, which speaks of "evil persons of Ephraim and Manasseh who seek to lay hands on the priest and on the men of his counsel at the time of trial that is coming upon them; but God will deliver them from their hand." Such references seem to refer to some persecution, but they are cryptic and tantalizing; they are not clear enough so that one can say definitely how or when the Teacher of Righteousness might have died.

It is also questionable whether this Teacher is the same as *něśî' hā'ēdāh*, "the prince of the congregation," or *něśî' kôl hā'ēdāh*, "the prince of the whole congregation." These variant titles occur in 1QSb 5:20; 4QpIsa^a (4Q161) 5-6:2; 1QM 5:1; CD 7:20. Conceivably they could refer to the Teacher of Righteousness, but more likely they refer to a community leader of a later date. See also the ambiguous text discussed in § 97.

49. Does any Qumran text mention crucifixion?

Certainly not of the Teacher of Righteousness, as Dupont-Sommer once alleged (see § 98 below). But there may be mention of crucifixion in two texts. One of them has been known for a long time, the Pesher on Nahum from Cave 4; the other came to light when the Temple Scroll of Cave 11 was published in 1977.

The relevant passage in 4QpNah (4Q169) quotes Nah 2:12–14, in which the prophet describes in poetic fashion the plundering of the treasures of Nineveh and the terror caused for its Assyrian inhabitants as a result of the attitude that the Lord assumed toward that rapacious city, when it fell in 612 B.C. The author of the Qumran pesher applies the prophet's words to the time of Judea in which he lived. The text of 3-4 i 6–12 reads:

> [and *he fills with prey*] *his cave and his dens with torn flesh*. The interpretation of it concerns the Lion of Wrath [who has found a crime punishable by] death in the Seekers after Smooth Things, whom he hangs alive [on the tree, as it was thus done] in Israel from of old, for of the one hanged alive on the tree (Scripture) re[ads], *Behold, I am against* [*you*], *say*[*s Yahweh of Hosts, and I will burn in smoke your abundance*]; *and the sword shall devour your young lions. And* [*I*] *will cut off* [*from the land*] *its* [*p*]*rey, and no* [longer] *sh*[*all the voice of your messengers be heard*. The interpretation of it: "Your abundance" means his warrior-bands wh[o are in Jerusa]lem; and "his young lions" are his nobles [   ], and "his prey" is the wealth, which [the prie]sts of Jerusalem have amas[sed], which they will give t[o   ].

The text alludes to events ca. 88 B.C., when enemies of the bellicose Sadducee priest-king Alexander Janneus invited the Seleucid ruler, Demetrius III Eucerus (95–78 B.C.), to come to their aid. After a fierce battle at Shechem Demetrius emerged as victor, but had to leave the country immediately and could not proceed to Jerusalem itself, having lost the support of the Jews who had invited him. Alexander Janneus then retook Jerusalem and brought there the Pharisees who had opposed him. Josephus tells how he put them to death: he "did a thing that was as cruel as could be: While he feasted with his concubines in a conspicuous place, he ordered some eight hundred of the Jews to be crucified, and slaughtered their children and wives before the eyes of the still living wretches" (*Ant.* 13.14.2 § 380). To this episode 4QpNah refers, calling Alexander Janneus "the Lion of Wrath," and referring to Pharisees as the "Seekers after Smooth Things." Yadin restores the lacuna in the third line with a slightly different wording, "[on the tree, as this is the law] in Israel as of old." He explains it by referring to Josh 8:23–29, the execution of the king of Ai, and to Deut 21:22, as used in the Temple Scroll quoted below ("Pesher Nahum (4QpNahum) Reconsidered," *IEJ* 21 [1971] 1–12 [+ pl. 1]).

The passage of the Temple Scroll from Cave 11 that is pertinent runs as follows:

> If a man has informed against his people and has delivered his people up to a foreign nation and has done evil to his people, you shall hang him on the tree, and he shall die. On the evidence of two witnesses and on the evidence of three witnesses, he shall be put to death, and they shall hang him ⟨on⟩ the tree. If a man has committed a crime punishable by death and has fled to the midst of the Gentiles and has cursed his people and the children of Israel, *you shall hang him* too *on the tree* and he shall die. Their bodies *shall not pass the night on the tree, but you shall indeed bury* them *that very day, for what is hanged upon the tree is accursed by God* and men; *and you shall not defile the land which* I am *giving to you for an inheritance. . . .* (11QTemple 64:6–13).

This text provides a halakhic interpretation of Deut 21:22–23. According to it, two crimes are punishable by death: (a) treason, by passing on information to an enemy, delivering one's people to the enemy, or doing evil to one's people; (b) flight from due process of the law, by fleeing to another country, cursing one's people. Again, Yadin applies the text to the event of Alexander Janneus and Demetrius III Eucerus.

When he refers to the incident of Alexander Janneus, Josephus (*Ant.* 13.14.2 § 380) uses the Greek verb *anastauroun,* which clearly means "crucify," and it gives the Qumran expression *ytlh 'nšym ḥyym,* "he hangs men alive" (4QpNah 3-4 i 7) that nuance, as it also does to *wtlytmh 'wtw 'l h'ṣ wymt,* "you shall hang him on the tree, and he shall die" (11QTemple 64:8). Yadin pointed out that, though both texts allude to Deut 21:22–23, the regulation about hanging the dead body of a criminal on a tree until sundown as a deterrent to crime, they reverse the order of the verbs, and so he interpreted the "dying as a result" as an allusion to crucifixion. Thus crucifixion was a form of punishment that the Hasmonean leader, Alexander Janneus, practiced, and 11QTemple seems to envisage it as a legitimate form of punishment to be used by (at least some) Jews against persons guilty of treason and evasion of the due process of law.

(In the NT, the crucifixion of Jesus is referred to as "hanging upon a tree" [*kremasantes epi xylou,* Acts 5:30; 10:39; cf. Acts 13:29; 1 Pet 2:24]. Indeed, Gal 3:13, speaking of Christ crucified, explicitly alludes to the same passage of Deuteronomy, translating *qillat 'ĕlōhîm tālûy* as *epikataratos pas ho kremamenos epi xylou,* "cursed be everyone hung on a tree," which is almost as it is translated in the LXX.)

In this matter, one must recall that there is no precise word for "crucify" in Hebrew or Aramaic. That is undoubtedly the reason why the circumlocution "hang on a tree" is used. But all of this shows that in Roman times crucifixion was understood as a form of punishment to which the words of Deut 21:23 could be applied.

The interpretation of the Qumran passages given above, which follows that of Yadin, the Israeli editor of the text, has been contested by J. M. Baumgarten, *JBL* 91 (1972) 472–81; *H. M. Orlinsky Volume* (Eretz-Israel 16; Jerusalem: Israel Exploration Society, 1982) 7*–16*. Cf., however, F. García Martínez, *EstBib* 38 (1979–80) 221–35.

50. Did the Qumran community think that its Teacher of Righteousness was to come back?

There is one text that has been so interpreted. The Damascus Document quotes Num 21:18 and proceeds to compose a pesher on it:

> *The well that the princes sank, that the nobles of the people dug with a staff* (Num 21:18). The "well" is the Law, and "those that sank it" are the returnees of Israel, who went out from the land of Israel and sojourned in the land of Damascus. God called them all "princes," because they sought him and their renown was not questioned by anyone. The "Staff" is the Interpreter of the Law, of whom

Isaiah said, '(He) makes a tool for his work' (54:16). "The nobles of the people" are those who come to dig the well with staffs, with which the Staff ordained that they should walk during all the time of wickedness; without them they will not succeed until there arises one who rains down righteousness at the end of days" (CD 6:3–10).

The problematic words are the last six in Hebrew: *'ad 'ămōd yôrēh haṣṣedeq bě'aḥărît hayyāmîm*. S. Schechter, who first published the CD, translated the clause, "until there will arise the teacher of righteousness in the end of days" (*Documents of Jewish Sectaries* [2 vols.; Cambridge, UK: University Press, 1910; repr. with a prolegomenon by J. A. Fitzmyer, New York: Ktav, 1970] 1. xxxviii). Similarly, A. Dupont-Sommer, "until the coming of the Teacher of Righteousness at the end of days" (*Essene Writings,* 131). In other words, they have read *yôrēh haṣṣedeq* as the equivalent of the title *môreh haṣṣedeq*. Dupont-Sommer's footnote explains, "The Teacher of Righteousness is dead but will reappear 'at the end of days', i.e. at the end of the world, when 'all the time of wickedness' will have ended. This expectation of the Teacher's return, formulated so clearly here, was one of the fundamental articles of belief in the credo of the New Covenant" (ibid.).

Geza Vermes, a reader in Judaic Studies at the University of Oxford, however, translates the words, "until he comes who shall teach righteousness at the end of days" (*Dead Sea Scrolls in English,* 87). This is clearly a more accurate translation, because it does not interpret *yôrēh haṣṣedeq* as the equivalent of the title *môreh haṣṣedeq.* It leaves the clause open to the expectation of someone, not necessarily the Teacher of Righteousness, who will teach righteousness in some future end-time. Yet not even that translation is certain, because the clause undoubtedly alludes to Hos 10:12, *'ad yābô' wěyôrēh ṣedeq lākem,* "till he comes and rains down righteousness upon you," which refers to Yahweh himself, mentioned in the preceding clause.

There are two Hebrew verbs with the root *yry,* one meaning "to teach" (cf. CD 3:8; 20:14), and the other meaning "to rain" (cf. 1QH 8:16). These possibilities have to be admitted even for Hos 10:12, which the Vg translates: "cum venerit qui docebit vos iustitiam" (when he comes who will teach you justice); similarly modern interpreters such as van Hoonacker, Ward, Weiser. But the vast majority of OT commentators understand *yôrēh* as "rains down" (so Andersen and Freedman, Cheyne, Craigie, Jacob, Keil, Knight, Lippl, Marti, Nowack, Pusey, Rudolph, Scholz, Sellin, Smith, Vawter); similarly modern versions (*RSV, NAB, KJV, SBJ, NRSV, NIV,* LutherBibel, Menge, Crampon). It seems to echo Isa 45:8. My translation of CD 6:10 (above) has used the latter meaning (following J. Carmignac, *RevQ* 1 [1958-59] 235-48, esp. 239-42), but I do not exclude the possibility of Vermes's translation. In any case, it is far from certain that the text talks about "the Teacher's return," as Dupont-Sommer would have had it.

51. But do not some texts mention the coming of the Interpreter of the Law at the end of days?

In § 47 above two texts were cited that mention the "Interpreter of the Law" (*dôrēš hattôrāh*). In one he is awaited as a companion of the coming "Sprout of David" (4QFlor [4Q174] 1-2 i 11-12), and in the other he is identified as the coming "star" of Balaam's Oracle (Num 24:17, used in CD 7:18). Though one of the functions of the Teacher of Righteousness was a special interpretation of the Law and the Prophets as one inspired by God (1QpHab 7:5), it is far from certain that the awaited "Interpreter of the Law" mentioned in these texts is the same as the Teacher of Righteousness, even though Allegro so interpreted that title (*JBL* 75 [1956] 175-76). The title *dôrēš hattôrāh* is developed from a phrase describing Ezra in Ezra 7:10, "Ezra set his heart on the study of the Law." Cf. 1 Macc 14:14. Without the article the phrase is used generically in Sir 32:15 (*dwrš twrh*). Indeed, the purpose of the existence of the community in the desert is explained by Isa 40:3, where the preparation of the way of the Lord is precisely the "study of the Law" (*midraš hattôrāh,* 1QS 8:15; cf. CD 20:6). Given the generic usage of the phrase in the OT and the QS, the title "Interpreter of the Law" would seem rather to refer to an expected figure who would be an ideal expositor, perhaps a high priest acceptable to the community, but it is far from clear that it is to be equated with the founding Teacher of Righteousness, who would be expected to return to life.

Given the fact that the Qumran community awaited the coming of Messiahs of Aaron and Israel (see § 45), it seems unlikely that they were also awaiting the coming of "the Sprout of David" and the "Interpreter of the Law" as two figures different from those Messiahs. It seems more likely that one should interpret "the Sprout of David" as another title for the "Messiah of Israel," the expected political Messiah, and "the Interpreter of the Law" as another title for the "Messiah of Aaron," the expected priestly Messiah.

52. Did entrance into the Qumran community require a period of testing or initiation?

Yes, for one was not a member of the Qumran community simply by being a Jew. The rule book often speaks of those who "freely pledge themselves" (e.g. 1QS 1:7, 11; 5:1, 6, 8, 10, 21, 22), using the reflexive form of the verb *nādab,* "offer voluntarily."

Concerning the entrance of an applicant into the community, the Manual of Discipline states,

> As for everyone from Israel who would freely pledge himself to join the council of the community, the Deputy at the head of the Many shall examine him concerning his understanding and his deeds. If he passes muster for the discipline, he will admit him into the Covenant, in order to turn to the truth and to turn from all iniquity. He shall instruct him in all the regulations of the community. Later, when he comes to stand before the Many, they shall inquire about everything concerning his affairs. As the decision is made according to the council of the Many, he shall enter or withdraw. When he enters the council of the community, he shall not touch the Purity of the Many {i.e. shall not share the common meal of the Many}, until they examine him about his spirit and his deeds at the completion of a full year. Nor shall he share in the property of the Many {i.e. his property shall not be mingled with that of the Many}. On his completion of a year, the Many shall

make inquiry about his affairs, about his understanding and his observance of the Law. If the decision favors him, according to the word of the priests and the majority of the men of their Covenant, to enter the core of the community, his property and his earnings (shall be given) to the Overseer over the revenues of the Many; but it shall be recorded to his account, and he {i.e. the Overseer} shall not use it on behalf of the Many. He shall not touch the Drink of the Many {i.e. the common meal} until his completion of a second year within the men of the community. On his completion of his second year, they shall examine him. According to the word of the Many, if the decision favors him to enter the community, they will inscribe him in the order of his rank among his brothers in what concerns the Law, equity, the Purity {i.e. the common meal}, and the mingling of his property. His counsel and his judgment shall be for the community (1QS 6:13–23).

Part of the entrance requirements seems to have been an oath mentioned in 1QS 5:7–8: "he shall undertake with a binding oath to turn with all his heart and all his soul to the Law of Moses" (see § 43).

53. Were the members of the Qumran community celibate?

In the Manual of Discipline there is no mention of women or children. The word *'iššāh,* "woman," occurs in the Manual only in the stereotyped phrase, "born of a woman": "What shall one born of a woman be accounted before You?" (1QS 11:21). All the rules and regulations in the Manual refer only to men. In 1QS 4:6–8, however, the author describes the blessings to come on those who are guided by the spirit of light: "These are the counsels of the spirit for the sons of truth (in the) world. As for the visitation of all who walk by it {by that spirit}, it will be healing, abundant peace, length of days, fruitfulness of seed, together with every everlasting blessing and eternal joy in life without end, a crown of glory, and a garment of honor in everlasting light." Is *pěrôt zera',* "fruitfulness of seed," a reference to children? It has been so understood by some interpreters, but it is not at all certain. Vermes and Dupont-Sommer translate it merely as "fruitfulness," and no one knows whether *zera'*, "seed," refers to human posterity or to an abundance of crops and produce for food. Yet apart from this possible cryptic reference, nothing in the rest of the text seems to reckon with the marriage of members of the group.

Moreover, the main cemetery on the eastern side of Khirbet Qumran contains about 1100 graves, arranged in regular and closely ordered rows, separated by three alleys. Of these regularly ordered graves thirty-one have been excavated, selected from different sectors, and all but one of them contained only male skeletons. By contrast, in the extensions of the cemetery over the hillocks to the east, to the north, and to the south of the Wadi Qumran, twelve other graves were opened; six contained a female skeleton, and four those of children. In all, over 1200 graves have been counted and 43 have been excavated. Because in the main and central part of the cemetery only male skeletons were found, the archaeologists have concluded that this evidence supports the celibate character of the Qumran community (see R. de Vaux, *Archaeology,* 45–47).

The appendix of the Manual of Discipline, however, does mention "children and women," who shall be assembled and instructed in the precepts of the Covenant (1QSa 1:4–5). Again, the same appendix ordains that a youth at the end of his period of training is not to approach a woman to know her sexually "before he is fully twenty years old" (1QSa 1:9–10). The Damascus Document also speaks of marriage: "If they dwell in camps according to the rule of the land and take wives and beget children, let them walk according to the word of the Law and according to the regulation of binding vows, according to the rule of the Law, as it says, '*Between a man and his wife, and between a father and his son*'" (CD 7:6–9, quoting Num 30:17).

The problem here is to interpret the nuances of both these rule books. Because the Manual of Discipline proper seems to envisage a celibate group, and its Appendix A and the Damascus Document reckon with marriage and children, it seems clear that there were two different forms of community life among the sectarians of Qumran, or at least different life-styles at different periods.

54. What was distinctive about the theological tenets of the Qumran community?

By and large, the theological tenets of the Qumran community would have agreed with those of the rest of Judaism, especially as they were based on the Hebrew Scriptures. But the community had its own way of interpreting those Scriptures, a way that it believed was inherited from the Teacher of Righteousness, whom God had inspired to understand the Scriptures in an esoteric way: "the Teacher of Righteousness, to whom God made known all the mysteries of the words of His servants the prophets" (1QpHab 7:4–5).

But also because of its belief in God's predestination of all things (see § 44) the community developed a very distinctive ethical dualism, consonant with its monotheistic belief. This dualism is expressed above all in the Manual of Discipline, in its teaching about the two spirits that God has put in human beings:

> From the God of knowledge comes all that is and will be, and before they came to be He established all the design of them. . . . He it is who created human beings for the governance of the world. He put in them two spirits that they should walk according to them until the time of His visitation: they are the spirits of truth and of iniquity. The origin of truth is in a fountain of light, and the origin of iniquity is from a source of darkness. Dominion over all the sons of light is in the hand of the prince of light: they walk in paths of light. But in the hand of the angel of darkness is all the dominion of the sons of iniquity: they walk in paths of darkness. On the angel of darkness (depends) the straying of all the sons of righteousness, all their sin, their iniquities, their guilt. Their deeds of transgression are because of its dominion according to God's mysteries until the end-time set by Him. All their afflictions and their seasons of distress are owing to the dominance of its malevolence. All the spirits of its lot are to cause the sons of light to stumble. But the God of Israel and His angel of truth have helped all the sons of light.

He has created the spirits of light and darkness, and upon
them he has based every deed, [and according to] their
[ways] every (form of) service. One (of them) God loves
everlastingly, and in all its deeds He takes delight forever.
As for the other, He abominates its counsel and hates all
its ways forever.

These are their ways in the world. It is ‹for the spirit of
truth› to enlighten the heart of a human being and to
make straight before him all the paths of righteousness
and truth, (to set) fear in his heart for the judgments of
God. (To it belong) a spirit of humility and forbearance,
of abundant mercy and everlasting goodness, of intelli-
gence and insight, of powerful wisdom that trusts in all
the deeds of God and finds support in His abundant grace.
(To it belong) a spirit of knowledge for every plan of
action, zeal for righteous ordinances, a resolve for holiness
with a firm inclination, abundant affection toward all the
sons of truth, and glorious purity that abhors all defiling
idols; walking modestly with prudence in every way and
discretion for the truth of the mysteries of knowledge.
These are the counsels of the spirit (of truth) for the sons
of truth ‹in the› world. As for the visitation of all who
walk by it, it will be healing, abundant peace, length of
days, fruitfulness of seed, together with everlasting blessing and eternal joy in life without end, a crown of glory,
and a garment of honor in everlasting light.

But to the spirit of iniquity belong covetousness, slackness
in the service of righteousness, wickedness and deceit,
pride and haughtiness of heart, falsehood and cunning,
cruelty and abundant hypocrisy, impatience and much
folly, jealous envy, and abominable deeds with a lusting
spirit, paths of defilement in the service of impurity, a
blaspheming tongue, blindness of eye and deafness of ear,
stiffness of neck and heaviness of heart, making one walk
in all paths of darkness with cunning wickedness. As for
the visitation of all who walk according to this (spirit) there
will be an abundance of affliction at the hands of all the
angels of destruction in the everlasting Pit because of the

furious wrath of the God of vengeance, with dread unend-
ing and shame without end, with the disgrace of destruction in the fire of absolute darkness. All their times will
be spent during all their generations in the sorrow of
chagrin and in the evil of bitterness, in the darkness of
calamity until they are destroyed without a survivor or
escapee.

By these (two spirits walk) the generations of all the sons
of man; by their divisions all their hosts inherit a share
from age to age. In their paths they walk, and all the reward
of their deeds is according to the divisions of (these spirits),
according to the inheritance of each one, whether much
or little, throughout all the ages. For God has set these
(two spirits) with equal influence until the end-time and
has put eternal hatred between their divisions. The deeds
of iniquity are an abomination to truth, and an abomination of iniquity are all the paths of truth. Envious contention (settles) on all their ordinances, for they walk not
together. But in His mysteries of understanding and in His
glorious wisdom God has set an end for the existence of
iniquity. At the time of (His) visitation He will destroy
it forever. Then will go forth forever the truth of the world.
But (the world) has defiled itself with paths of wickedness
under the dominion of iniquity until the time of judgment
that has been decreed. Then God will purge by his truth
all the deeds of human beings, refining {i.e. by fire} for
himself some of mankind in order to remove every evil
spirit from the midst of their flesh, to cleanse them with
a holy Spirit from all wicked practices, and to sprinkle
them with a spirit of truth like purifying water from all
abominations of deceit and wallowing in the spirit of
defilement. Then the upright shall come to understand the
knowledge of the Most High and the wisdom of the sons
of heaven. For God has chosen them for an everlasting
Covenant, and all the glory of Adam is theirs. Iniquity
shall exist no more or shame for all deceitful deeds. Until
such time the spirits of truth and iniquity will contend for
the heart of man. People shall walk in wisdom or in folly

each according to his share in truth and righteousness. So shall each hate iniquity. But according to his inheritance in the lot of iniquity he will do evil by it, and so he will abominate truth. For God has set them {the two spirits} with equal influence until the end-time that is decreed, the time of renewal. He reckons the reward of their deeds throughout all ages, and He has apportioned them {the two spirits} for the sons of man that they may know good [and evil, that] lots may be cast for every creature according to his spirit within [him until the season for vis]itation (1QS 3:15–4:26).

What one reads in these paragraphs is not something that was commonly taught among the Jews of ancient Palestine. It constitutes rather the distinctive theological tenets of this sect of Jews, of the Qumran community. This dualistic treatise on the spirits of truth and iniquity provides the background of the names "sons of light" and "sons of darkness" that are found in various QS, especially in the War Scroll.

55. What do the QS tell us about the ritual life of the community?

Several of the Qumran texts refer to rites that characterized the communal life of the sectarians. There seems to have been some sort of entrance rite, described in the Manual of Discipline as follows:

All who embrace the rule of the community shall enter into the Covenant before God to act according to all that He has commanded and not to turn away from Him out of any fear, dread, or temptation that shall come to pass during the dominion of Belial. On entering the Covenant, the priests and the levites shall bless the God of salvific deeds and all his faithful works; all those entering the Covenant shall say after them, "Amen, amen!" Then the priests shall recount God's righteous deeds (manifest) in his powerful works and shall make known all His merciful favors to Israel, and the levites shall recount the

iniquities of the children of Israel and all their guilty transgressions and sins during the dominion of Belial. After
them [all] those who enter the Covenant shall confess, saying, "We have acted wickedly, [we have transgressed, we
have si]nned, we have done evil, we and our [fa]thers before
us, in walking [counter to the commands of] truth and
righteous[ness.] His judgment against us and against [our]
fathers" (1QS 1:18–26).

Again,

The priests shall bless all the men of God's lot, who walk
perfectly in all his ways, and say, "May He bless you with
all that is good, and may He keep you from all evil! May
He illumine your heart with life-giving understanding and
favor you with eternal knowledge! May He lift His gracious countenance toward you for everlasting peace!" Then
the levites shall curse all the men of Belial's lot, taking
up the word and saying, "Cursed be you with all your
wicked, guilty deeds! May God make you tremble at the
hands of all vengeful avengers! May He visit you with
destruction at the hands of who recompense (evil) deeds!
Accursed be you without mercy according to the darkness
of your deeds, and may you be damned in the deep
darkness of everlasting fire! May God not be gracious to
you when you call upon Him and not pardon you by
wiping away your iniquities! May He turn an angry face
to take vengeance on you! May there be no "Peace" for
you on the lips of all those who hold fast to the fathers!"
And after those blessing and those cursing, all those who
enter the Covenant shall say, "Amen, amen!" (1QS 2:1–10).
The priests and the levites will continue and say again,
"Cursed be the one who has entered this Covenant with
the idols of his heart (set) to transgress, who sets before
him the stumbling-block of his iniquity to turn back on
it! It will happen that, when he hears the words of this
Covenant, he will bless himself in his heart and say, 'Peace
be with me, even though I walk in the stubbornness of my

heart' (Deut 29:18-19), but his spirit, thirsty or watered, shall be without pardon. May God's wrath and His zeal for His regulations consume him in utter destruction. May all the curses of this Covenant cling to him, and may God set him apart for evil. May he be cut off from the midst of the sons of light in his turning back from God because of his idols and the stumbling-block of his iniquity. May He set his lot with those cursed forever!"

And all those who enter the Covenant shall take up the word and say after them, "Amen, amen!" So they shall do, year after year, during all the days of the dominion of Belial. The priests shall enter first, in order one after the other according to their spirits, and the levites shall enter after them, and thirdly all the people shall enter, one after the other in their Thousands, Hundreds, Fifties, and Tens, so that every Israelite will know his place in God's community according to (His) everlasting design (1QS 2:11-23).

The end of the last quotation seems to refer not only to an entrance ritual, but one that was renewed each year, the renewal of the Covenant, which may have taken place at the Feast of Weeks (Pentecost). Again, a fragmentary collection of blessings is found in appendix B of the Manual of Discipline, which is too long to quote here (1QSb 1:1-5:29). The text begins, "Words of the blessing for the Master" (*lam-Maśkîl*), when he is to bless the God-fearers {=members of the community}, the high priest, the sons of Zadok, the priests, the prince of the congregation (*něśî' hā'ēdāh*)."

In addition, the community apparently had various purification rites, since some very fragmentary prayers associated with these rites have been recovered. They mention days of purification, feasts, ritual washings, donning of clean clothing, offering of holocausts, defilement, blood, etc. (see 4Q512).

There is also a text called a marriage ritual by the modern editor, but it is so fragmentary that its character is not certain (4Q502).

Even though it is not possible to give more details under this topic, it is clear that the Qumran community life was governed by many ritual practices.

56. Do the QS give us any information about the sectarian communal meals?

In speaking of the communal life that the sectarians lived at Qumran, the Manual of Discipline prescribes that "they shall eat in common, they shall bless in common, and they shall take counsel in common. In every place where there are ten men from the council of the community, there shall not be lacking among them a priest" (1QS 6:2–4). Ten as a quorum is mentioned in other QS (CD 13:1–2; 1QSa 2:22), probably as some sort of liturgical requirement. The same passage in the Manual continues, "And it shall be that, when they set the table in order to eat or to drink new wine, the priest shall first stretch forth his hand to bless the first-fruits of the bread and the new wine" (1QS 6:4–5).

A more elaborate description is given in appendix A of the Manual:

> [This shall be the as]sembly of the men of renown [sum-moned] to the meeting of the council of the community, when/if [God] begets the Messiah among them. There shall enter [the priest], the head of the whole congrega-tion of Israel, and all [his] bro[thers, the sons of] Aaron, the priests [summoned] to the meeting of the men of renown. They shall sit be[fore him, each] according to his dignity. Afterwards there sh[all take his seat the Mes]siah of Israel. And the head[s of] the Th[ousands of Israel] shall sit before him, [ea]ch according to his dignity, according to [his stat]us in their camps and according to their stations. All the heads of fa[milies of the con]grega-tion with the sag[es of the holy congregation] shall sit before them, each according to his dignity. And [when they] meet together [at tab]le [or to drink the ne]w wine and (when) the table is prepared and [the] new wine is [mixed] for drinking, [no] one shall [stretch forth] his hand to the first-fruits of the bread and [the new wine] before the priest; for [he it is who shall bl]ess the first-fruits of the bread and the new win[e and he shall stretch forth] his hand to the bread first. Afterwa[rd] the Messiah of

Israel [will stre]tch forth his hand to the bread. [And then]
all the congregation of the community [shall utt]er a blessing, ea[ch according to] his dignity. According to this
regulation [they] shall act at every meal-prepar[ation when]
at least ten me[n are ga]thered (1QSa 2:11-22).

What is striking here is the importance given to this meal by the
community and its belief that the Messiah of Israel is somehow present at the partaking of the communal meal. But it must be recalled
that this regulation for the communal meal stands in the appendix
of the Manual of Discipline, the title of which is given in 1:1: "This
is the rule for all the congregation of Israel at the end of days." For
this reason it is sometimes called "the Messianic Rule." This may explain the belief about the presence of the Messiah of Israel. Yet it
is also striking that "the priest" takes precedence over him. Just who
this priest is in this context is not easily determined; some interpreters
have thought that it refers to the priestly Messiah, the Messiah of
Aaron, which would mean that the priestly Messiah was seen to be
somehow superior to the Davidic Messiah. But that is far from clear.
In any case, there is a communal meal at which a priest presides and
blesses bread and new wine in the presence of the Messiah of Israel.

That this meal is somehow a prefigurement of the Christian
eucharist is not impossible; at least it provides a Palestinian Jewish
context for the understanding of the Christian meal. But it also lacks
the essential interpretative utterances of the NT eucharistic narratives
and the obvious Passover connotations of the latter.

57. Do the QS tell us anything about the dietary habits of the community?

The ritual of the common meal mentions "bread" and "wine,"
the staples of Palestinian diet (1QS 6:6; 1QSa 2:19-21). In these cases,
however, mention is actually made of tîrôš, "must, fresh wine," which
may even mean unfermented grape juice. Though yayin, "wine," is
mentioned in CD 8:9-10; 19:22-23, it is in a quotation from Deut 32:33
and is symbolically interpreted. It tells us nothing about the consump-
tion of "wine" by the members of this community.

In 11QTemple the Feast of New Wine (19:14) mentions *yayin ḥādāš*, lit. "new wine," but later on it is called *mô'ēd hattîrôš*, "Feast of Must" (43:8–9). When there is mention of the offering of wine in the Temple, priests, levites, "princes of the 'standards,'" and "all the people, great and small, shall begin to drink new wine (*yayin ḥādāš*) and not eat any sour grapes from the vine, for on this day they shall make expiation for the must (*hattîrôš*); and the children of Israel shall rejoice before the Lord" (21:4–8; cf. *Jub.* 7:6). Later there is mention of a libation of *šēkār, yayin ḥādāš*, "strong drink, new wine," to be poured upon the altar of the Lord (21:10). Just what such regulations are to be taken to mean is puzzling.

Whereas in Gen 14:18 Melchizedek is said to have brought out to Abram and his men returning from the battle with the kings *leḥem wāyayin*, "bread and wine," the Genesis Apocryphon translates this phrase as *mē'kal wĕmištēh*, "food and drink" (1QapGen 22:15), thus understanding the Hebrew phrase in a generic sense.

Time after time the Temple Scroll gives regulations for the sacrifice of goats, bulls, oxen, sheep, rams, and lambs as offering to the Lord; presumably the people who offered these animals partook of them in some way at times. In one instance it speaks of "the firstling of your flock, (which) you shall eat before me year by year in the place that I shall choose" (52:8–9).

There are, however, other proscriptions about foods that should not be eaten: "Let no one defile himself with any animal or creeping thing by eating of them, either the larvae of bees or any living creature that creeps in the waters. As for fish, let them not be eaten, unless they have been slit open alive and their [blood] has been dr[ai]ned out. As for locusts in all their variety, let them be put into fire or water while they are alive, for this is the determination of their nature" (CD 12:11–14). "According to these regulations (they are) to distinguish between the unclean and the clean, in order to make known the sacred from the profane" (CD 12:19).

There were also regulations about fasting or abstention from food. "(They are) to distinguish between the unclean and the clean and to make known (the distinction) between the sacred and the profane, and to observe the sabbath according to its exact determination and the feast days and the Day of Fasting {the Day of Atonement} according to the findings of those who have entered the New Covenant in the land of Damascus" (CD 6:17-19). The regulations for the celebration of *yôm kippûrîm,* "Day of Atonement," are found in 11QTemple 25:10-27:10:

> On the tenth in this month is the Day of Atonement, on which you shall afflict yourselves {i.e. fast}, for every person who does not afflict himself on this very day shall be cut off from his people. You shall offer a holocaust on it to Yahweh, one bull, one ram, seven male lambs a year old, one male goat for a sin offering, besides the sin offering for expiation and their cereal offering and their libation according to the regulation for the bull, the ram, the lambs, and the goat. For the sin offering for expiation you shall offer two rams for the holocaust. The high priest shall offer one for himself and for his father's house (25:10-16).
> ... The [high prie]st [shall cast lots over the two goats], o[ne] lot [for Yahweh, and one lot for Azazel. And] he shall slaughter the goat [on which the lot] fel[l for Yahweh and lift up] its blood in the golden basin, which is in [his] ha[nd, and d]o with [its] bl[ood as he did with the blood of] the bull which (he offered) for himself, and he shall make expiation with it for all the people of the assembly. Its fat and the cereal offering (with) its libation he shall burn upon the altar of holocaust; its flesh, its skin, and its dung they shall burn beside his bull, (for) it is a sin offering for the assembly. With it he shall make expiation for all the assembly, and they shall be pardoned. He shall wash his hands and his feet of the blood of the sin offering and come to the live goat; he shall confess over its head all the iniquities of the children of Israel, with all their guilt, all their sin. He shall put them all on the head of the goat and send it off to Azazel in the desert by the hand of a man in readiness. The goat shall bear all the iniquities ... (26:3-13).
> ... for all the children of Israel, and they shall be pardoned. Afterwards he shall make (an offering of) the bull, the ram, and [the lambs according to] their [regu]lations on the altar of holocaust, and the [ho]locaust shall be

accepted for the children of Israel. (These are) perpetual statutes for their generations. Once a year this day shall be for them a memorial; they shall do no work on it, for it will be [for th]em a sabbath of sabbaths. As for any man who shall do work on it or who shall not fast on it, they shall cut ⟨him⟩ off from the midst of his people. A sabbath of sabbaths, a holy convocation shall this day be for you. You shall consecrate it as a memorial in all your dwellings, and you shall do no work (27:2-10).

The phrase *mô'ēd hatta'ănît* also occurs in 4QpPs^a 1-2 ii 9, but it is not certain whether one is to translate it "Feast of Fasting" or, more probably, "time of affliction."

58. Do the QS tell us anything about how the community functioned and was governed?

Many details are given in various scrolls about the governance of the community, but they are not clear, and it is not easy to get a coherent picture from them. Part of the difficulty is that details in the Manual of Discipline do not always agree with those in the Damascus Document; in this one has the usual problem of distinguishing the groups to which these rule books may refer.

The Manual of Discipline seems to describe a structured assemblage, variously called *yahad,* "community," *'ēdāh,* "congregation," or *'ăṣat hayyahad,* "council of the community," whereas the Damascus Document uses *yahad* only in CD 20:1, 14, 32 (where it is spelled *yhyd,* perhaps the result of a medieval copyist's confusion of *yahad,* "community," with *yāhîd,* "beloved"). Otherwise, it often uses *'ēdāh,* "congregation," but also *'ēṣāh* once in the strange phrase, *'ăṣat hibbûr yiśrā'ēl,* "council of the Association of Israel" (CD 12:8). The Damascus Document describes a structured common life in "camps," in which there were priests and levites, but lay members, men and women, seem to predominate. In the War Scroll and the Messianic Rule (1QSa) details are laid down for a future type of communal existence. The name *yahad* never occurs in the War Scroll, nor does *'ăṣat hayyahad,* but both often occur in the Messianic Rule. In the

War Scroll the group is designated only as *'ēdāh,* "congregation."

In general, in all the scrolls the community uses divisions derived from the OT. There are priests, levites, and lay persons divided into groupings called Thousands, Hundreds, Fifties, and Tens (1QS 2:21–22; CD 13:1–2), designations that seem to be more symbolic than factual, used perhaps in imitation of Exod 18:21, 25; Deut 1:15.

The Manual of Discipline describes "the council of the community" or "the community," which has withdrawn "from the midst of the habitation of men of iniquity to go into the desert to prepare there the way of Him" (1QS 8:13). In its communal activity it engaged in work, meals, prayer, study, and deliberation. It was a community in which all the members had pooled "their knowledge, their strength, and their wealth" (1QS 1:11). They pledged themselves to "keep vigil in common for a third of every night in the year, to read the Book, to study the law, and to bless in common" (1QS 6:7–8). An important element in their communal life was the observance of feasts and "appointed times" (1QS 1:14–15).

It is not clear whether "the council of the community" is the same as "the community." In 1QS 8:1 there is mention of "twelve men and three priests" in "the council of the community," but interpreters are not agreed as to the meaning of this line. According to some, it might be a description of the original nucleus of the community at its founding. Others have tried to ascribe certain tasks to this "council," a sort of oligarchy within the greater structure of the community. The community itself also decided things "according to the word of the Many" (1QS 6:21), which seems to suggest that all of its full members had a deliberative vote on some issues. Yet in many places "the council of the community" seems to be only another way of saying "the community."

In this community, as described in the Manual, each member had an assigned position or rank: "they will inscribe him in the order of his rank among his brothers in what concerns the Law, equity, the Purity {i.e. the common meal}, and the mingling of his property" (1QS 6:22–23). The sons of Zadok, the priests, took precedence; of their number was undoubtedly the *mĕbaqqēr,* "Overseer," a sort of superior, who is said to be *'al hārabbîm,* "over the Many," i.e. over the whole group (1QS 6:12). The person described as *hā'îš happāqîd bĕrô'š hārabbîm,* "the Deputy at the head of the Many" (1QS 6:14), is almost certainly the same as that Overseer. He may also be the same as the one called *hammĕbaqqēr 'al mĕleket hārabbîm,* "the Overseer over the income of the Many" (1QS 6:20); the latter, however, is taken by some interpreters as a distinct administrator in the community, a sort of treasurer or bursar.

Another figure is called *maśkîl,* probably "the Instructor, Master," whose task was "to instruct and teach all the sons of light about the generations of all humanity, each according to the kinds of spirits they possess and their deeds in their lifetime . . ." (1QS 3:13–14; cf. 9:12, 21). The Manual itself was actually intended to be his guidebook (1QS 1:1), especially for his instructions about the spirits of light and darkness that dominate human life. What his relation to the *mĕbaqqēr* was is not easy to determine; most likely *maśkîl* is simply another name for the Overseer.

At times, *zĕqēnîm,* "elders," are mentioned, who outrank "the rest of the people" (1QS 6:8–9). But just what their function was is not clear. Levites were also part of the community, but their function is mentioned only in connection with the blessings and curses of the entrance rite (1QS 1:19–2:20).

According to the Damascus Document, the community lived rather "in camps according to the rule of the land and they take wives and beget children; they were to conduct themselves according to the Law, according to the regulation of binding vows, and according to the rule of the Law" (CD 7:6–8). For them the observance of "the sabbath, appointed times, and the day of fasting" (CD 6:18) was also important. From this text it is clear that members of the community lived in cities and villages, but separately from other Jews and from Gentiles. This rule book mentions the raising of children, the employing of servants, trade with outsiders, the tending of cattle, and agricultural produce.

In this form of communal life there was again a *mĕbaqqēr,* "Overseer," one who was expected to adjudicate in cases of delinquent conduct (CD 9:18–22) and to instruct a priest in a case of leprosy (CD 13:6). His general duty is spelled out in the following passage:

> This is the rule of the Overseer of the camp. He shall instruct the Many about God's deeds, teach them about

His marvellous mighty works, and recount before them
the events that came to pass of old. . . . He shall have pity
on them, as a father on his children, and he shall bri[ng]
(them) back in all their distress as a shepherd his flock.
He shall untie all the bonds that bind them that there may
be no one oppressed or broken in his congregation. As
for whoever joins his congregation, he shall examine him
concerning his deeds, his understanding, his strength, his
power, and his property; and they will inscribe him in his
place according to his rank in the lot of li[ght]. Let no one
of the camp-members take the authority to introduce
someone into the congregation [again]st the decision of
the Overseer of the camp. . . . Let no one make an association to buy or sell without making it known to the Overseer
who is over the camp (CD 13:7–16).
On the day on which he speaks with the Overseer of the
Many, they shall appoint him by the oath of the Covenant, which Moses concluded with Israel, the Covenant
to tu[rn t]o the Law of Moses with all his heart [and with
all] his soul, to whatever is found to be done during al[l
the ti]me of [wickedness]. Let no one make known to him
the regulations until he has stood before the Overseer, lest
he [the Overseer] be deceived by him when he is examin-
ing him. But when he takes it upon himself to turn to the
Law of Moses with all his heart and with all his soul
[   ] and (to) all that is revealed by the Law for knowl-
ed[ge   ] and he is worthy of it [   ], the Overseer
shall [examine] him and give orders about him, and he
shall [   ] for a whole year (CD 15:7–15).

But the same text also speaks of *hammĕbaqqēr 'ăšer lĕkol ham-
maḥănôt,* "the Overseer, who is for all the camps," and it thus seems
to imply that the *mĕbaqqēr* mentioned in the above paragraph was
one found in every camp, but that there was a still higher superior
over all the camps:

The Overseer, who is for all the camps, shall be a person
thirty to fifty years old, one who has mastered all human

counsel and the language of all their clans. Those who
enter the congregation shall do so at his word, each in his
turn. For everything that a man has to say, let him say it
to the Overseer concerning every dispute and regulation.
This is the rule of the Many, to provide for all their needs.
The earnings of at least [t]wo days of every month they
shall deposit with the Overseer and the Judges. From it
they shall provide for [or]phans, and from it they shall
support the poor, the needy, and the elderly who [are about
to d]ie; and the man who wanders (homeless) or who is
taken captive by a foreign people, and the virgin who has
[no] kin or the youn[g girl wh]om no one seeks (CD
14:8–16).

In this instance it is not clear whether *hammĕbaqqēr* is the same as
the "Overseer who is for all the camps" or simply the Overseer of
each camp.

Mention is also made here of "Judges," who also played a role
in the governance of this community:

This is the rule for the Judges of the congregation. (They
shall be) up to ten in number, men chosen for a time, four
of the tribe of Levi and Aaron, and six from Israel, (men)
well learned in the Book of Meditation and in the con-
stitutions of the Covenant, from twenty-five to sixty years
old. Let no one sixty years old or older take office to judge
the congregation, for because of man's faithlessness his
days have been shortened, and in the heat of wrath against
the inhabitants of the earth God has ordained that their
understanding should decline even before they have completed their days [allusion to *Jub.* 23:11?] (CD 10:4–10).

Unfortunately, little is said here about the matters about which such
Judges were to sit in judgment and how their governance worked
within the community. Only a hint is given in CD 15:4, where the
Judges are those before whom members of the community swear their
oaths. There is mention also of *nĕśîʾ kol hāʿēdāh,* "Prince of the whole
congregation" (CD 7:20; cf. 5:1), but this is used in pesher-like

explanations of OT passages that are cited, and it is not clear to whom such a title is applied. It is conceivably a symbolic title for the Overseer, but that is not certain.

In the War Scroll, which describes the community preparing for the holy war of the end-times, there is no mention of an Overseer or Instructor of any sort, but the *něśî' kôl hā'ēdāh,* "Prince of the whole congregation," again appears as one on whose shield special names are to be inscribed (1QM 5:1); unfortunately, it says nothing about his function in the community or the war. The title *nāśî'* is used a number of times for a leader of a tribe or company (1QM 3:3, 15, 16; 4:1). But the important figure in this scroll is *kôhēn hārô'š,* "the head priest" (1QM 2:1; 15:4; 16:13; 18:5; 19:11), who marshalls the troops for battle and exhorts them to fight.

In the Messianic Rule of the Congregation, the priests, the sons of Zadok, are given the primary role; they are to assemble the community and instruct its members, "from the toddler to the women" (1QSa 1:4). Regulations are set down for the youth in the community, who can be numbered in the community's census, when he is twenty years old (1QSa 1:8–9), and is only then allowed to marry (1:10). When he is twenty-five, he is allowed to join the officials of the community (1:12–13); when he is thirty he may arbitrate and take his place with the heads of the Thousands, Hundreds, Fifties, and Tens and with the Judges (1:13–15). The role of the levites is also described: they are the ones who summon the community to an assembly and see that they sit in proper order (1:23–25), "in the presence of the sons of Zadok, the priests" (2:3). From the *qěhal 'El,* "the assembly of God," (2:4) certain persons are excluded: those with "human impurities," such as those smitten in their flesh, paralyzed in feet or hands, the lame, blind, or deaf, the tottering aged, "because holy angels are [in] their [congre]gation" (2:5–9), and such angelic beings were not supposed to gaze on such deformities. The order of rank in the assembly is this: the Priest, the heads of the sons of Aaron, the Messiah of Israel, the chiefs of the tribes of Israel; then the heads of families and the sages (2:11–17). After this follows the description of the common meal, quoted in § 56.

The important Temple Scroll of Cave 11, however, gives us little information about the community and its governance. Neither *yaḥad* nor *'ăṣat hayyaḥad* are used, and *'ēdāh* may be used twice in a specific sense (11QTemple 22:[02]; 42:14), but *kôl 'ă[d]at běnê yiśrā'ēl,* "all the congregation of Israelites" (39:6–7) is scarcely specific. The noun *qāhāl,* "assembly," occurs in 16:15, 16, 18; 26:7, 9bis, where it is clearly influenced by Lev 4:21 or 16:33; only in 18:7 is it used without such influence. There is mention, however, of "the elders of the congregation, the princes, the heads of ancestral houses of the Israelites, leaders of Thousands, and leaders of Hundreds" (42:13–15), but no information is supplied about who these people might be or what their functions are. Yet this is owing to the nature of the Temple Scroll, which is not specific in supplying information about the community that made use of it.

The various pesharim are of little help in this regard, even though they do mention under figurative names various historical characters ("Teacher of Righteousness," "Wicked Priest," "Man of the Lie").

59. Do the QS tell us anything about how members of the community settled their differences?

Not exactly, but there are instructions in their rule book about how they are to conduct themselves in some cases. For instance,

> They shall inscribe them in order one before the other (each) according to his intelligence and his deeds that they may all be obedient to one another, the lesser to the greater. They shall examine their spirits and their deeds year after year to move up an individual according to his comprehension and the perfection of his conduct or move one down according to his guilty conduct. Let them reprove each other with tru[th], humility, and loving kindness toward the other. Let no one speak to his ‹brother› in anger or ill-temper or obduracy or with the envy of a malicious spirit. Let no one hate another [in] his [uncircumcised] heart. Rather let one reprove his companion (the same) day lest he incur a fault because of him. Moreover, let no one bring a matter against another before the Many without first reproving him before witnesses (1QS 5:23–6:1).

Other instructions are given for their conduct in an assembly:

> Let no one interrupt the words of another before his
> brother has finished speaking. Let no one speak before
> him who is inscribed before him. The one who is ques-
> tioned shall speak in his turn. In a session of the Many
> no one shall say a word without the consent of the Many,
> unless he is the Overseer of the Many. As for anyone who
> has something to say to the Many but who is not in a posi-
> tion to ask the council of the community, let him rise to
> his feet and say, "I have something to say to the Many."
> If they order him, he shall speak (1QS 6:10–13).

The Damascus Document has similar regulations:

> Anyone of those entering the Covenant who shall bring
> up a matter against his companion without reproving him
> before witnesses or brings this matter up in the heat of
> anger or recounts it to his elders in order to discredit him
> is one who takes vengeance and bears a grudge, whereas
> it is written, "*He* {God alone} *brings vengeance on His
> adversaries and lays up wrath for His enemies*" (Nah 1:2).
> If one has kept silent about his (companion) from one day
> to another {without reproof} and has (then) spoken out
> against him in the heat of his anger, he has born witness
> against himself in a matter liable to death that he has not
> fulfilled the commandment of God, who has said to him,
> "*You shall indeed reprove your companion and not incur
> sin because of him*" (Lev 19:17) (CD 9:2–8).

Again, it specifies:

> As for every infraction that one commits against the Law
> and that a companion sees, even though alone, if it is a
> matter liable to death, (the witness) shall make him known
> to the Overseer with a reproof in his presence. The Overseer
> should record it with his own hand (against him) until he

does it again before one (witness, who) again makes it known to the Overseer. If he should repeat and be caught in the act before one person, the case (against him) is complete. If there are two (witnesses) and they testify about the same matter, that man shall be excluded from the Purity {i.e. the common meal}, only if they are trustworthy and they make the matter known to the Overseer on the very day of their seeing him. If it is a matter that concerns property, they shall accept (the testimony of) two trustworthy witnesses, but on (the testimony of) one (it is permissible) to exclude ‹from› the Purity (CD 9:17-23).

60. What is known about the Qumran community's calendar and celebration of festivals?

Calendaric interests and the celebration of festivals were of great importance to this Jewish community. The initial statement about its purpose in col. 1 of the Manual of Discipline mentions among other aims, "to walk before Him perfectly ‹according to› all that has been revealed about their determined feasts" (1QS 1:8). This is a cryptic reference to what has been called the community's "unorthodox" calendar, which set them apart from other contemporary Jewish groups. For they regarded it as a sacred duty "not to make a single step away from all God's words about their times, either to advance the times or to delay them for any of their feasts" (1QS 1:13-15).

The Qumran community, in fact, clung to an ancient solar calendar, said to be of priestly origin, which did not normally use the Canaanite or Babylonian month-names, but simply numbered the months. Traces of this calendar are found in Ezek 45:18-20, and also in *Jub.* 6:29-33; *1 Enoch* 74:11-12; 82:6, 11, 15, 18. This calendar of 364 days insured absolute regularity, with each of the four seasons of three months of 30, 30, 31 days or thirteen weeks yielding a yearly cycle of 52 weeks. This meant that each festival in the calendar fell each year on the same day of the week. Thus Passover, beginning at sundown on the fourteenth day of the first month, always fell on the fourth day of the week (what we call Wednesday); the Feast of Weeks, the fifteenth day of the third month, fell on the first day of the week

(= our Sunday); the Day of Atonement, the tenth day of the seventh month, fell on the sixth day of the week (= our Friday); and the Feast of Tabernacles, the fifteenth day of the seventh month, fell on the fourth day of the week (= our Wednesday). Unfortunately, the QS give us no idea of how the community, which used this calendar, coped with the missing 29 hours, 48 minutes, and 48 seconds to keep their calendar in proper cycle with the movement of the earth about the sun.

That the Qumran community used this calendar is seen in 11QPs^a 27:6-7, in the prose insert called "David's Compositions." Here it is recorded that David composed "song ⟨s⟩ to sing before the altar over the holocaust of the daily *tamid* for all the days of the year, 364." The broken text of 1QM 2:1-2 seems to allude also to 52 weeks: "[the heads of] the ancestral [houses] of the congregation are fifty-two. They shall arrange the heads of the priests after the head priest and his representative, twelve heads to be serving constantly before God; and the heads of the twenty-six courses shall serve in their courses." Cf. the course-regulations in 4QMišm A-H (B. Z. Wacholder and M. G. Abegg, *A Preliminary Edition of the Unpublished Dead Sea Scrolls: Fascicle One* [Washington, DC: Biblical Archaeology Society, 1991] 60-95).

The use of this calendar is also confirmed by the regulations for the sacrifices given in the Feast-Day Calendar of 11QTemple 13:8-30:2, according to which we learn that the community also celebrated feasts not recognized by other Jews. The list of sacrifices and feasts given in this scroll is as follows: the Daily Tamid, the Sabbath Offering, the Offering at priestly Ordination, I/2-10 (*Millû'îm,* 11QTemple 15:13-17:5), the feasts of New Year, I/1 (14:9-15:?), Passover, I/14 (17:6-9), Unleavened Bread, I/15-22 (17:10-16), Sheaf-Waving or First Fruits of Barley, I/26 (18:?-18:10), Feast of Weeks or First Fruits of Wheat, III/15 (18:10-19:9), First Fruits of New Wine, V/3 (19:11-21:10), First Fruits of Oil, VI/22 (21:12-23:9), the Wood Festival, VI/23-29 (23:?-25:2), the Seventh Month, VII/1 (25:2-10), the Day of Atonement, VII/10 (25:10-27:10), Tabernacles, VII/15-23 (27:10-29:2). The Feast of Oil is also mentioned in 4QMišm Eb 1 ii 4-7 as occurring on VI/22, which agrees only with the 364-day calendar.

What is striking here is the celebration of three Pentecosts: the Pentecost of Wheat, the Pentecost of Wine, and the Pentecost of Oil, each clearly marked as "fifty days" from the preceding feast, beginning with the Sheaf-Waving or First Fruits of Barley. *Pentēkostē* is the Greek name for the "fiftieth" day, which the LXX of Tob 2:1 describes as "the sacred (festival) of the Seven Weeks." Its postbiblical Aramaic name was *'ăsartā'*, or in Greek *Asartha,* as used by Josephus (*Ant.* 3.10.6 § 252), which means "(the feast of) the Gathering" or "Assembly." It was to be fifty days from Passover, but reckoned according to Lev 23:15-16, "from the morrow after the sabbath (*mimmoḥŏrat haššabbāt*), from the day that you brought the sheaf of the wave offering: seven full weeks shall they be, counting fifty days to the morrow of the seventh sabbath." Debate ensued, however, among Palestinian Jews about the meaning of "sabbath" in that formula. For Sadducees that "sabbath" was understood as the "feast day" itself (I/15), and fifty days from its "morrow" resulted in the Feast of Weeks being celebrated on III/6. Pharisees counted from the sabbath after Passover, whenever that would come. Still others, like the Qumran community, which used the 364-day calendar, reckoned the fifty days from the morrow of the sabbath after the Passover octave, thus beginning from Sheaf-Waving or the First Fruits of Barley (I/26). As a result, the first Pentecost, the Feast of Weeks, First Fruits of Wheat, fell on III/15.

Particularly important for the Qumran community was the celebration of this Feast of Weeks on III/15, because according to Exod 19:1 Israel arrived in its exodus-wandering at Mt. Sinai in the third month after leaving Egypt, i.e. after Passover. Thus in time the giving of the Sinai Covenant was commemorated yearly, and this commemoration may be reflected in the "assembly" of Jews in Jerusalem in the fifteenth year of King Asa, recorded in 2 Chr 15:10-12. Later the renewal of the Covenant came to be celebrated on the Feast of Weeks (see *Jub.* 6:17: "It is ordained and inscribed in heavenly tablets that they are to celebrate the Feast of Weeks in this month once a year, so as to renew the covenant each year"). This yearly celebration became part of the Qumran community's life; the rite of renewal of their Covenant is described in 1QS 1:16-2:25, most of which is quoted as the entrance rite in § 55 above.

The consequence of the use of this calendar is that the Qumran community's celebration of the main feast days did not coincide with those of the rest of Judaism, and for that reason its calendar was regarded as "unorthodox." Other Jews were using a lunar calendar of 12 months of 29½ days, which made a year of 354 days and which did not correspond to the four seasons, determined by the sun, the solstices, and the equinoxes; so every three years an extra month had to be intercalated, Second Adar, which followed Adar (= our February/March). The Qumran community found serious fault with this lunar calendar-observance and hence broke with the rest of Judaism. It maintained: "With those who held fast to the commandments of God {the Qumran community}, who were left (as a remnant) from them {the rest of Judaism}, God established his 'covenant for Israel' forever, to reveal to them {the community} the hidden things in which all Israel had strayed: His holy sabbaths, His glorious feast days, His righteous testimonies, and His faithful ways, the desires of His good pleasure, which man must do and by which he shall live . . ." (CD 3:12–16). This explains why "all who have been brought into the Covenant are not to go to the sanctuary to kindle in vain (a sacrifice) on its altar" (CD 6:11), i.e. why the community took no part in the sacrificial offerings of the Jerusalem Temple, because the sacrifices would be offered on the wrong days (cf. CD 6:17–20). Similarly, the priests and levites of the rest of Judaism served in the Temple in twenty-four courses (1 Chr 24:7–19; *m. Taanith* 4:2). But according to the Qumran community they were to serve in twenty-six, each course serving for a week in each half-year; to this practice the passage quoted above from 1QM 2:1–2 refers.

This explains why the Wicked Priest was able to come from Jerusalem to the Teacher of Righteousness "in his place of exile" on the feast of "the Day of Atonement" to devour them and "cause them to stumble on the Day of Fasting" (1QpHab 11:6–8; see § 48 above).

61. What do the QS tell us about the community's observance of the sabbath?

Because it is prescribed in the Decalogue, "Remember to keep holy the sabbath day" (Exod 20:8; Deut 5:12), the observance of this day was of supreme importance in the Qumran community. Though nothing is said about the observance of the sabbath in the Manual of Discipline, there is extensive regulation that heightens its observance in the Damascus Document:

Concerning the sab[b]ath, that (they may) observe it according to the regulation for it: Let no one do any work on the sixth day from the time when the sun's disc is distant (by) its fullness from the gate {wherein it sets}, for this is what it {Scripture} says, *"Observe the sabbath day to keep it holy."*

On the sabbath let no one utter a foolish or vain word; let no one lend anything to his companion. Let them not adjudicate matters of property or profit. Let them not discuss matters of work or the labor that is to be done on the morrow. Let no one walk in the field to carry out his business labor on the sabbath. Let no one walk beyond a thousand cubits outside his town. Let one eat on the sabbath day only that which has been prepared (beforehand); and from that which has been lost in the field let no one eat. Let one drink only in the camp. . . . Let no one draw water in any vessel. Let no one send a stranger to carry out his business on the sabbath day. Let no one put on himself soiled garments or those brought to a closet unless they have been washed in water or rubbed with incense. No one shall fast at his own pleasure on the sabbath. No one shall walk beyond two thousand cubits after a beast to pasture it outside his town. Let no one raise his hand to hit it with his fist; if it is stubborn, let him not (try to) bring it out of his house. No one may bring anything outside the house or take anything into (it). If one is in a booth, let him not bring anything out of it or bring anything into it. No one shall open a sealed vessel on the sabbath. No one shall carry medicaments with him when coming or going on the sabbath. No one shall pick up in his dwelling place a stone or clod of dirt. A foster-father shall not carry an infant when coming and going on the sabbath. Let no one aggravate his manservant, maidservant, or hireling on the sabbath. No one shall assist a beast to give birth on a sabbath day; if it should fall into a cistern or into a pit, no one shall lift it out on a sabbath. On the sabbath no one shall spend the sabbath-rest in a place near to Gentiles. On the sabbath let no one profane the sabbath-rest for the sake of property or profit. As for every human being who falls into a place of water or a place of ‹fire›, let someone bring him up with a ladder or a rope or (some other) object. No one shall offer anything on the altar on the sabbath but the sabbath holocaust, for thus it is written, *"Apart from your sabbath-offerings"* (Lev 23:38) (CD 10:14–11:18).

62. What was the community's attitude toward the Temple in Jerusalem?

During the time of the Qumran community, Jerusalem Jews were still using as the Temple the shabby building that had been constructed on the return of Jews from the Babylonian Captivity at the end of the sixth century B.C. The Temple was eventually reconstructed under Herod the Great, who began work on it in the eighteenth year of his reign (20–19 B.C.). By that time the Qumran community had been in existence for over a century. The Temple Scroll of Cave 11 contains an elaborate description of the Temple. This is obviously the way the people who composed this text toward the middle of the second century B.C. thought that the Temple should be reconstructed.

These things [you shall offer on your feast days   ] for your holocausts and your libations [   ] in the house on which I [shall cause] my name to dwell [   ], burnt offerings, [each] on its [proper] day according to the law of this regulation, continually from the children of Israel, besides their freewill offerings for everything that they shall offer, for all their libations and all their gifts, which they shall bring to me for acceptance. And I shall accept them, and they shall be my people, and I shall be theirs forever, and I shall dwell with them for ever and ever. I shall consecrate my [te]mple with my glory, (the temple) on which I shall cause my glory to dwell until the day of blessing, when I shall create my (own) temple and establish it for all times, according to the covenant which I made with Jacob at Bethel (11QTemple 29:2–10).

In this passage one reads the command given by God Himself to reconstruct the Jerusalem Temple, a place where God will make his glory dwell until "the day of blessing," when He would create His own eschatological Temple. This was the conviction about the Temple, by which the Qumran community lived. This accounts for the elaborate description of how it should be built. Herod's reconstruction of the Temple unfortunately did not follow their plans.

But long before Herod's work began, the Qumran community had expressed its opposition to the Jerusalem Temple and its cult. It is not that they were against the Temple, its sacrifices, and its cult as such, but they did not approve of the priests who were serving in the Temple, because of their failure to carry out their duties according to traditional practices and purity regulations and because of the calendar that they were following.

The Qumran community seems to have originally been formed of a nucleus of Jewish priests, the sons of Zadok, as they are often referred to (1QS 5:2, 9; 1QSa 1:2, 24; 2:3; 1QSb 3:22). They were descended from the priesthood that formerly served in the Temple. But they apparently broke with those Jerusalem priests and would not have approved of their Temple cult in the decades after the Maccabean revolt, for some of them apparently even became temporizers with the Roman occupiers after 63 B.C.

Moreover, the QS speak of *hakkôhēn hārāšāʻ*, "the Wicked Priest," the adversary of the Teacher of Righteousness. He is usually thought to have been Jonathan Maccabee, who succeeded his brother ca. 162 B.C. but usurped the high priesthood about 152 B.C. and reigned until his death in 143 B.C. The Pesher on Habakkuk describes him thus: "The interpretation of it concerns the Wicked Priest, who was called in the name of truth at the beginning of his rise [i.e. 162 B.C.]. But when he came to rule over Israel, his heart became haughty [i.e. 152 B.C.], and he abandoned God and betrayed the precepts because of riches. He stole and heaped up the riches of violent men who had rebelled against God" (1QpHab 8:8–11). This Wicked Priest also persecuted the community, disturbing its festive Day of Atonement (see § 48 above). For the Qumran community this priest epitomized all that was wrong with the Temple. Yet his colleagues in the Temple were no better. The Pesher says of them: "The interpretation of it concerns the last priests of Jerusalem (kôhănê yĕrûšālayim hā'aḥărônîm) who heaped up riches and gain by plundering the people. But at the end of days their riches and their booty will be handed over to the army of the Kittim, for they are the remnant of the peoples" (1QpHab 9:4-7; cf. 4QpNah 1:11).

The disapproval of the Jerusalem priesthood was undoubtedly the main reason why the community withdrew to the desert, to prepare there the way of the Lord (1QS 8:13-15) by studying the Law. Instead of the Temple, the Qumran community regarded itself as having built bayit ne'ĕmān bĕyiśrā'ēl, "a trustworthy house in Israel" (CD 3:19). In contrast to the priests in Jerusalem, the community was established in truth, as "an everlasting planting, a house of holiness for Israel" (1QS 8:5).

Commenting on 2 Sam 7:10-11, the Qumran author explains,

> This is the house that [He will build for them at the e]nd of days, as it stands written in the book of ['In the sanctuary which] Your hands have [er]ected, [O Lord], Yahweh shall reign forever and ever!' (Exod 15:17-18). This is the house into which [the unclean] shall never enter, never an Ammonite, a Moabite, a bastard, a foreigner, or a sojourner, for there shall my holy ones be. [My glory] sh[a]ll be there forever; it shall be seen above it perpetually. Strangers shall not lay waste to it, as they formerly laid waste the sanctua[ry of I]srael because of their sin. He has commanded them to build for Him a sanctuary of men, that they may offer the deeds of the Law as incense to Him in it" (4QFlor [4Q174] 1-2 i 2-7).

Thus the Qumran community regarded itself as the replacement of the Jerusalem Temple and its sacrifices. In a word, it was "the Temple of God."

It is a matter of debate whether the Qumran community offered sacrifices in their desert retreat. The excavations at Khirbet Qumran turned up thirteen deposits of animal bones carefully stored and covered with sherds or pitchers and pots or sometimes placed in jars with lids on them. When analyzed, the bones proved to be of sheep, goats, calves, and oxen. They were the remnants of meals; the bones were clean, but some had been charred. The care with which the bones were set apart after the flesh had been cooked and eaten is puzzling. Were they the remains of some sacrifices? No one can answer that question. No remains of any altars have been found in the excavations, and nothing in any of the QS explains this peculiar deposit of animal bones.

All of this serves to show why the Qumran community had a very definite stance toward the Jerusalem Temple and its priests and cult.

63. What do the QS tell us about the community's dealings with Gentiles?

The members of the Qumran community were expected to avoid dealings with other Jews; so it is not surprising that they would avoid dealings with Gentiles too. First, the QS refer to the Roman occupiers of the country as the *Kittîm* or *Kittî'îm,* a name derived from Greek *Kition,* a town on the southeast coast of Cyprus (modern Larnaka). Though Kittim are mentioned among the descendants of Javan in Gen 10:4, the name came to denote in Jer 2:10 the people of "coasts" in the far western Mediterranean. In 1 Macc 1:1; 8:5 it is used more properly of the Macedonian Greeks, from whom came Alexander the Great, but in Dan 11:30 it designates the Romans who forced Antiochus IV Epiphanes to withdraw from Egypt. From this Danielic usage, the Qumran writers adopt Kittim as a code-word for the Romans. In 1QpHab 2:12 the Kittim are described as "quick and valiant in battle, causing many to perish," under whose dominion the whole earth falls; "fear and dread of whom extends over all the nations" (3:4), for "they trample the earth with their horses and beasts" (3:9; cf. 4:5,10; 6:1,10; 9:7). The holy war described in the War Scroll is to be waged against the Kittim (1QM 1:2, 3, 6, 9, 12, etc.). Thus the pesharim and the War Scroll manifest the community's attitude toward the Roman occupiers.

Second, the word *gôyim* occurs in the QS not just in the generic sense of "nations" (1QM 2:7; 4:12), but in the specific sense of "Gentiles." An ambiguous regulation is found in the Damascus Document: "Everyone who puts another human being under a deadly curse is to be put to death by the laws of the Gentiles" (CD 9:1); or it may mean, "Everyone who puts another human being under a deadly curse by the laws of the Gentiles is to be put to death." (It is not clear with what *bĕḥûqqê haggôyim*, "by the laws of the Gentiles," is to be taken; but the first translation seems more likely.)

Again there are some very specific regulations, "Let no one stretch out his hand to shed the blood of one of the Gentiles for the sake of property or profit. Let no one carry off any of their property, lest they utter blasphemies, unless by the consent of the association of Israel. Let no one sell clean beasts or birds to the Gentiles, lest they sacrifice them. Let no one sell them anything from his granary or his winepress under any circumstances. Let no one sell to them his slave or his maidservant, who have come with him into the covenant of Abraham" (CD 12:6–11).

In the broken text of 4QpHos^a 2:16 there may be reference to a Gentile calendar: "they will cause ‹them› to walk by the festivals of the Gentiles."

The Temple Scroll has a very specific rule for Jews who in a war take captive a beautiful woman from among Israel's enemies:

> When you go out to war against your enemies and I give them into your hand, and you take them captive and see among the captives a woman beautiful in appearance, whom you covet and would take as a wife, you shall bring her into your house, shave her head, and pare her nails. You shall take off her captive-garb, and she shall dwell in your house and bewail her father and her mother for a full month. Then you may go in to her and be her husband, and she shall be your wife. But she may not touch your Purity for seven years, nor may she consume a peace-offering until seven years pass. Afterwards she may eat (63:10–15).

64. What relation do the QS have to the Pharisees or Sadducees mentioned in the NT?

It is not easy to answer this question, because the last text mentioned in § 15, 4QMMT, which may have a bearing on it, has not yet been officially published (a preliminary, unauthorized publication of the text has appeared in the *Qumran Chronicle* 2 [1991] appendix); and it will take some time before scholars agree about its nature and relation to the Qumran community. But it seems to refer to Pharisees.

The question is also complicated by the history of the Qumran community. As we have already indicated, the community members have some relation to the Zadokite priesthood. They are called at times in the QS *bĕnê ṣādôq,* "sons of Zadok" (1QS 5:2, 9; 1QSa 1:2, 24; 1QSb 3:22; 4QFlor [4Q174] 1-2 i 17; CD 3:21; 4:3), thus related to the priestly line named after Zadok mentioned in 1 Kgs 1:26 (cf. Ezek 40:46; 44:15; 48:11). This is probably also the source of the title *Saddoukaioi* of NT writings (Mark 12:18; Matt 3:7; 16:1,6, 11, 12; 23:23, 34; Luke 20:27; Acts 4:1; 5:17; 23:6, 7, 8). But there is no certainty that the "sons of Zadok" mentioned in the QS are related to these Sadducees. One reason for this is the community's negative attitude toward "the last priests of Jerusalem," mentioned above in § 62. The opponent of the community's Teacher of Righteousness is called the "Wicked Priest" (*hkwhn hrš‘,* 1QpHab 8:8; 9:9; 11:4). These terms seem to refer to the priests of the Jerusalem Temple, who would apparently have been Sadducees, "the party of the high priest" (Acts 5:17). Josephus depicts the Sadducees as influential among the rich, but with little influence among the ordinary people (*Ant.* 13.10.6 § 298; 18.1.4 § 16–17). The Sadducees first emerged about the middle of the second century B.C. As sons of Zadok, they should have opposed the Hasmoneans who usurped the high priesthood, but they apparently supported them and so won the opposition of the "sons of Zadok" of the Qumran community.

As for the Pharisees, they may be referred to in the QS as *dôrĕšê ḥălāqôt,* "seekers after smooth things" (4QpNah 1:2, 7; 1QH 2:[15], 32), a derogatory name used of some adversaries in the QS. These adversaries are thought to be Pharisees, for these Jews had a great interest in *ḥălākôt,* "(halakhic) regulations," a term which may be reflected in the derogatory name, "seekers after smooth things," a pun on what they advocated. The Qumran community clearly considered itself stricter in observing regulations of the Mosaic law than such adversaries, and the Temple Scroll of Cave 11 as well as the rule books reveal in what regard their regulations were stricter. So in this way the QS may reflect opposition to the Pharisees.

Because of this opposition to both the Sadducees and the Pharisees, if such allusions to them in the QS are rightly interpreted, many scholars today are inclined to identify the Qumran community with the Essenes. But the main reasons for this identification are not solely such "opposition."

65. Who were the Essenes?

Though the Essenes are not mentioned in the NT, various ancient writers name them as a group of Palestinian Jews in pre-Christian times. They are called by the Jewish historian, Flavius Josephus, *Essēnoi* (*J.W.* 2.8.2 § 119) or *Essaioi* (*Ant.* 15.10.4 § 371). He mentions them when he speaks of the three kinds of "philosophy" that exist among the Jews of Judea. Josephus is trying to explain the different kinds of Jews to Greek-speaking Romans and thus calls their different *haireseis,* "sects" (*Life* 2 § 10) "philosophies."

The Essenes are first mentioned by Josephus in connection with events in the mid second century B.C., about the time of Jonathan, son of Mattathias, brother of Judas Maccabee. The Essenes have been related by some scholars to the Hasidim or Hasideans (1 Macc 2:42; 7:13), those Jews who at first sided with the Maccabees' revolt against Antiochus IV Epiphanes, but broke off from them when the Maccabees became too involved in the politics of the time. These scholars even see the name "Essene" related to an Aramaic form of Hasidim, "pious ones." But other interpreters think that the Qumran community emerged from Jews who returned to Palestine from Babylon toward the end of the second quarter of the second century B.C., having heard of the success of the Maccabean revolt (167–165 B.C.). For them "Damascus," which is mentioned in the CD, would be a code-name for Babylon. But they would have refused to support the rest of the house of Judah at that time because they found that the Judean Jews were not living strictly according to the ancient traditions of the fathers, and so they broke with such lax Jews and retired to the desert of Qumran as Essenes. Their name has been explained at times as "Healers," related to the Aramaic noun *'āsayyā',* "physicians" (so G. Vermes). Other scholars try to explain it as a Greek corruption of Hebrew *'ôśê hattôrāh,* "doers of the Law" (see 1QpHab 7:11), Greek

Ossaioi becoming *Essaioi,* since the former is attested as a spelling for "Essenes" in some patristic writers.

No matter which theory about the emergence of the Essenes is correct, there can be no doubt that there was a group of Judean Jews so called in the mid-second century B.C. who differed with the Sadducees and the Pharisees, especially in view of their strict mode of interpreting the Law. So they stand a good chance to be the Jews we know of from the QS as the Qumran community.

The Damascus Document seems to speak of the community being formed about 390 years after the capture of Jerusalem by Nebuchadnezzar in 587 B.C.: "then God made a new planting grow forth from Aaron and Israel" (CD 1:5-7). That should refer to about 197 B.C., but the number 390 may be figurative, derived from Ezek 4:5 and intended only to express a long time after Nebuchadnezzar's conquest. Another passage in the QS may refer to the independence of Jerusalem first gained from the Seleucids: from the time of Antiochus IV Epiphanes until the rise of the rulers of the Kittim (=the Romans; see 4QpNah 1:3-4). From the standpoint of the writer, who has composed this commentary on the prophet's words in the time of the Romans, this would refer to the beginning of the community, sometime toward the end of the reign of Antiochus IV Epiphanes (175-164 B.C.). This is more or less the time about which Josephus mentions the Essenes for the first time.

The community itself may have supported the Maccabean revolt against Antiochus, if its origin is to be sought in the Hasidim mentioned above, but later have broken off from the Maccabees. The period of this break may also be referred to in the Damascus Document, which speaks of the community as "blind men, groping to seek their way for twenty years," for whom God finally "raised up a Teacher of Righteousness to lead them in the way of his heart" (CD 1:9-11).

Josephus speaks of the Essenes as following "a way of life taught to Greeks by Pythagoras" (*Ant.* 15.10.4 § 371), which would characterize their life as communal, ascetic, and religious. Though such a comparison with the Pythagoreans is often queried by modern scholars, the Qumran community did lead that kind of life. As we have already seen, the Qumran sectarians regarded themselves as the New Covenant (see Jer 31:31; cf. CD 6:19; 8:21; 19:34; 20:12; 1QpHab 2:[3]), and their community was restricted to Jews, who voluntarily

joined the group to live in common according to a strict interpretation of the Mosaic law.

In a similar way Josephus speaks of the Essenes, who adopted
the children of others, while yet pliable and docile, and trained them
in their way of life (*J.W.* 2.8.2 § 120), who practiced a community of
goods and whose new members merged their property with the community and used all in common like "brothers" (2.8.3 § 122).

> For those who seek to join their sect entrance is not
> immediate. For one year he remains outside the sect, and
> they present him with a way of life, a small hatchet, the
> aforementioned loin-cloth, and white garments. When he
> gives proof of his discipline during this time, they bring
> him closer to their way of life and allow him to share in
> the holiness of their purer waters, but he is not yet accepted
> into the meetings of the community. After such a display
> of steadfastness, for two more years his character is tested,
> and having appeared worthy, he is enrolled in the com-
> munity. But before he may touch the common food, he
> swears to them terrifying oaths, that he will reverence the
> Deity, that he will observe justice toward (other) human
> beings, that he will wrong no one either by his own judg-
> ment or at the behest of someone else, that he will always
> hate the wicked and struggle with the upright, that he will
> always keep faith with all others, especially with author-
> ities, since no ruler comes to rule apart from the will of
> God . . . ; that he hide nothing from the sectarians and
> not reveal any of their secrets to others . . . ; that he will
> abstain from robbery and likewise preserve the books of
> the sect, as well as the names of the angels (2.8.7 § 137–42).

Josephus also tells of the common meal of the Essenes, who after
their work until the fifth hour of the day and a bath of purification
don linen clothes and assemble in a private apartment, which none
of the uninitiated is permitted to enter.

> Pure now themselves, they repair to the refectory, as to
> some sacred shrine. Having seated themselves in silence,
> the baker places loaves before them in order and the cook

sets before them one plate with a single course. The priest prays over the food first, and it is not allowed to taste the food before the prayer. When the meal is finished, he prays again. Thus as they begin and as they end they give homage to God as the sustainer of life" (*J.W.* 2.8.5 § 129–31).

Philo, Pliny the Elder, and Josephus all know of the celibate character of the Essenes. Pliny (*Nat. Hist.* 5.17.4) and Philo (*Hypothetica* 11.14 § 380) are categorical about Essene abstention from marriage. Josephus (*J.W.* 2.8.2 § 120) speaks of the Essene "disdain" for marriage but also knows that there was "another order of Essenes," which differed from the rest in its view of marriage and which did marry, because they considered "the propagation of the race" as "the chief function of life" (2.8.13 § 160). So if the Qumran community is indeed to be identified with the Essenes of whom these ancient writers speak, then the evidence from the QS and the ancient writers indicates that these Jews of Qumran were celibate at least at some stage of their existence. Since the community seems to have lived at Qumran from roughly mid-second century B.C. until about A.D. 68, there could well have been both celibate Essenes and those that married. It is, however, not impossible that the Essenes at Qumran were celibate, whereas those that lived in towns and villages throughout Judea, about whom Josephus also tells us (*J.W.* 2.8.4 § 124), were married. These would then have been those living in "camps" and "according to the rule of the land," as the Damascus Document puts it. Philo maintains that they lived in villages and avoided the contaminating influence of cities (*Quod omnis prob. liber* 12 § 76); but even he knows of Therapeutae in Egypt, related to the Essenes of "Palestinian Syria" (*De vita contemp.* 1 § 1–2).

Josephus in his discussion of the Essenes tells us further, "They do ‹not› send votive offerings to the Temple, but carry out their sacrifices with a difference of purity rites, which they consider (important). For this reason barring themselves from the common court of the people, they carry out their sacrifices by themselves" (*Ant.* 18.1.5 § 19). This text of Josephus is difficult to interpret, for the negative adverb "not" is not read in all the manuscripts. But Philo (*Quod omnis probus liber sit* 12 § 75) also says of the Essenes, "They have shown themselves especially devout in the service of God, not by sacrificing living animals, but by deeming it proper to prepare their own minds as befits their sacred calling." Whatever we are to make of these two quotations about the Essenes and their attitude toward sacrifices, they do not contradict the data in the QS themselves.

The evident similarity of details in the passages quoted from such ancient writers to that given above from the QS is the main reason for identifying the Qumran community with the Essenes about whom Josephus, Philo, and Pliny report.

66. What other ancient writers tell us about the Essenes?

The main ancient writers who mention the Essenes are Pliny the Elder (*Nat. Hist.* 5.17.4 § 73), Flavius Josephus (*J.W.* 1.3.5 § 78–80; 2.7.3 § 113; 2.8.2–13 § 119–61; 2.20.4 § 567; 3.2.1 § 11; 5.4.2 § 145; *Life* 2 § 7–12; *Ant.* 13.5.9 § 171–72; 15.10.4–5 § 371–79; 18.1.5 § 18–22), and Philo of Alexandria (*Quod omnis prob. liber* 12–13 § 75–91; *Hypothetica* 11.1–18 [quoted in Eusebius, *Praepar. evang.* 8.6–7]; on the Therapeutae of Egypt: *De vita contemp.* 1 § 1–2; 2–4 § 11–40; 8–11 § 63–90).

The Essenes have also been mentioned by Dio Chrysostom, quoted in Synesius of Cyrene, *Dio* 3.2; Hegesippus, *Hypomnemata,* quoted in Eusebius, *HE* 4.22.7; Hippolytus of Rome, *Refutatio omnium haeresium* 9.18.2–9.28.2; Epiphanius of Salamis, *Panarion* 10.1–5; 19.1.1–4, 10; 5.1, 6–7; 20.3.1–4; *Constitutiones Apostolorum* 6.6.1–8; Jerome, *De vir. illustr.* 11; *Adv. Iovinianum* 2.14; Philastrius of Brescia, *Diversarum haereseon liber* 9; Nilus of Ancyra, *Tractatus de monastica exercitatione* 1–4; Isidore of Seville, *Etymologiae* 7.4.5; Suidas, *E* 3123; Michael I of Antioch, *Chronikon* 6.1.

See further A. Adam, *Antike Berichte über die Essener* (2d ed.; Berlin/New York: de Gruyter, 1972); G. Vermes, *The Essenes according to the Classical Sources* (Oxford Centre Textbooks 1; Sheffield, UK: JSOT, 1989).

67. Is the identification of the Qumran community with the Essenes certain?

No, it is not. The identification of the Qumran community with the Essenes was apparently first proposed by Eleazar Lipa Sukenik;

he has been followed by A. Dupont-Sommer, Y. Yadin, G. Vermes, J. T. Milik, F. M. Cross, and many others. In fact, the identification of the Qumran community with the Essenes is currently the opinion of the majority of scholars who have been studying the QS. But there have always been interpreters who have contested that identification, e.g. G. R. Driver, C. Roth, S. Zeitlin, M. H. Gottstein, N. Golb, L. Schiffman, R. H. Eisenman.

Josephus, in speaking of the Essenes in Judea, mentions them for the first time in the reign of Jonathan Maccabee, who usurped the high priesthood about 152 B.C. Josephus himself tried out their way of life sometime in the second quarter of the first century A.D., as he tells us in his *Life* (2 § 10–11). This span of time, from the mid-second century B.C. to the mid-first A.D., is precisely the time when the community mentioned in the DSS was in existence, living at Qumran until the first revolt of Palestinian Jews against Rome (A.D. 66–70). This is also precisely the time when the archaeologists date the strata of Periods Ia, Ib, and II of Khirbet Qumran (roughly 150 B.C. to A.D. 68).

Pliny the Elder, who died in the eruption of Vesuvius (A.D. 79) and who wrote sometime after the destruction of Jerusalem (A.D. 70), which he mentions, locates the *Esseni* in the Judean desert, living along the western shore of the Dead Sea somewhere south of Jericho and north of En-gedi (*Nat. Hist.* 5.17.4 § 73). Since the only place that Pliny could have referred to in that desert area, which is known to have been inhabited in Roman times, is Khirbet Qumran, this is the best reason for identifying the Qumran community with the Essenes. This is the reason given by R. de Vaux, the excavator of Khirbet Qumran (*Archaeology,* 133–38) and has been confirmed by the studies of E.-M. Laperrousaz (*Qoumrân,* 229).

What is now known about the Qumran community from the QS agrees in general with the information given about the Essenes and their organized way of life, doctrines, and practices described by both Josephus (*J.W.* 2.8.2–13 § 119–61; *Ant.* 18.1.5 § 18–22) and Philo (*Quod omnis prob. liber* 12–13 § 75–91; *Hypothetica* 11.1–18).

There are, indeed, some conflicting details in the various accounts and texts. Yet Josephus himself knows of different kinds of Essenes, and the site of Khirbet Qumran reveals that the community lived there for roughly two centuries; so there could have been an evolution in the structure and life of the community. See T. S. Beall, *Josephus' Description of the Essenes Illustrated by the Dead Sea Scrolls* (SNTSMS 58; Cambridge: University Press, 1988).

The question recently raised about the identification of the community depends on the interpretation of 4QMMT, the text mentioned in § 15 above. Until that is fully published and its relationship to the community is clarified, the majority opinion will undoubtedly hold sway. On the basis of that text some have tried to maintain that the Qumran community was not Essene, but Sadducee, but that has also been contested. See J. C. VanderKam, "The People of the Dead Sea Scrolls: Essenes or Sadducees?" *Bible Review* 7/2 (1991) 42–47; J. M. Baumgarten, "Some Remarks on the Qumran Law and the Identification of the Community," in *Qumran Cave IV and MMT: Special Report* (ed. Z. J. Kapera; Cracow: Enigma Press, 1991) 115–17.

68. How does the Qumran understanding of God differ from that in the NT?

In the NT Jesus is depicted as repeating the Shema, the ancient basic Israelite creed: "Listen, O Israel, the Lord our God, the Lord is One" (Mark 12:29), formulated as in the LXX, but echoing the original of Deut 6:4, "Listen, O Israel, Yahweh is our God, Yahweh alone." Jesus thus affirmed the monotheism of Israel, the God of his forebears.

Such a notion is basic to the Christian view of God in the NT. In this there would be no difference from that of the Qumran community (see § 43 above).

The NT, however, depicts Jesus as "the Son of God" (Rom 1:3; Mark 1:1, 11; John 1:18; 3:17; Heb 1:2–5), using of him a title, which has roots in the OT (see § 74 below). But such a title is given to no identifiable individual in the QS, nor to any member of the Qumran community.

Moreover, the NT portrays Jesus addressing God as "Father," again with a title that has roots in the OT. In the OT, however, when "Father" is used of God, it has a different connotation. It is used of God, when Israel is spoken of as his children or his first born (Exod 3:22–23; Deut 14:1; Isa 30:9; Hos 11:1–3); when God is considered as creator (Deut 32:6; Mal 2:10), as Lord of his chosen people who are expected to obey him (Jer 3:19; 31:9; Isa 63:16), as the one against whom Israel sins (Jer 3:4–5; Mal 1:16), and as the one from whom come mercy, assistance, and forgiveness (Ps 103:13; Isa 64:7–8). Thus God is acknowledged by Israel as "our Father" (Isa 63:16; 64:8), and David or its king addresses him as "my Father" (Ps 89:27). Yet in all these passages God is viewed as the Father of corporate or national Israel.

The use of "Father" by an individual Palestinian Jew in addressing God is rare. It may be attested in deuterocanonical Sir 23:1,4: "O Lord, Father and Ruler/God of my life." But that address is found only in the Greek translation of Sirach, whereas the Hebrew text has "Say to one who fashioned you, 'God of my father and Lord of my life.'" Joachim Jeremias once thought that such an address might be found in two deuterocanonical writings: Tob 13:4, which reads, "because he is the Lord our God, our Father and God forever," and Sir 51:10, "I extolled the Lord, 'You are my Father.'" The first, however, is again an instance of the corporate sense, whereas the second may be a valid example.

Two examples of it have now turned up in Qumran texts: *'ābî wĕ'lōhay, 'al ta'azbēnî bĕyad haggôyim*, "My Father, my God, do not abandon me to the Gentiles" (4QJoseph [4Q372] 1:16); see E. Schuller, *RevQ* 14 (1989–90) 352, who reports that there is another text as yet unpublished, 4Q460 5:6, which reads, *'ābî wa'ădônî*, "My Father and my Lord." This is new important evidence. In one of the Qumran Thanksgiving Psalms we also read: "For you are Father to all [the sons of] your truth, and You take delight in them as one who gives birth in her child" (1QH 9:35–36), which is possibly an echo of Prov 23:25. Here God is again acknowledged as father in a corporate sense, as the Father of the Qumran community. Similarly, in *Jub.* 1:28; 19:29 "father" is used, echoing 2 Sam 7:14, now applied to "the children of Israel."

In contrast to this OT and Qumran usage, there is the clear address of God as *abba* by the individual Jesus of Nazareth in Mark 14:36, echoed in Gal 4:6; Rom 8:15, which makes of it a prayer for individual Christians. Hence the sonship of Jesus in the NT is something intimately related to his concept of God as Father (see Luke 10:21-22; Matt 11:25-27). The Johannine Gospel makes much of this relationship, regarding it specifically as the notion of God that Jesus has been sent to reveal (John 5:36-37, 43; 15:15-16).

In addition to such NT verses that speak of a special sense in which Jesus of Nazareth is the Son of God, a sense not common to others (Christians), who are regarded as adopted "sons of God" or "children of God" (Rom 8:14-17, 21), there are also verses that predicate the title *theos* of Jesus (John 1:1; 20:28; Heb 1:5-8; possibly also Rom 9:5, depending on how the verse is punctuated). Such a usage is not found at all in the QS. The closest that one comes to anything like that is found in 11QMelch 10-11, where Pss 82:1 and 7:8-9 are predicated of Melchizedek, now considered a heavenly figure, and to whom *'Elôhîm* or *'El* from the psalms is applied. But this, in effect, equates Melchizedek with an "angel," since that is the meaning of these words in these psalms.

So the notion of God found in the NT differs somewhat from that of the QS. After all, the Qumran community was not Christian. In the NT one finds the elements that lead eventually to the Trinitarian understanding of "God" in the Christian sense. The NT formulation is not yet explicit in this regard, for the NT writers have not yet sought to unpack the idea of *theos* or *deus,* as it would later be understood in the patristic period, when the notion of the Triune God becomes explicit. Here it is a question of distinguishing ideas of God, the history of which is not yet mature. But the QS contains none of those elements that one finds in the NT.

69. How do the QS help in the study of the NT?

The NT writings were composed in Greek, by early Christians who lived roughly a generation or two after Jesus of Nazareth. They date from roughly A.D. 50-110, in other words from the second half of the first Christian century. The QS, however, written mostly in Aramaic or Hebrew and dating roughly from the mid-second century B.C. to A.D. 68, have proved to be very important in the study of the NT, because they shed light on the very matrix in which Christianity itself was born. Though the vast majority of the NT writings were composed outside of Judea, at various places in the eastern Mediterranean world, yet the movement to which those writings are related began in Judea and among the Jews of the period of the QS. Hence it is not surprising that in the Greek text of the Gospels and Acts, in particular, one detects many echoes of Palestinian Jewish life, language, and literature. Moreover, it is not surprising that characteristic Jewish phrases, now known from the QS, turn up in Greek dress in the NT writings. Whereas there was the tendency, before the discovery of the DSS, to explain Jewish-sounding phrases in such writings by comparison with later rabbinic literature (e.g. the great commentary of P. Billerbeck, *Kommentar zum Neuen Testament aus Talmud und Midrasch* [6 vols.; Munich: Beck, 1926-63]), now one realizes that there is Palestinian Jewish literature available for comparison that is slightly prior to or almost contemporaneous with Jesus of Nazareth and slightly prior to the composition of NT writings. For this reason the QS lend themselves more properly than the rabbinic literature of the third to the sixth centuries as the corpus of Jewish writings with which such comparison should preferably be made. This does not mean that the rabbinic literature is wholly replaced; it is not, but it now has to be used with greater care and circumspection. One has to have some other control to guide in the selection of comparable material from the rabbinic corpus. Sometimes, some of the material that occurs in the QS is also found in the rabbinic tradition; in such a case the QS themselves provide the control and show that what is used from the rabbinic tradition was indeed characteristic of Judaism of the first century A.D. Or a literary tradition attested in the rabbinic literature may be known from either Philo or Josephus; in such a case there is again a first-century control that reveals that the rabbinic tradition was already in vogue.

To give an example of the differences. Years ago Bruce M. Metzger, of the Princeton Theological Seminary, studied the formulas used to introduce explicit OT quotations that are found scattered through most of the NT books; he compared them with similar formulas in the Mishnah, the earliest of the rabbinic corpus ("The Formulas Introducing Quotations of Scripture in the NT and the Mishnah," *JBL* 70 [1951] 297-307; slightly revised in his *Historical and Literary Studies: Pagan, Jewish, and Christian* [NTTS 8; Leiden: Brill, 1968] 52-63). After the discovery of the DSS, I made a similar comparison of the NT introductory formulas with those scattered in a similar way in the QS. What emerged was that the NT introductory formulas were invariably closer to the Qumran formulas than to the Mishnaic formulas, sometimes even a literal translation of the Qumran formulas. For instance, *houtōs gar gegraptai*, "for thus it is written" (Matt 2:5; 1 Cor 15:45), is a literal translation of Hebrew *kî' kēn kātûb* (1QS 5:15; CD 11:18; 2Q25 1:3). *Kathōs gegraptai en biblō tōn prophētōn*, "as it was written in the book of the Prophets" (Acts 7:42), is a translation of Hebrew *ka'ăšer kātûb běsēper [Môšeh]* (4QFlor [4Q174] 1-2 i 2; cf. 4QpIsa^c 1:4). *Kathōs eirēken*, "as it said" or "as He said" (Heb 4:3; 3:7), is a literal translation of Hebrew *ka'ăšer 'āmar* (CD 7:8, 14, 16). This was significant because both the QS and the Mishnah used the same verbs, "say" or "write," but it was a rare Mishnaic formula that corresponded exactly with a NT formula. It was even more significant that not one formula found in Metzger's list corresponded to any formula in the list composed from the QS. Moreover, it was not just a question of the NT introductory formulas, but even some of the modes and techniques of quotation in the NT paralleled those in the QS (see "The Use of Explicit Old Testament Quotations in Qumran Literature and in the New Testament," *ESBNT*, 3–58).

There are likewise many phrases and ideas in the QS that sound familiar to the student of the NT. Some of these will be mentioned below (see § 73–82).

70. Is John the Baptist mentioned in the QS? Could he have been a member of the Essene community at Qumran?

John is not mentioned in any of the QS, but it is not unlikely that he was a member of the Qumran community. This is a plausible hypothesis, but one can neither prove it nor disprove it. He may have been at Qumran, until "a message came from God to John, the son of Zechariah, in the desert" (Luke 3:2), when he then went forth to preach "a baptism of repentance for the remission of sins" to all Jews. He would thus have severed himself from the esoteric community that regarded contact with outsiders as a source of ritual defilement.

Since Josephus tells us (*Life* 2 § 10–11) that he himself had spent some time among the Essenes, trying out their way of life, the same sort of temporary connection might have been had by John, the son of Zechariah. Born of elderly parents (Luke 1:7,57), John is located by the gospel tradition "in the desert" (Luke 1:80) until God's call came to him. That would have been the turning point, when he broke off from the Essenes. Part of the reason for this hypothesis is that, though John was born into a priestly family (Luke 1:5), he is never depicted in the Gospels as serving as a priest in the Temple or as associated with it in any way, as his father Zechariah is portrayed in Luke 1:5-23. Perhaps after the death of his elderly parents, he may have been adopted by the Essenes, who were known to take "other men's children, while yet pliable and docile . . . and mold them according to their ways" (Josephus, *J.W.* 2.8.2 § 120).

Moreover, all the Gospels (Mark 1:3; Matt 3:3; Luke 3:3-6; John 1:23) make use of Isa 40:3 ("the voice of one crying in the wilderness") to explain why John is in the desert. But the same text is used in the Manual of Discipline (1QS 8:12-16) to explain why the Qumran community is in the desert. This may be sheer coincidence, but the use of the same text and the presence of the Essenes in the desert provide an intelligible matrix for John's stay there.

Again, John's baptism acquires a likely explanation as a development of the ritual washings of the Essenes; the difference is that his baptism was one "of repentance for the forgiveness of sins" (Mark 1:4; Luke 3:3). Yet this is illustrated by the Essene conception of their ritual washing: to "enter into the Covenant" was to "enter into water" (1QS 5:8, 13). Again, "let him not enter the water, to use the purification of holy men, for they will not be purified, unless they turn from their wickedness" (1QS 5:13-14). So the community thought of its ritual washings in relation to sin. It was not a washing which did away with sin, as John's baptism seems to imply; but his conception could well have developed from theirs. Finally, the relation of John's baptism to "water, spirit, and fire" (Luke 3:16) is plausibly explained by a passage in the Manual of Discipline, which juxtaposes "water," "holy Spirit," and "refining (by fire)":

> Then {at the season of visitation, when the truth of the world will forever appear} God will purge by his truth all the deeds of human beings, refining {i.e. by fire} for himself some of mankind in order to remove every evil spirit from the midst of their flesh, to cleanse them with a holy Spirit

from all wicked practices, and to sprinkle them with a spirit
of truth like purifying water (1QS 4:20–21).

Moreover, the traditional spot along the Jordan River, where John
is said to have baptized, is within a few hours' walk of Khirbet
Qumran.

The one thing that militates against this hypothesis is that John
came from a priestly family that served in the Jerusalem Temple; hence
he would have been related to "the Jerusalem priests," of whom the
Qumran community did not approve (1QpHab 9:4; 4QpNah 1:[11]).
Yet would such opposition have prevented the Essenes from adopt-
ing the son of a priest affiliated with the service of the Temple so
tainted in their eyes to train him in their way of life? See now O. Betz,
"Was John the Baptist an Essene?" *Bible Review* 6/6 (1990) 18–25.

71. Is Jesus of Nazareth mentioned in any of the QS?

So far there is no mention of him in any known texts. Since most
of the QS date from the second and first centuries B.C., it is not
surprising that he is not mentioned in them. Those too that are dated
palaeographically to the first century A.D. usually come from so early
a time in that century that there is again little likelihood that they
would mention him.

While he was still director of the Jordanian Department of
Antiquities. G. Lankester Harding wrote an article about the excavations at Qumran and the work on the QS in *The Illustrated London
News* (3 September 1955, pp. 379–81), which bore the title, "Where
Christ Himself May Have Studied: An Essene Monastery at Khirbet
Qumran." Lankester Harding reported that "more than 400 coins give
us the maximum and minimum dates for the history of the building
{at Khirbet Qumran}, which can be briefly summarised as beginning
about 125 B.C., destroyed by earthquake in 31 B.C., rebuilt about 5 B.C.,
and finally destroyed by the Tenth Roman Legion in A.D. 68." He adds,
"Many authorities consider that Christ himself also studied with them
{the Essenes} for some time. If that be so, then we have in this little
building something unique indeed, for alone of all the ancient remains
in Jordan, this has remained unchanged—indeed, unseen and

unknown, to this day. These, then, are the very walls He looked upon, the corridors and rooms through which He wandered and in which He sat, brought to light once again after nearly 1900 years."

That, of course, is speculation. That Jesus of Nazareth knew of the Qumran community is not unlikely. That he taught some of the same things that they espoused is not impossible (see § 82 for a good example). But there is always the problem that, though he is depicted in our Christian Gospels as reacting to Pharisees and Sadducees, there is no mention whatsoever of the Essenes, about whom we now know from the QS and from what Josephus and Philo have passed on to us. Did Jesus know of this Jewish settlement on the west side of the Dead Sea? Did he ever visit it? Who knows?

At times it has been suggested that one saying or other of Jesus recorded in the Gospels hints at his awareness of the Qumran community. For instance, in Matt 24:24 Jesus speaks of the coming of false Christs and says, "So if they say to you, 'Look, he is in the desert,' do not go out. If they say, 'He is in the inner rooms,' do not believe it" (24:26). Could the Matthean Jesus be referring to the Qumran community and its messianic beliefs? Obviously, it is possible, but how can anyone be sure that this refers to an Essene Messiah? Again, Jesus' saying about those who "have made themselves eunuchs for the sake of the kingdom of heaven" (Matt 19:12) might seem to refer to the celibate community of Qumran. But once more, who can say for sure that it does? One could easily multiply such speculative suggestions. (See B. Hjerl-Hansen, "Did Christ Know the Qumran Sect?" *RevQ* 1 [1958–59] 495–508.)

72. Is there mention of anything Christian in the QS?

Again, the answer is no. At least, not yet. There is always the possibility that Bedouins will discover another cave in which something will come to light that mentions disciples of Jesus or early Christians.

There are, of course, certain interpreters of Qumran texts who have tried to interpret them as referring to Christians. For instance, Robert H. Eisenman, professor at the State University of California, Long Beach, thinks that James, the brother of the Lord (Gal 1:19), was the Qumran Teacher of Righteousness and that Paul the Apostle was "the Man of the Lie" (1QpHab 2:2).

Another interpreter is Barbara Thiering of Australia, who thinks that John the Baptist is the Teacher of Righteousness and Jesus the Wicked Priest.

Such opinions, however, ride roughshod over the archaeological, palaeographical, and radiocarbon dating of the evidence that clearly pinpoints most of the QS to the pre-Christian centuries. Recently Eisenman has been quoted as objecting to the radiocarbon dating because "neither he nor any other outsider was included in the group managing and monitoring the tests" (*BARev* 17/6 [1991] 72). By "outsider," he means someone not part of the "consensus" convinced — a priori, in his opinion — about the Essene identification of the Qumran sect and the pre-Christian dating of most of the material.

The vast majority of NT books are judged by scholars today to have been composed outside of Judea. This is certainly true of the four Gospels, the Acts of the Apostles, the seven uncontested letters of Paul, the Deutero-Pauline writings (Colossians, Ephesians, 2 Thessalonians), and the Pastoral Epistles (Titus, 1–2 Timothy). The same is usually held for Hebrews, 2 Peter, Jude, 1–3 John, and Revelation. Years ago, a Dutch scholar, J. N. Sevenster, toyed with the idea that 1 Peter and James might have been composed in Greek in Palestine itself (*Do You Know Greek? How Much Greek Could the First Jewish Christians Have Known?* [NovTSup 19; Leiden: Brill, 1968] 2–21). Again, this is not impossible, but it is a highly speculative hypothesis. In any case, there is little echo of Qumran phrases or writings in these two letters, although Eisenman finds Qumran echoes in the Epistle of James.

73. Have genuine parallels to NT ideas and phrases been discovered in the QS?

The amount of NT phrases that can be shown to be at home in Palestinian Judaism as a result of the discovery of the QS is almost numberless. In 1956 shortly after the publication of Cave 1 materials, R. E. Murphy wrote an article, "The Dead Sea Scrolls and New Testament Comparisons" (*CBQ* 18 [1956] 263–72), in which he listed about

175 Qumran parallels. A year later Krister Stendahl edited *The Scrolls and the New Testament* (New York: Harper & Brothers). In 1966 Herbert Braun published two volumes, *Qumran und das Neue Testament* (Tübingen: Mohr [Siebeck]), in which he gathered and critically discussed all the suggestions that had been made up to that time about such parallels in the QS. Two other volumes, *Paul and the Dead Sea Scrolls* (ed. J. Murphy-O'Connor and J. H. Charlesworth) and *John and the Dead Sea Scrolls* (ed. J. H. Charlesworth [see Select Bibliography]) discuss a number of Pauline and Johannine topics illumined by the discovery of the QS. From the mention of these and other such books it is clear that many, many parallels to NT ideas and phrases have turned up in the QS.

One has to be wary of such "parallels," however, because of the danger of parallelomania. Parallels in literature are legion, and S. Sandmel once warned against them in his presidential address before the Society of Biblical Literature ("Parallelomania," *JBL* 81 [1961] 1–13). There is also the oft-quoted dictum of E. R. Goodenough about such parallels: a parallel by definition consists of two straight lines in the same plane which never meet, no matter how far they are produced in either direction. Yet that definition is derived from mathematics. When it is applied to literature, it cannot be taken too literally. To repeat the dictum as if it closes off all discussion or absolves one from investigating literary relationships is only a form of obscurantism, something worse than parallelomania. It enables one to avoid asking the question when a literary parallel might cease to be a parallel and actually prove to be a contact.

The greatest number of parallels or literary contacts have turned up in the Gospels of Matthew and John, in the Pauline corpus, and in the Epistle to the Hebrews. Because Mark's Gospel is usually judged to be the earliest and is considered to have more Semitisms than the other Gospels, one might have expected that the parallels would be greater in this case. But it is not so.

74. Do the QS shed any light on christological titles used in the NT?

Yes, they do. The most significant of them is "Son of God." This title is used already in the OT; so one has to be precise in distinguishing the sense in which the phrase is used. In the OT, for instance, it is a mythological title given to angels (Gen 6:2; Job 1:6; 2:1; 38:7; Ps 29:1; Dan 3:25); a title of predilection for the people of Israel collectively (Exod 4:22; Deut 14:1; Hos 2:1; 11:1; Isa 1:2; 30:1; Jer 3:22; Wis 18:13); a title of adoption used for a king on the Davidic throne (2 Sam 7:14; Ps 2:7; 89:27); a title for judges (Ps 82:6); for an individual upright Jew (Sir 4:10; Wis 2:18). It is often said to have been a messianic title, but there is no clear instance of its use of an expected Messiah either in the OT or in any pre-Christian Jewish writing now known. Not even Ps 2:7 is to be understood as "messianic" in pre-Christian times. It is a royal psalm, in which the king on the Davidic throne is called Son: "You are my son; this day I have begotten you." But it has none of the connotations of an expected messianic figure. That psalm acquires a messianic connotation from the use of it in the NT, when it is applied to Jesus, the Christian Messiah. It has sometimes been thought that the title *huios theou* (e.g. Mark 1:1; Luke 1:35; John 19:7) or *ho huios tou theou* (e.g. Acts 8:37; Gal 2:20; Eph 4:13; Heb 4:14), as used of Jesus, was a borrowing of the title given, at first, to Augustus and then to many Roman emperors, *divi filius,* or *theou huios* (see A. Deissmann, *Light from the Ancient East* [London: Hodder and Stoughton, 1927] 350). Given the frequency of this title in the Greco-Roman world of the NT, one cannot wholly dismiss the influence that it might have had on early Christians, who may have reacted to the Greco-Roman usage by asserting that for them Christ Jesus was the "Son of God."

That such a Greco-Roman usage was not alone in influencing the Christian usage is now apparent from a striking Aramaic text, discovered in Cave 4 and acquired by the Palestine Archaeological Museum on 9 July 1958. It is officially known as 4Q246; it has not yet been fully published, but the crucial six and half lines of it are known. Unfortunately, it is a broken text, and the subject of whom the titles used in it are predicated is unknown. That person will be long debated, when the text is finally published in full. At any rate, the crucial lines run thus:

> [X] 7shall be great upon the earth. 8[O King! All shal]l make [peace], and all shall serve 9[him, and he] shall be called [son of] the [gr]eat [God], and by his name shall

he be named. (Col. 2) ¹He shall be hailed the Son of God, and they shall call him Son of the Most High. As comets (flash) ²to the sight, so shall their kingdom. For (some) year[s] they shall rule upon ³the earth and shall trample everything (under foot); people shall trample upon people, city upon ci[t]y, ⁴(*vacat*) until there arises the people of God, and everyone rests from the sword.

No one who reads this text fails to see its importance. It not only shows that the title *bĕrēh dî 'ēl*, "Son of God," was current in Palestine in the first century B.C. or A.D. (the text is written in Herodian script), but it uses the same titles "Son of God" and "Son of the Most High" (*bar 'elyôn*) with the same verb "be called" that is used in the Lucan infancy narrative, when Gabriel informs Mary of the birth of Jesus (1:32, 35). The impact of this text has yet to be fully studied.

Similar light has been shone on the title *Kyrios*, "Lord," used of the risen Christ many times in the NT (e.g. 1 Cor 12:3; Rom 10:9), *Kyrion Iēsoun*. Ever since W. Bousset (*Kyrios Christos* [3d ed.; Göttingen: Vandenhoeck & Ruprecht, 1926; Engl. tr., Nashville, TN: Abingdon, 1970] 119–52), many NT scholars (R. Bultmann, P. Vielhauer, H. Conzelmann) have maintained that the title *Kyrios* was derived from a Hellenistic background, where it was used for pagan gods or human rulers. It is said that when the Palestinian kerygma was carried by Christian missionaries into the eastern Mediterranean world, they adopted this title and so proclaimed Jesus Christ as the *Kyrios*. Proof for this understanding was sought in 1 Cor 8:5–6: "For though there are many so-called gods in heaven and on earth, just as there are many 'gods' and 'lords,' for us there is one God, the Father, from whom are all things and for whom we exist, and one Lord, Jesus Christ, through whom are all things and through whom we exist." As support for this position, Bultmann even maintained:

At the very outset the un-modified expression "the Lord" is unthinkable in Jewish usage. "Lord" used of God is always given some modifier; we read: "the Lord of heaven and earth," "our Lord" and similar expressions. Used of Jesus, therefore, at least "*our* Lord" or something similar would be required (*Theology of the New Testament* [2 vols.; London: SCM, 1952–53] 1. 51 [his italics]).

But the unmodified term has turned up in at least two texts in the QS. The first emerged in the Targum of Job from Cave 11, where the unmodified Aramaic *mārê'*, "Lord," stands in parallelism with *'ĕlāhā'*, "God." In Elihu's poetic discourse, he addresses Job and says to him (according to the original Hebrew), "Indeed, God will not act wickedly; the Almighty will not pervert justice" (Job 34:12). The targum renders this in Aramaic as "Now will God really prove faithless, and [will] the Lord [distort judgment]?" (11QtgJob 24:6–7).

A second clear instance is found in 4QEn^b 1 iv 5, where we read, "[And to Gabriel] the [L]ord [said], '[Now] g[o to the bastards . . .'].'" The text is unfortunately broken here, but apart from the missing initial letter *m*, which is easily restored, the emphatic state of the Aramaic noun *māryā'*, "the Lord," is clearly attested. This part of *1 Enoch* is also extant in Greek, and its text reads *ho Ks*, an abbreviation for the unmodified *ho Kyrios*.

There is also a clear instance of Hebrew *'ādôn*, "Lord," used of God in 4Q403 1 i 28: *bārûk [hā]'ād[ô]n, mele[k hak]kôl*, "Blest be [the] L[o]rd, Kin[g of the Uni]verse." Again, there may be another instance of *'ādôn* in 11QPs^a 28:7–8, "and who can mention and who can recount the deeds of the Lord? Everything has God seen, everything has he heard, and he has listened." In this case, the interpretation is contested, because *'ādôn* may not be absolute and unmodified; perhaps it should be taken with the following word as *'ădôn hakkôl*, "Lord of the Universe."

In any case, such Qumran evidence is precious indeed. Yet it has to be taken in conjunction with two instances in the writings of Josephus. Whereas the historian usually uses *despotēs* as the Greek equivalent for the tetragram, on two occasions he employs *Kyrios*, clearly with no dependence on NT usage (*Ant.* 20.4.2 § 90 and 13.3.1 § 68). Lastly, one should note that there is a clear instance in the Hebrew Psalter itself, which has long been overlooked, "Tremble, O earth, before the Lord, before the God of Jacob" (*millipnê 'ādôn*, Ps 114:7).

These are now clear examples of the use of the unmodified title "(the) Lord" for Yahweh in Jewish usage. From such usage it would not have been impossible for Greek-speaking or Aramaic-speaking Jewish converts to Christianity to derive the title "Lord," which they then extended to the risen Christ.

Hence at least these two important NT christological titles have now to be explained against the background of this clearly Jewish usage found in the QS.

75. Does the title "Son of Man," which appears so frequently on the lips of Jesus in the Gospels, occur in the QS?

The phrase "son of man" does occur, but in no case is it a title, such as it is in the NT.

First, one should recall that the NT phrase that is translated as "Son of Man" is a strange Greek expression, *ho huios tou anthrōpou,* which should mean "the son of the man," or "the man's son." The arthrous form of the phrase (i.e. with the definite article) occurs abundantly in the Synoptic tradition (e.g. Mark 2:10; Matt 9:6; Luke 5:24; Mark 2:28; Matt 12:8; Luke 6:51; also in "Q" passages, Matt 8:20; Luke 9:58; Matt 11:19; Luke 7:34).

Second, the anarthrous form (i.e. without the definite article), *huios anthrōpou,* is used in Rev 1:13; 14:14 (in an allusion to Dan 7:13); Heb 2:6 (in a quotation from Ps 8:5); and John 12:34a,b. It is less strange, because it can be regarded as a Semitism, reflecting either Hebrew *ben 'ādām* or Aramaic *bar 'ĕnāš.* The Hebrew *ben 'ādām* occurs 93 times in Ezekiel, as a form of address, a quasi-vocative (e.g. 2:1, 3; 3:1, 3, 4, 10); it means something like "O mortal being." In Ps 144:3 one finds an equivalent form *ben 'ĕnôš,* and in 1QS 11:20 the definite article has been added to it above the line, *ben hā'ādām,* but it is not clear what the meaning would then be (compare 1QH 4:30, where *lbn 'dm* stands in parallelism with *l'nwš*). In fact, it has often been queried whether such a phrase ever existed in Aramaic.

Third, apart from a very early occurrence of the phrase in an eighth-century Aramaic inscription (Sefire 3. 16–17), where it is used in a generic sense, "human being," it is known to appear in Dan 7:13, again in the generic sense of a "human being." Now Aramaic *bar 'ĕnāš* has turned up in the QS. In 1QapGen 21:13, it is used in the indefinite sense, "I shall make your descendants as numerous as the dust of the earth that no one can number" (lit. "that a son of man cannot number," a paraphrase of Gen 13:16, where *bar 'ĕnôš* translates Hebrew *'îš*, "man, human being," into Aramaic). It also occurs in 11QtgJob 26:2-3, "Your sin affects a man like yourself, and your righteousness (another) human being" (a translation of Job 35:8). The speech of Elihu is here contrasting God and a human being. Again, the generic sense is found in 11QtgJob 9:9, where the fragmentary phrase is [*b*]*r 'nš twl'*[*t'*], "[s]on of man, (who is) a wor[m]," translating *ben 'ādām* of Hebrew Job 25:6.

These few phrases reveal that the phrase "son of man" was in use in Palestine of the first century B.C. or A.D., both in the indefinite sense of "someone" or in the generic sense of "human being." But there is no instance so far of the titular sense (as it is used on the lips of Jesus or about him in the NT), or of the surrogate sense (as a substitute for "I" or "me," as it occurs in the targums of later date: in Neofiti 1 and Cairo Targum B of Gen 4:14), or as a form of direct address (like *ben 'ādām* in Ezekiel).

Hence the NT titular sense of the expression is still unique. Whether such a use was current in the days of Jesus is a moot question. This means, of course, that the theory that Jesus is depicted in the Gospels using at times the phrase as the title for an expected figure different from himself is highly questionable.

76. Is the "Servant of Yahweh" theme used in the QS?

The title *'ebed,* "servant," is given in the QS to the prophets (1QpHab 2:9; 7:5; 1QS 1:3; 4QpHos^a 2:5), to Moses (4QDibHam^a 1-2 v 14; 6:12; 4QDibHam^b 122:1), and to David (1QM 11:2), and it is often employed with the second person singular suffix, "your servant," in prayers addressed to God, where it is the substitute for "I" or "me" (1QH 5:15; 7:16; 9:11; 11:30). But there is as yet no place in any of the QS that exploits the *'ebed Yahweh* figure of Deutero-Isaiah.

This is said despite the attempts that W. H. Brownlee once made to find reference to a "Suffering Messiah in the Isaiah Scroll," which he thought would "indicate the sect's belief that the highest embodiment of the Servant of the Lord would be in the Messiah" (*BASOR*

132 [1953] 10). Brownlee proposed this idea, because 1QIsaᵃ 44:2 reads the form *mšḥty* instead of the MT's form *mšḥt,* and so he wanted to translate Isa 52:14b, "I so anointed his appearance beyond any one (else)," which would thus make the prophet speak of the "anointing" of the Servant. But scholars have long since forgotten about this misguided attempt and explain the anomalous Hebrew form *mšḥty* otherwise, as a scribal variant for *mšḥt,* "marring," rendering Isa 52:14 rather: "so marred was his appearance beyond that of a man."

There are, however, passages that allude to the Servant of Yahweh Songs and make use of some phrases from them, but most of these uses are insignificant or ordinary. One of the Thanksgiving Psalms, which is formulated in the first person singular and which many commentators admit may refer to the Teacher of Righteousness himself, reads thus: "For you have known me from (the time of) my father; from the womb [you have called me]; you have dealt bountifully with me [from the belly of] my mother; from the breasts of her who conceived me your mercies (have come) to me" (1QH 9:29–31). These utterances remind one of the Servant Song of Isa 49:1b; cf. Jer 1:5. They do not make of the Teacher another Servant of Yahweh, but they formulate the divine protection, which the community realized had blessed him. Again, in 1QH 8:26–27. "[There was given me] a place to sojourn with the sick and a s[our]ce of [affliction] with plagues; I have become like a man abandoned [   ] without a refuge for me," the terminology is reminiscent of Isa 53:5. But these are at most fleeting allusions.

It should also be recalled that there is no "Suffering Messiah" motif in the OT; so it is unlikely that it would turn up in the QS. It occurs in the NT only in the Lucan writings (Luke 24:26, 46; Acts 3:18; 26:23). Hence, it is a Lucan theologoumenon.

77. What sort of parallels have been found to the Matthean Gospel?

The Matthean Sermon on the Mount begins with a list of nine beatitudes (5:3–11). Though the beatitude-form is found in the OT, especially in its wisdom literature (e.g. Ps 1:1; 2:12; Prov 3:13; 8:32,34; Qoh 10:17; Wis 3:13), and there are even paired beatitudes (1 Kgs 10:8; 2 Chr 9:7; Ps 32:1–2; 84:5–6; 119:1–2; 137:8–9; 144:15), an extended collection of beatitudes is not found there, such as one has in the Sermon on the Mount.

Now, however, such a distinct literary form has turned up in the QS. In 4Q525 one reads:

> [Blessed is the one who speaks truth] with a pure heart
> and slanders not with his tongue.
> Blessed are those who cling to her statutes and cling not
> to paths of iniquity.
> Bles[s]ed are those who rejoice in her and babble not about
> paths of iniquity.
> Blessed are those who search for her with clean hands and
> seek not after her with a deceitful heart.
> Blessed is the man who has attained wisdom and walks
> by the law of the Most High and fixes his heart on her
> ways, gives heed to her admonishments, delights al[wa]ys
> in her chastisements, and forsakes her not in the stress of
> [his] trou[bles]; (who) in time of distress abandons her
> not and forgets her not [in days of] fear, and in the
> affliction of his soul rejects [her] not. For on her he
> meditates, and in his anguish he ponders [on the law];
> and in [al]l his existence [he considers] her [and puts her]
> before his eyes so as not to walk in the paths of [   ] . . .
> (4QBeat [4Q525] 1–6).

Here in a clearly sapiential text there is a collection of five beatitudes. Since the text is broken one cannot say how many more would have preceded this quintet. The feminine suffix that occurs throughout undoubtedly refers to "wisdom" (a feminine noun, *ḥokmāh*), mentioned at the beginning of the fifth beatitude; it could also refer to "the law of the Most High," since *tôrāh*, "law," is also feminine. Since for such a community "the law of the Most High" was the supreme "wisdom," it makes little difference.

Another feature that should be noted in this collection of beatitudes is the mention of different parts of the body: heart, tongue, hands. It resembles the catchword bonding that links OT quotations in the *testimonia*-list in Rom 3:10–18.

In any case, it is an interesting Palestinian Jewish parallel to the stringing together of beatitudes in the Matthean Sermon on the Mount, showing that the evangelist was aware of such a literary form. It differs from the Matthean collection in that the beatitudes are all sapiential, and not eschatological as are the Matthean beatitudes. (Luke 6:20-22 also has a list of four beatitudes, with four parallel woes; but there is no parallel to such a composition in the QS.)

The Matthean form of the first beatitude, "Blessed are the poor in spirit" (*ptōchoi tō pneumati,* 5:3), finds a verbal parallel in the Qumran phrase *ʿanwê rûăḥ* (1QM 14:7; 1QH 14:3), but it is debated whether its meaning is the same as in the Matthean Gospel. There it seems to refer to those who are spiritually poor, in contrast to the Lucan form, "Blessed are you poor" (6:20), i.e. those who are economically poor. In the Qumran phrase it seems rather to mean "those who are humble in spirit," the opposite of *rāmê rûăḥ,* "those who are haughty in spirit" (1QS 11:1).

In 5:43 the Matthean Jesus says, "You have heard that it was said, 'You shall love your neighbor and hate your enemy.'" The first clause has always been understood as a reference to Lev 19:18, "You shall love your neighbor as yourself," where "neighbor" refers to a "fellow countryman," i.e. a fellow Jew. But one has always looked in vain in the OT or in any other pre-Christian Jewish literature for "hate your enemy." Now, however, such a parallel to Jesus' words may occur in the purpose of the community stated in 1QS 1:9-10, "to love all the sons of light, each according to his lot in the council of God, and to hate all the sons of darkness according to his guilt in the vengeance of God." Again, "these are the norms of conduct for the Instructor in those times, about what he must love and what he must hate: everlasting hatred for all the men of perdition . . ." (1QS 9:21-22). This regulation for the members of the Qumran community and their attitude for all who disagree with or oppose them may thus provide a background for Jesus' reference to what had been taught of old.

Again, Jesus' injunction, "You, then, must be perfect as your heavenly Father is perfect" (5:48) may find a counterpart in the goal of the Qumran community, "to walk perfectly before Him" (1QS 1:8); they are "all the men of His lot, who walk perfectly in all His ways" (1QS 2:2; cf. 3:9). So if perfection is a goal for the sectarian, the Qumran prescription at least lacks the designation of God as "heavenly

Father," which is a characteristically Matthean title for God in any case.

The two "ways" or "paths" of Matt 7:13–14 may reflect the Qumran "paths of light" and "paths of darkness" (1QS 3:20–21), but the Qumran mention is dualistically formulated, whereas the Matthean is not.

Commentators have at times seen a parallel between Jesus' words about building his church on Peter, the rock, against which the gates of Hades would not prevail (Matt 16:16–19), and the following passage from the Manual of Discipline:

> When these things come to pass in Israel, the council of the community shall be established in truth, as an everlasting planting, a holy house for Israel, and a foundation of the Holy of Holies for Aaron. (They shall be) witnesses to the truth at the judgment, the chosen ones of His good will to make expiation for the land and to render the wicked their recompense. It shall be a tested wall, that precious cornerstone, the foundations of which none shall rock or sway from their place (Isa 28:16). It shall be a dwelling-place for the Holy of Holies for Aaron with everlasting understanding for the covenant of justice, in order to offer up an odor of sweet fragrance. It shall be a house of perfection and truth in Israel to set up a covenant with everlasting precepts (1QS 8:4–10).

The parallelism is interesting, but it cannot be pressed, because the terminology is not identical and the crucial word *qāhāl,* usually understood to be the Hebrew word behind Greek *ekklēsia* in Matt 16:18, is not found here. Nor is there anything to parallel the pun on Simon Peter's name: "You are *Petros,* and on this *petra* I will build my church." The Aramaic proper name *Kēphā'* is now attested in a fifth-century B.C. Aramaic text from Elephantine (*BMAP* 8:10) and the common noun *kēphā',* "rock, crag" is now attested in 11QtgJob 32:1 (=Hebrew 39:1); 33:9 (=Hebrew 39:28). So the pun is clearly seen to have been possible. There is nothing in the QS about building a community *on* a person, even though 4QpPs^a 1,3–4 iii 15–16 interprets Ps 37:23–24 to refer to "the priest, the Teacher of [Righteousness],

[whom] God ordered to arise and [whom] He set up to build for Him a congregation [of His chosen ones]." Others have tried to use 1QH 6:20–31 and 7:6–12 as parallels to this Matthean passage, but the similarities are too superficial to be convincing.

In Matt 18:15–17 one reads of Jesus' words on fraternal correction: "If your brother sins against you, go and rebuke him, between you and him alone. If he listens to you, you have gained your brother. If he does not listen, take one or two others along with you, in order that every word may be confirmed by the statement of two or three witnesses. If he refuses to listen, tell it to the church; let him be to you as a Gentile and a toll collector." This three-stage reproof has a parallel in the Qumran community's rule book: "Let one rebuke his companion in tru[th], humility, and loving kindness; let him not speak to him in anger or ill-temper or obduracy or with envy prompted by a spirit of wickedness. Let him not hate him [because of] his [un-circumcised] heart. Rather let him rebuke him (that same) day, lest he incur guilt because of him. Moreover, let no one bring a matter against his companion before the Many without having (first) ad-monished him before witnesses" (1QS 5:24–6:1). The wording, of course, is not the same, but the idea of proper fraternal correction is similar to that of the Matthean Jesus. A regulation in the Damascus Document can also be cited: "(If) anyone among those who enter the Covenant brings up a matter against his companion without (first) rebuking him before witnesses, and (if) he denounces him in the heat of his anger or reports him to his elders to cause him disdain, he is one that takes vengeance and cherishes rancor, even though it is written, '*An avenger is He for His adversaries, and He cherishes rancor toward His enemies*'" (CD 9:2–5, quoting Nah 1:2).

78. What sort of parallels have been found to Johannine writings?

Though both the QS and the Johannine literature are heavily dependent on the OT and its themes, there are distinctive parallels that one can cite, which are not already formulated in the OT.

First of all, there is the pervasive Johannine ethical and eschato-logical dualism of light and darkness (John 1:4–5; 3:19; 12:35; 1 John 1:5–6), truth and falsehood (John 3:21; 8:44; 1 John 2:21, 27; 4:6:

"From this we know the spirit of truth and the spirit of error"). This dualism is now clearly seen to be closer to the Qumran ethical dualism, which reckons with monotheism, than with dualistic notions of Mandaean writings, Philo, or the Hermetic Corpus (sources for the Johannine usage once invoked by R. Bultmann, C. H. Dodd, and others).

In the QS, the dualism is expressed as two spirits created by God to struggle within human beings and to dominate them until the time of God's visitation, for "He created the spirits of light and darkness" (1QS 3:25). They are called (a) "the spirit of light" (1QS 3:25) or "the spirit of truth" (1QS 4:21, 23; 1QM 13:10) or "the prince of light" (1QS 3:20; CD 5:18; 1QM 13:10) or "the holy spirit" (1QS 4:21; 9:3; 1QH 7:7; 9:32; 12:12; 14:13; 16:12); and (b) "the spirit of iniquity" (1QS 3:18–19; 4:20, 23) or "the angel of darkness" (1QS 3:20–21) or "the prince of the dominion of evil" (1QM 17:5). As a result, all humanity is divided into two groups or lots: (a) "the sons of light" (1QS 1:9; 2:16; 3:13, 24, 25; 1QM 1:1, 3, 9, 11, 13; 4QFlor 1–2 i 8–9; 4Q177 10–11:7; 12–13 i 7, 11) or "the sons of truth" (1QS 4:5, 6; 1QM 17:8; 1QH 7:30; 9:35), "the lot of light" (1QM 13:9; CD 13:12), "the lot of God" (1QS 2:2; 1QM 17:7); and (b) "the sons of darkness" (1QS 1:10; 1QM 1:1, 7, 10; 3:6, 9; 13:16; 14:17) or "the sons of iniquity" (1QS 3:21), "the lot of darkness" (1QM 1:11; 13:5), "the lot of iniquity" (1QS 4:24), "the lot of Belial" (1QS 2:5; 1QM 1:5; 4:2; 13:2; 11QMelch 12–13). Noteworthy too is the idea of a battle or struggle that is to take place between "the sons of light" and "the sons of darkness." Whether one is to understand the spirits as opposing cosmic beings or as expressions of psychological tendencies within human beings is debated, but in any case the Qumran community tried in this way to explain the problem of evil in human life.

What is distinctive here is the use of Semitic *běnê*, "sons of," together with the symbolism of light and darkness. *Ben* is used in the OT to designate groups (e.g. 1 Kgs 20:35, "sons of the prophets," the prophetic guild; 2 Chr 25:13, troopers). "Light" and "darkness" are likewise OT symbols of good and evil (Isa 5:20; 45:7). Such symbols, however, are never combined in the OT with "sons of," and the combination is never employed as a means of dividing all humanity into two groups. Hence one finds neither "sons of light" nor "sons of darkness" in the OT or in later rabbinic literature. Its use, then, in the QS scrolls is distinctive and significant.

Some of this dualistic terminology turns up in a Johannine form in the NT, applied to Jesus, who is described as "the light shining in darkness" (John 1:5), "the light of the world" (John 8:12), "the truth" (John 14:6). Or the Paraclete that Jesus will send is described as "the holy Spirit" (John 14:16) or "the Spirit of truth" (John 15:26). The Johannine writings also express a struggle that exists between light and darkness: "The light shines in the darkness, and the darkness has not overcome it" (John 1:5; cf. 3:19; 12:35). Jesus also speaks of his disciples becoming "sons of light" (12:36). Hence, the QS supply precious Palestinian Jewish evidence of and background for such abstract and symbolic language that the Johannine Jesus uses. It eliminates the need to try to explain it from some Greek or Hellenistic background.

The Jewish sectarian thought revealed in the QS thus provides a contemporary and intelligible Palestinian matrix for specific aspects of Johannine dualism. There are, however, some minor differences in the dualistic thinking, such as the Johannine use of "above" and "below." This sort of dualist expression is not paralleled in the QS and seems to be more Platonic in its conception.

Second, there is a remarkable affinity in affirmations about God as creator and his wisdom or knowledge in creation in the QS and Johannine writings: All things exist and happen as they do because the wisdom and knowledge of the Creator have so ordained. The Qumran sectarian acknowledges:

> From the God of knowledge is everything that exists or will exist; before they come to be, He has established all their design. As they come into being according to their determination, they fulfill their function according to His glorious plan, and there is no change (from it). In His hand are the regulations of all things, and He upholds them in all their needs. He it is who created man to govern the world (1QS 3:15–18). By His knowledge all is brought into being, and everything exists by His thought; He establishes it, and without Him nothing is made (1QS 11:11)

The Qumran Psalmist similarly sings:

> In Your wisdom [You] ha[ve established all from] of old,
> and before You created them, You knew all their works
> for all ages, [for without You no]thing is made; nothing
> is known without Your good pleasure (1QH 1:7–8).
> In the wisdom of Your knowledge You have esta[bl]ished
> the deter[min]ation of them before they came to be; and
> according to [Your good pleasure] everything has been
> [broug]ht into being. Without You nothing is made (1QH
> 1:19–20).

No one who reads such lines fails to note the similarity of formulation, thought, and ideas expressed here with such Johannine
statements as, "All things were made through it [the *Logos*], and
without it was made nothing that came into being" (John 1:3). Even
if one detects in the Johannine prologue some influence of the wisdom
thinking of Prov 8:22–25, the similarity in the formulation of this
verse of the prologue with the Qumran writings is distinctive.

There is a major difference, of course, for the QS do not speak
of "the Word" personified as does the Johannine prologue, or of the
influence of someone who enables human beings to become "children
of God" (1:12). Nothing in the QS resembles the way the Johannine
Jesus speaks of himself as "the way, the truth, and the life; no one
comes to the Father but by me" (14:6). No one would expect such distinctively Christian ideas to turn up in the QS, but the secondary
elements that do have parallels in these Qumran writings make one
realize today the Palestinian matrix from which the distinctively
Johannine teaching has emerged.

79. Is not the phrase "sons of light" used elsewhere in the NT too?

Yes, Christians are designated by the Semitic phrase, *huioi phōtos,*
"sons of light," in 1 Thess 5:5; John 12:36. Luke improves the Greek,
writing *hoi huioi tou phōtos* (16:8). In Eph 5:8 one finds an equivalent
phrase, *tekna phōtos,* "children of light." The NT use reveals, then,
that in this regard it is tributary to a genuine Palestinian Jewish usage,
even though it gives to the phrase a distinctively Christian nuance.
The counterpart, "sons of darkness," is, however, never found in the

NT; the closest one comes to it is *ho huios tēs apōleias,* "son of perdition," used of Judas Iscariot in John 17:12 and of the unnamed "man of lawlessness" in 2 Thess 2:3. So the characteristically Qumran division of all humanity into two groups is not taken over as such in the NT.

80. What sort of parallels have been found to Pauline letters?

One of the most important teachings of the Apostle Paul, justification by faith (Rom 3:21–31), has been shown to have a remarkable background in the teachings of the Qumran community. The Qumran doctrine is not identical, but it has such a striking similarity to the Pauline teaching that one has to see the latter against the background of it.

In the hymn that closes the community rule book, the Manual of Discipline, one reads:

> As for me, I belong to wicked humanity, to the assembly of perverse flesh; my iniquities, my transgressions, my sins together with the wickedness of my heart belong to the assembly doomed to worms and walking in darkness. No human being sets his own path or directs his own steps, for to God alone belongs the judgment of him, and from His hand comes perfection of way. . . . And I, if I stagger, God's grace is my salvation forever. If I stumble because of a sin of the flesh, my judgment is according to the righteousness of God, which stands forever. . . . In His mercy He has drawn me close (to Him), and with His favors will He render judgment of me. In His righteous fidelity He has judged me; in His bounteous goodness He expiates all my iniquities, and in His righteousness He cleanses me of human defilement and of human sinfulness, that I may praise God for His righteousness and the Most High for His majesty (1QS 11:9–15; cf. 1QH 9:32–34; 14:15–16).
>
> Who is righ[te]ous before You when he is judged? No answer can be made to Your rebuke! All (human) glory

is (like the) wind, and no one is able to stand before Your wrath. Yet You bring all Your faithful children to pardon before You, [to clean]se them of their transgressions with much goodness and in the abundance of Your me[r]cy (1QH 7:28–30).

As for me, I know that righteousness belongs not to a human being, nor perfection of way to a son of man. To God Most High belong all the deeds of righteousness, whereas the path of a human is not set firm. . . . And I said, It is because of my transgression that I have been abandoned far from Your covenant. But when I recalled Your mighty hand along with the abundance of Your mercy, then was I restored, and I stood up; my spirit strengthened my stance against blows, because [I] have based myself on Your graces and on the abundance of Your mercy. For you expiate iniquity to clean[se a human be]ing from guilt by Your righteousness (1QH 4:30–38).

Here one finds an admission of the utter sinfulness of the sectarian who praises God in such hymns. That admission finds a striking parallel in Paul's utterance, "all alike have sinned and fall short of the glory of God" (Rom 3:23). Moreover, the sectarian realizes that judgment of him is rooted in the same quality of God that Paul extols, "the righteousness of God" (see Rom 1:17; 3:21). Again, the sectarian is convinced that that judgment of God is a mark of his grace: "And by your grace you judge them with an abundance of mercy" (1QH 6:9; cf. 7:27). In such ideas one finds the Palestinian matrix for the Pauline idea of God's righteousness and of justification by grace. In both writings God's judgment is involved, and the sinner stands before his tribunal and finds himself or herself acquitted by the grace of God.

There is a big difference, however, in that for Paul justification is an effect of the Christ-event: Christ Jesus has brought it about that the godless sinner stands acquitted before God's tribunal: "It is credited to us who believe in him who raised from the dead Jesus our Lord, who was handed over (to death) for our trespasses and raised for our justification" (Rom 4:24–25). Another difference is the role of "faith," for Pauline justification takes place by God's grace through faith. There is in the QS no counterpart to this element in justification.

In this regard one has to beware of the tendentious translations sometimes given to such passages in the QS. At times the word *mišpāṭ,* "judgment," is translated as "justification" (e.g. A. Dupont-Sommer, *Essene Writings,* 102; G. Vermes, *Dead Sea Scrolls in English,* 79). In such cases, the Pauline nuance of the term has been read into the Qumran texts.

Similarly, one cannot fail to note the way in which the Pesher on Habakkuk interprets Hab 2:4, "The one who is righteous shall find life through fidelity," the verse that Paul builds into the thesis of the Epistle to the Romans (1:17). The community's interpretation runs this way: "The interpretation of it concerns all the doers of the law in the house of Judah, whom God will rescue from the house of judgment because of their striving and their fidelity to the Teacher of Righteousness" (1QpHab 8:1-3). This Qumran interpretation of the verse of Habakkuk, which is so important for Paul in his teaching on justification, is highly significant, because it shows that in Palestinian Judaism prior to Paul the verse had already been understood in terms of a relationship to a person, to a renowned teacher. Herein one finds a remarkable parallel and a significant background to Pauline teaching. But again there is a difference, because Paul understands the OT word *'ĕmûnāh,* not merely as "fidelity," the sense it has in Habakkuk and also in the Qumran commentary, but as "faith" (*pistis*), faith in his own sense, viz. faith in the risen Christ. "Life" also takes on a new meaning for Paul. It is not just deliverance from invaders and oppressors, as it meant in the context of the prophet Habakkuk, or "rescue from the house of judgment," as in the Qumran pesher, but "life in Christ Jesus," a share in the risen life of Christ, a share in "eternal life." (Again, one should beware of the tendentious translations of 1QpHab 8:1-3 in A. Dupont-Sommer, *Essene Writings,* 263; and G. Vermes, *Dead Sea Scrolls in English,* 287; both translators make the Qumran phrase too Christian, when they speak of "faith in the Teacher of Righteousness.")

Related to such teaching on justification is the Pauline phrase, *erga nomou,* "the deeds of the law," i.e. deeds prescribed or required by the Mosaic law (Gal 2:16; 3:2, 5, 10; Rom 2:15; 3:20, 27, 28). Paul insists that these are not a means to justification. Yet the way he uses the phrase, when he inveighs against it, makes it sound as though he were quoting a well-known slogan in Jewish life. But it is never found as such either in the OT or in later rabbinic literature. It has now, however, turned up in Qumran writings, as *ma'ăśê hattôrāh*, "the deeds of the law" (4QFlor [4Q174] 1–2 i 7 [quoted in full in § 62 above]; 4QMMT C 29). Indeed, its meaning in the last named document is precisely what Paul has meant by it, "deeds prescribed by the law," i.e. the basic acts that the Qumran community thinks that its opponents should be performing if they were really Jews.

One passage in the Apostle's writings has been called "a meteor fallen from the heaven of Qumran into Paul's epistle" (P. Benoit, commenting on 2 Cor 6:14–7:1 [*Paul and the Dead Sea Scrolls*, 5]). I myself analyzed this paragraph in the light of Qumran writings and regarded it as a non-Pauline interpolation into 2 Corinthians (*ESBNT*, 205–17). The paragraph has always seemed to interrupt the sequence of Paul's thought in 2 Corinthians, where he is otherwise making an eloquent plea for reconciliation.

> Do not be misyoked with those who are unbelievers. For what partnership do righteousness and iniquity have? Or what fellowship does light have with darkness? What accord has Christ with Beliar? Or what has a believer in common with an unbeliever? What agreement has the temple of God with idols? For we are the temple of the living God; as God has said, "I will dwell with them and move among them, and I will be their God, and they shall be my people. Therefore, come out from them and separate yourselves from them," says the Lord. "Touch nothing unclean; then I will welcome you, and I will be a father to you, and you will be sons and daughters to me," says the Lord Almighty. Since we have such promises, beloved, let us cleanse ourselves from every defilement of flesh and spirit, making holiness perfect in the fear of God (2 Cor 6:14–7:1).

This strongly worded admonition is self-contained and independent of its preceding and following context, and it contains six key-words that are not otherwise used by Paul, some of them used only here in the whole Greek Bible: *heterozygein*, "yoke with something different," *metochē*, "partnership," *symphōnēsis*, "accord," *synkatathesis*, "agreement," *Beliar,* "Belial," and *molysmos,* "defilement."

What makes it sound like a Qumran paragraph is the combination of the following five elements: (a) The triple dualism, of righteousness/ iniquity, of light/darkness, of Christ/Beliar. Compare 1QS 1:9-11, "love all the sons of light . . . hate all the sons of darkness"; 1QS 2:16-17, "may he be cut off from the midst of the sons of light because he swerved from following God for the sake of his idols and that which casts him into iniquity" (also 1QS 3:3, 13, 19-20, 24-25; 1QM 1:1, 3, 9, 11, 13; 13:5-6, 9, 15-16; 1QH 12:6). Compare too the ideas of "the lot of light" (*gôral 'ôr,* 1QM 13:9; 4QCatena^a 1-4:8), or "the lot of God" (*gôral 'El,* 1QS 2:2; 1QM 1:5, 15; 13:5), or the destruction of all "iniquity and wickedness" by God, whose "righteousness" will be made manifest (1QH 14:16). Christ does not appear in the QS, of course, but there is the contrast of God and Belial: "Blest be the God of Israel . . . , but cursed be Belial" (1QM 13:1-4), as well as "all the men of Belial's lot" (1QS 2:4-5).

(b) Opposition to idols. Compare 1QS 2:16-17 (cited above).

(c) The temple of God. Compare 1QS 9:5-7, where the men of the community are set apart to be a "sanctuary for Aaron," "a Holy of Holies," and "a community for Israel"; or "a sanctuary for Israel and a foundation of the Holy of Holies" (1QS 8:4-6).

(d) Separation from all impurity. Compare CD 6:17, "to make a distinction between the clean and the unclean"; 1QS 9:8-9; 5:13-14.

(e) Catena or string of OT texts, which emphasizes the elect character of the people of God's lot. It strings together quotations conflated from Lev 16:12; Ezek 37:27; Isa 52:11; Ezek 20:34; 2 Sam 7:14. This is a sort of *Testimonia*-list, a literary form known from 4QTestim (4Q175).

The trouble with this analysis of 2 Cor 6:14-7:1 is that it is not admitted by all who have studied the text. Though G. Grossouw, K. G. Kuhn, J. Gnilka, H. D. Betz, P. Benoit have tended to regard it as interpolated, others have sought to understand it as integral to the letter (G. Fee, J. Lambrecht, J. Murphy-O'Connor). Whether the literary similarities are sufficient to label the paragraph as a non-Pauline interpolation or not, they at least manifest the striking Palestinian Jewish parallels to such Pauline thinking.

What Paul says in Rom 12:19 about not seeking revenge, but leaving to God the recompense for evil done has an interesting parallel in 1QS 10:17–18: "I shall return to no one a recompense for evil; I shall pursue him with goodness, for the judgment of all the living is with God, and He will render to each one his reward."

Lastly, we mentioned indirectly above the dualism that also turns up at times in Paul's writing, a dualism that is not as pronounced as the Johannine, but that is similar to that of Qumran: "sons of light" (1 Thess 5:5); the lack of fellowship of "light and darkness" (2 Cor 6:14); "Satan" and "an angel of light" (1 Cor 11:14); "deeds of darkness" and "armor of light" (Rom 13:12).

81. What light have the QS shed on the Epistle to the Hebrews?

Yigael Yadin once thought that the enigma of the addressees of the Epistle to the Hebrews was finally solved, now that the QS had been discovered. For it seemed to him that, now that new light had been shed on "sectarian Judaism," the addressees "must have been a group of Jews originally belonging to the DSS sect who were converted to Christianity, carrying with them some of their own beliefs" ("The Dead Sea Scrolls and the Epistle to the Hebrews," *Aspects of the Dead Sea Scrolls* [Scripta hierosolymitana 4; Jerusalem: Magnes Press of the Hebrew University, 1958] 36–55). Others have agreed with him (C. Spicq, H. Kosmala, J. Betz, J. Daniélou). Still others have queried such an identification of the addressees (F. F. Bruce, H. W. Attridge). Whether Yadin's interpretation is correct or not, there are many points that show how sectarian tenets in the QS help in the interpretation of this important NT epistle.

In this NT writing Jesus is presented as the heavenly *hiereus* or *archiereus,* "priest" or "high priest," indeed as one superior to Aaron and the Aaronid priestly line (Heb 7:4–10). This may reflect an esteem among converts from a form of Judaism that held the Aaronids in high regard, an esteem that the author seeks to correct. There is no doubt that the Qumran nucleus community, coming from priestly families and called "the sons of Zadok," would have shared such an esteem for the Aaronids. Part of that esteem, as we have already seen, led to the opposition of the Qumran community against the "priests of Jerusalem" and the "Wicked Priest."

For the author of the Epistle to the Hebrews Jesus is "a priest forever, according to the order of Melchizedek" (Heb 5:6, quoting

Ps 110:4), or, as he puts it in 7:15, "according to the likeness of Melchizedek" (*kata tēn homoiotēta Melchisedek*), hence a priest of a superior sort. To support his contention, the author insists that Jesus, like Melchizedek, is *agenealogētos,* "without a genealogy." The verses in Genesis, which refer to Melchizedek, are 14:18-20, an insert into the story of Abram's meeting with the king of Sodom on his return from the defeat of the kings. The insert, in effect, serves to adopt Melchizedek, originally a Canaanite priest-king of Salem, into Israelite tradition. Because nothing more is ever said about Melchizedek in the OT (save the snippet in Psalm 110), those three verses do not explain really who he was or where he came from. In Genesis 14 they upset the contextual sequence and are regarded as rootless. This character of vv. 18-20 gave rise to much speculation in ancient Judaism: How could one who was called "a priest of God Most High" (14:18) be without a genealogy recorded in the OT? Every priestly family was supposed to be able to trace its lineage from Levi via Aaron and Zadok. Aaron's lineage itself was known from Exod 6:16-19, but Melchizedek's lineage was unknown.

The author of the Epistle to the Hebrews undoubtedly reworks a Jewish legend and formulates it in a four-line poem (7:3):

> *apatōr, amētōr, agenealogētos,*
> *mēte archēn hēmerōn mēte zōēs telos echōn,*
> *aphōmoiōmenos de tō huiō tou theou,*
> *menei hiereus eis to diēnekes.*
> Without father, without mother, without genealogy,
> having neither beginning of days nor end of life,
> but made to resemble the Son of God,
> he remains a priest forever.

The author of Hebrews, having written the first two lines, inverts the roles of Melchizedek and Jesus. For him Jesus is really the one who has "no end of life," because he is now exalted to heavenly glory and reigns in heaven as "a priest forever." This strange inversion enables the author to describe the priesthood of Melchizedek, in whose "likeness" Jesus is a priest. As Melchizedek's priesthood is "untransferable" (7:24), because it is not passed on in a family lineage like Aaron's, so too is Jesus' priesthood, and so it is superior to Aaron's.

Now this "strange inversion" has been clarified by an important document in the QS. A fragmentary text, called 11QMelchizedek, strings together OT quotations (Lev 25:13; Deut 15:2; Isa 61:1; Lev 25:10; Ps 82:1; Ps 7:8–9; Ps 82:2; Isa 52:7; and Lev 25:9) and comments on them in the manner of a Qumran pesher; it is sometimes called "an eschatological midrash." Leviticus 25 deals with the jubilee year, and into the Qumran discussion of it Melchizedek is introduced. He is given a special role in the execution of divine judgment related to the jubilee. In this year of "release" and "liberation" Melchizedek is depicted as a heavenly being, apparently given even the name "Elohim," and is said to "have taken his stand in the assembly of El, in the midst of gods" (*'ĕlôhîm*, understood as angels). This he does "to atone in it {the jubilee year} for all the sons of [light and] the men [of the l]ot of Mel[chizedek]" (11QMelch 10,7). Melchizedek, who is thus associated with the deliverance of divine judgment on a Day of Atonement and in a jubilee year, has become in this Palestinian Jewish tradition a heavenly being, with a role that exalts him above the angelic assembly of heaven itself. Indeed, though the text is broken and hence precludes certainty, it may even identify Melchizedek as the *mĕbaśśēr,* "herald" of good news of salvation according to Isa 52:7, perhaps even as an anointed figure like that of Dan 9:25. In any case, the text clearly speaks of Melchizedek exalted as a heavenly redemption-figure, bringing atonement to the men of his "lot."

The author of Hebrews alludes to such a tradition about Melchizedek, who is "made to resemble the Son of God" and "remains a priest forever." Thus the exalted status of Melchizedek presented in this Qumran text as a heavenly being, provides a background for the understanding of the christology of the Epistle to the Hebrews. The way the author of Hebrews reads Genesis, he is concerned to present Melchizedek as superior to Abraham, and consequently to Abraham's descendants, Levi and the Aaronid priesthood, "still in the loins of his ancestor," Abraham, "when Melchizedek met him" (Heb 7:10). (See *ESBNT,* 221–67.)

Another detail may be cited. When Heb 1:6 quotes Deut 32:43, "and let all the angels of God worship him," it does so quoting neither the LXX, which includes a similar but not identical clause ("and let all the sons of God worship him"), nor the MT, which lacks the whole clause. Now, however, a form of Deut 32:43 has turned up in 4QDeutq:

whšthww lw kl 'lhym, "and let all the elohim worship Him," a Hebrew clause borrowed from Ps 97:7. But the Greek phrase in Hebrews corresponds exactly to this Qumran addition to Deut 32:43.

Among minor phrases of the Epistle to the Hebrews said to reflect terminology of the QS are the following:

(1) "at the end of these days" (Heb 1:2): Save for the addition of the demonstrative, that phrase could echo the commonly used Qumran eschatological phrase, *bě'aḥărît hayyāmîm*, "at the end of days" (1QSa 1:1; 1Q14 6:2; 4QpIsaᵃ 8–10:17; 4QFlor [4Q174] 1–2 i 12, 19; 4QCatenaᵃ [4Q177] 1–4:5, 7; 9:[2]). (This phrase, however, turns up in the OT, often in passages dealing with eschatological hopes: Gen 49:1; Num 24:14; Deut 4:30; 31:29; Hos 3:5; Ezek 38:16; Dan 10:14.)

(2) "the knowledge of the truth" (Heb 10:26): *da'at 'ĕmet* (1QS 9:17; 1QH 10:29).

(3) "a new covenant" (9:15): *habbērît haḥădāšāh* is the name given to the community by "the men who entered" it "in the land of Damascus," a designation derived from Jer 31:31 (CD 6:19; 8:21; 19:34; 20:12; 1QpHab 2:3).

(4) "the fruit of the lips," as a sacrifice of praise (13:15): *těrûmat śěpātayim*, "an offering of lips" (1QS 9:5, 26; 10:6).

(5) "at the end of the ages" (9:26): *lēkôl qiṣṣê 'ôlāmîm* (1QS 4:16, 25–26; 1QM 1:8).

Yet, when all is said and done, the author of the Epistle to the Hebrews is not directly tributary only to the writings of the Qumran community, because we have learned from the discovery of the DSS that Christianity was born in a variegated Jewish matrix, that included much that is known not only from the OT, but also from many intertestamental writings, not to mention the Philonic Jewish tradition.

82. In the NT Jesus forbids divorce. Is there anything like that in the QS?

The prohibition of divorce is ascribed to Jesus in five different places in the NT: 1 Cor 7:10–11; Mark 10:2–12; Luke 16:18; Matt 5:31–32; 19:3–9. In these five places there are seven sayings about the dissolution of marriage.

The earliest record is preserved in 1 Cor 7:10–11 (written ca. A.D. 57), where Paul attributes the saying to "the Lord": "To the married I give command, not I but the Lord, that the wife should not be separated from her husband (but if she is separated, let her remain single, or else be reconciled to her husband) — and that the husband should not divorce his wife." This formulation of the prohibition is undoubtedly Pauline and reflects the situation of the Hellenistic world of Paul's missionary activity, in which the woman could divorce her husband (note that in v. 13c he says, "let her not divorce her husband"). In any case, the prohibition of divorce as recorded is absolute; it stands in contrast to what Paul himself, not the Lord, permits in vv. 12–15: a believing woman is "not bound," if an unbelieving husband divorces her.

The most primitive form of the prohibition is found in Luke 16:18, where Jesus says, "Everyone who divorces his wife and marries another commits adultery, and he who marries a woman divorced from her husband commits adultery." In this form the saying is not only a prohibition of divorce, but a judgment about a husband's marriage after the divorce, equating it with adultery, which was proscribed in the decalogue (Exod 20:14; Deut 5:18). This Lucan form of the saying is regarded as the "most primitive" because it is formulated completely from the OT or Jewish point of view: it comments on the action of the husband who would divorce his wife and marry again, or who would marry a divorced woman. Underlying it are the notions of the husband as the owner (Hebrew *ba'al*) of the wife, implied in such passages as Exod 20:17; 21:3, 22; Jer 6:12; Num 30:10–14; Esth 1:20–22; and above all Sir 23:22–27. Divorce is allowed to the husband according to Deut 24:1–4. What is new here is the branding of the man's action as adulterous. This form of the prohibition comes to Luke from "Q," which has recorded an isolated dominical saying that Luke uses as part of his Travel Account.

The same "Q" saying is found in Matt 5:31–32, as part of the Sermon on the Mount, forming one of the six antitheses of 5:21–48, in which Jesus reacts to the righteousness of the scribes. The "Q" form is evident in that both Matt 5:32 and Luke 16:18 have the participial form, *pas ho apolyōn,* lit. "everyone divorcing." The Matthean formulation reads: "It was said too, 'Whoever divorces his wife, let him give her a document of divorce.' But I say to you, 'Everyone who divorces his wife, except on the ground of illicit union, makes her an adulteress; and whoever marries a divorced woman commits adultery.'" Here the saying proper (v. 32) is couched in the typical Matthean antithetical form, which uses a quotation from Deut 24:1 as an introduction to the saying. Yet the Matthean form of the saying not only has an added exceptive phrase, *parektos logou porneias,* "except on the ground of *porneia*" (which will be explained below), but it lacks the second clause in Luke 16:18b, "and marries another." It also relates divorce itself, and not divorce and remarriage, to adultery. Whereas the Lucan formulation expresses a judgment about the husband's subsequent marriage as adulterous, the Matthean formulation regards divorce itself as the cause of adultery (lit. "makes her to be adultered"). It is probably Matthew who has modified the formulation of "Q," which is preserved in more primitive form in Luke. Once again, the prohibition is stated from the viewpoint of the man, as in the Lucan form.

In Mark 10:2–12, the passage is composite: vv. 2–9 form a pronouncement-story, which, having quoted Gen 1:27 and 2:24, ends with the apophthegm, "What then God has joined together, let not man put asunder." This is Jesus' answer to the Pharisees who have asked whether "it is lawful for a man to divorce his wife" (10:2), an absolute, unqualified prohibition of divorce. Joined to this pronouncement is a dominical saying, addressed to the disciples later on in a house (vv. 10–12). Hence in this Marcan form there are two prohibitions of divorce in Jesus' sayings: (a) "What then God has joined together, let not man put asunder" (v. 9); (b) "Whoever divorces his wife and marries another commits adultery against her; and if she divorces her husband and marries another, she commits adultery" (vv. 11–12). The first brings God into the prohibition, echoing a view of marriage recorded in Tob 6:18 (LXX, mss. BA), and is based on Gen 1:27 and 2:24. The second, the dominical saying, echoes the judgmental form of prohibition found in "Q." The first part of this saying is not well transmitted, having other forms in some Greek manuscripts. But it has two noteworthy items: first, the addition of the phrase *ep' autēn,* "against her," almost certainly a Marcan addition, which makes adultery against a woman something that now has to be considered, something that differs from the OT tradition; and v. 12, which is a Marcan extension of the prohibition in v. 11b,c to suit the contingencies of Gentile Christian communities in areas where Roman and Greek law prevailed and where a woman could divorce her husband. This possibility was not envisaged in the OT or in ancient Palestine, but apparently was possible in fifth-century B.C. Egypt, where Jewish marriage contracts mention it explicitly. But in both cases the prohibition of divorce attributed to Jesus is absolute or unqualified.

In Matt 19:3–9, the parallel to Mark 10:2–12, the evangelist casts the Pharisees' question in terms of the famous Hillel-Shammai dispute, making them ask whether it be lawful for a man to divorce his wife "for any cause," and introduces the dominical saying into the controversy itself. Like Mark, then, Matthew has preserved two prohibitions of divorce: (a) "What then God has joined together, let not man put asunder" (v. 6); (b) "Whoever divorces his wife except for an illicit union and marries another commits adultery" (v. 9). The first saying repeats the absolute prohibition of divorce, as in Mark; the second, which adds an exceptive phrase, takes over from Mark only 10:11 and omits "against her," thus adapting the saying to Matthew's Jewish-Christian concerns.

It has often been thought that the Matthean formulation of the Pharisees' question, "Is it lawful for a man to divorce his wife *for any reason*?" is more primitive than the Marcan form, "Is it lawful for a man to divorce his wife?" because it reflects the Palestinian Jewish controversy between two rabbinical schools. The school of Shammai interpreted Deut 24:1, "because he finds in her something indecent," to mean that a man could divorce his wife only because he discovered her involved in "unchastity" (*dēbar 'erwāh*), but the school of Hillel permitted divorce "for anything" (even if she spoiled a dish for him; see *m. Gittin* 9:10). Yet now the evidence from the QS sheds new light on the question as formulated in Mark, and it may have a different nuance. But, before we consider that new evidence, a few words of explanation are necessary about the Matthean exceptive phrases and the meaning of *porneia* in them.

Could the exceptive phrases be authentic or original? Most interpreters are reluctant to admit that they are an authentic part of the primitive prohibition, because of the greater difficulty of explaining how the absolute, unqualified form of the prohibition recorded in Paul, Luke, and Mark would have arisen, if Jesus had actually used the exception. Again, there is Matthew's tendency, otherwise detected, to add things to the sayings of Jesus (e.g. two petitions in the Our Father

[6:10b,13b; cf. Luke 11:2–4]; additions to the Beatitudes [5:3a,6a; cf. Luke 6:20b–21]; Peter's secondary confession [16:16b–19; cf. Mark 8:29]). Hence, Matthew, faced with a problem in the mixed Jewish-Gentile Christian community for which he was writing, added the exceptive phrases.

What is meant by *porneia*? It occurs elsewhere in Matthew only in 15:19, "murder, adultery, *fornication*," where it is lined up with *moicheia,* "adultery," and hence is distinct from it. Etymologically, it means "fornication, prostitution, harlotry," being an abstract noun related to *pornē,* "harlot," or the verb *porneuein,* "fornicate, act as a harlot." But historically, it was used of "every kind of unlawful sexual intercourse" (BAGD, 699). And it was also used in a very specific sense, since it is found lined up with several dietary tabus that early Gentile Christians who lived in close contact with Jewish Christians were expected to avoid: "what was sacrificed to idols, blood, what was strangled, and *porneia*" (Acts 15:20, 29). These are four of the things that the Holiness Code of Leviticus 17–18 proscribed, not only for "any man of the house of Israel," but also for "the strangers that sojourn among them" (Lev 17:8). These were meat offered to idols (Lev 17:8–9), the eating of blood (Lev 17:10–12), the eating of strangled, i.e. not properly butchered, animals (Lev 17:15; cf. Exod 22:31), and intercourse within close degrees of kinship (Lev 18:6–18).

What is meant by *porneia* in Matt 5:32 and 19:9? For many commentators it means "adultery." But why, then, would not Matthew have used *moicheia,* the proper word for it, which he uses elsewhere? Again, the Matthean Jesus is speaking of something that he equates with adultery; so he must mean something else. For other commentators it means merely prostitution in general, "unchastity" (as the *RSV* has rendered it). Still others use the specific meaning of *porneia* found in Acts 15:20, 29, understanding it as a reference to Lev 18:6–18 and translating it as "illicit marital union." If the last is correct, as I think it is, Matthew would have added the exceptive phrases, because he was writing for a mixed community, one which was predominantly Jewish Christian, but which Gentile converts had joined, who were already living in such marital unions proscribed by Leviticus. In this case, Matthew would have added the exceptive phrases to allow for the dissolution of marital unions of Gentile converts that should not have taken place to begin with from the Jewish point of view.

Two texts from the QS have now to be considered, which help in the interpretation of these NT passages about the dissolution of marriage. The first is found in the Temple Scroll of Cave 11, which among other things has a section called "the statutes for the king and his army." One of the statutes begins with a quotation of Deut 17:14–17, in which Israel is instructed to set up as a king over it one "whom the Lord your God will choose, one from among your brethren," and which ends with the injunction, "He shall not multiply wives for himself lest his heart turn away; nor shall he greatly amass for himself silver and gold" (Deut 17:17). This injunction becomes in 11QTemple 57:17–19: "He shall not take in addition to her another wife, for she alone shall be with him all the days of her life; and if she dies, he shall take for himself another (wife) from his father's house, from his clan." The first part of this injunction precludes polygamy, echoing Deut 17:17; but the reason that is further added makes it clear that the king is not to divorce his wife, "for she alone shall be with him all the days of her life."

Commentators on this text usually note that what is legislated in this Second Torah for the king is also legislated for the commoner. If that is correct, and I think it is, then we have in this Qumran text a clear example of the prohibition of divorce from a Palestinian Jewish context, something that was unknown prior to the discovery of this scroll. In light of this injunction, the question posed to Jesus by the Pharisees in the Marcan pronouncement story, instead of reflecting the Hillel-Shammai debate as the Matthean form does, would then be asking Jesus whether he agreed with the Pharisaic view, which permitted divorce according to Deut 24:1, or with the Essene view, now known from 11QTemple, which did not permit divorce. So the Temple Scroll sheds important light on the question posed to Jesus in the Marcan passage.

The second text has been known for a long time, being a section of the Damascus Document, but its meaning was not clear until the Temple Scroll from Cave 11 became known. In CD 4:12b–5:14a there is part of an Essene missionary document, an admonition addressed to Jews of Judea who were not members of the Essene community. It seeks to explain God's attitude toward mankind as revealed in history, extolling the role of the privileged remnant to which the author belonged, i.e. the Essene community, and warning other Jews about their situation. The text levels against current Palestinian Jewry a harsh indictment: Israel has become ensnared in various traps laid by Belial, of which Isa 24:17 speaks. These "traps" are explained as three nets of Belial in which Israel is caught: *zĕnût,* usually translated merely "unchastity," *tammē' hammiqdāš,* "defilement of the sanctuary," and *hahôn,* "wealth." The last named net seems to be an allusion to Deut 17:17b, quoted above, viz. the amassing of silver and gold. The second net, the defilement of the sanctuary, is explained by the failure to avoid intercourse with the woman considered unclean in Lev 15:19, i.e. the woman who is in a state of impurity for seven days because of a menstrual flux.

The first net, *zĕnût,* is explained "in two ways": (a) "by taking two wives in their lifetime" (CD 4:20–21); and (b) "they take (as wives) each one (of them), the daughter of his brother, and the daughter of his sister" (CD 5:7–8). The second way is marriage with a niece, a contravention of forbidden degrees of kinship (cf. Lev 18:15), but the first way is seen as a contravention of Gen 1:27 ("male and female he created them"); Gen 7:9 ("two by two they entered the ark"); and Deut 17:17, quoted above.

But the meaning of the clause in CD 4:21, "by taking two wives in their lifetime," has always been controverted, because the last word *bĕḥayyêhem,* "in their lifetime," has a third plural masculine suffix. Does it forbid polygamy and divorce (the majority opinion), or only divorce (G. Vermes), or any second or further marriage (J. Murphy-O'Connor)? Now that we have the text of 11QTemple 57:17, quoted above, we see that it is stipulating the same thing: a prohibition of polygamy and divorce.

This text of the Damascus Document, understood in the light of the Temple Scroll of Cave 11, not only shows that some Jews of Palestine in pre-Christian times viewed divorce as forbidden, but also understood *zĕnût* in a very specific sense. This word, an abstract formation of the root *zny,* etymologically means the same as Greek *porneia,* "fornication, harlotry." But here *zĕnût* is understood specifically in the second sense as illicit marriage within forbidden degrees of kinship. This, then, makes *porneia* in the specific sense of "illicit union" very plausible in Matt 5:32 and 19:9, especially in the sense of a marital union within forbidden degrees of kinship.

Hence these two texts from the QS clarify in an unexpected way

the NT passages about Jesus' prohibition of divorce. To answer the
question, they also show that the Qumran community did, indeed,
forbid divorce, as did Jesus. (See further *TAG*, 79–111.)

83. Did the subsequent history of the Qumran sect contribute in any way to Jewish Christianity?

Once the community center at Qumran was destroyed by the
Romans in the summer of A.D. 68 on their way to the siege of
Jerusalem, little was left to give us any information about either the
community or what may have happened to its members. The excavation of Khirbet Qumran revealed that after the destruction of the
community center the Romans continued to occupy the area and
established a small military post on the site. This was apparently to
enable them to keep watch on the shores of the Dead Sea. After the
fall of Jerusalem in A.D. 70, other Jewish sites were also captured,
e.g. Herodium and Machaerus. But the Jews still held the fortress of
Masada, which overlooked the Dead Sea itself and was situated about
45 kilometers to the south-southwest of Khirbet Qumran. This did
not fall until April of A.D. 74. To control the area on the west side
of the Dead Sea the Romans set up this small military encampment
on the ruins of the Qumran community center. The tower of the center
was reutilized, the wall extending to the east was doubled in thickness,
and the rooms to the northeast of the tower were slightly altered. The
Romans also modified the supply of water from the wadi to one
cistern. It is not certain how long this Roman encampment lasted.
A few coins from Ashkelon of A.D. 72–73 were found in the stratum
connected with the camp, as well as four inscribed *Judaea Capta* of
uncertain date. It must have been occupied at least until A.D. 74, the
fall of Masada.

In the Acts of the Apostles Luke records in one of his summary
statements that "the word of God increased, and the number of
disciples multiplied greatly in Jerusalem, and a great many of the
priests became obedient to the faith" (6:7). Were some of the priests
of the Qumran community among this number of priests converted
to Christianity? It is not impossible, but who can say for sure?

Some scholars have speculated that, because the Qumran community refers to itself in some of the scrolls as *'ădat hā'ebyônîm,*

"the congregation of the poor" (4QpIsaᵃ 1-2 ii 9; 1, 3-4 iii 10; cf. 1QpHab 12:3, 6, 10), remnants of it after the destruction of the center and of Jerusalem may have become Christians and were eventually known as the Ebionites, Jewish Christians, about whom patristic writers such as Justin Martyr, Irenaeus, Tertullian, Origen, Hippolytus, Eusebius, Jerome, and Epiphanius give us some information. This was the suggestion of Oscar Cullmann in the early days of DSS debate (1954). There were also some scholars who even wanted to identify the Qumran community itself with the Ebionites (so J. L. Teicher, H.-J. Schoeps). There is little evidence, however, beyond speculation for Cullmann's position, and so many difficulties with the suggestion that it is hardly likely. As for the outright identification of the Qumran community with the Ebionites, that is contradicted by the pronounced Jewish character of the QS and the lack of anything in them that would point to the community as Jewish Christian. (See further *ESBNT,* 435-80.)

84. What relation did the Qumran community have to later Christian monasticism?

Per se, it had no relation to Christian monasticism, which has usually been said to be "a creation of Christian Egypt. Its founders were not the philosophers of the Hellenistic world but the fellahin of the country of the Nile, who were untouched by Greek ideas. Its beginnings are intimately connected with the history of asceticism, which was inherent in Christian teaching from the first" (J. Quasten, *Patrology* [Westminster, MD: Newman], 3 [1960] 146).

The origin of anchoritic monasticism is normally traced to Antony (251?-356), who withdrew as a hermit to the Egyptian desert ca. A.D. 285, attracted followers, and ca. 305 organized them into a community of hermits living under a rule. Historians of Christian monasticism have always known about the Essenes in Palestine and the Therapeutae in Egypt, but the influence of these groups on Antony and his movement or on other forms of monasticism, such as cenobitism, has never been clearly worked out.

When, however, one reads the Manual of Discipline and the Damascus Document today and realizes that these documents stem from Jews in pre-Christian times, one notes how there was already in pre-Christian Palestinian Judaism a communal, ascetic mode of religious life that was previously unknown, at least unknown in such detail. For it is not merely a question of a mode of common life, described to some extent in § 52–62 above, but innumerable minor details that are strikingly similar to those of later Christian monastic and religious communities in the Christian church.

The Judaism of the OT already knew of vows, even of Nazirite vows (Num 6:2, 5, 21). The Damascus Document uses the noun *nēder*, "vow," once and the cognate verb twice (CD 6:15; 16:13, 18), but always in the sense of vowing contributions to the altar or to a sacrifice. Though celibacy was practiced in this pre-Christian Jewish community, and all members contributed their knowledge, their strength, and their property to the good of all, and their communal life was lived in obedience to an Overseer, the mode of life was not yet conceived of as lived under vows of poverty, chastity, and obedience, as in Christian monasticism. There were, however, the binding oaths that the members who entered the Covenant did make; they were obviously the antecedents of the Christian vows. Hence one sees in the Qumran community many antecedents of things that did develop in the Christian form of monastic life. Even the retreat to the desert of Qumran itself and the effort there to live a common life in obedience to the Law of Moses provide analogies for the later Christian movement. Not to mention the procedures that the Qumran community worked out for the admission, testing, and training of candidates who voluntarily offered themselves to such a mode of life. See V. Desprez, "The Roots of Christian Monasticism: The Jewish Bible and Ancient Religions," *American Benedictine Review* 41 (1990) 357–77.

85. Why have the scrolls from Cave 4 created such a problem as was recently described in news media?

Since no complete scroll was discovered in Cave 4 and only thousands of fragments, the problem that first confronted the seven scholars assembled to work on the fragmentary texts was a giant jigsaw puzzle. Those fragments often had to be unfolded and cleaned; they had to be sorted out and grouped, according to papyrus or skin; they had to sorted according to the color of the skin and according to the form of their handwriting; they had to be pieced together as best they could be, when joins were possible. Since many pieces were missing, it was sometimes possible to relate, say, twenty different pieces to a given text by color of skin and form of handwriting, but without making any joins, because intervening pieces were lacking. All of this identification and joining of fragments took time, patience, and a great deal of skill.

Once fragments of a given text were assembled, they had to be photographed, often with infrared photography to make the writing on especially dark pieces of skin more legible.

The fragments so assembled and photographed could then be studied and identified. Of course, sometimes the identification of words on fragments often led to their being joined or related to other fragments. So the reading, joining, and identification of fragments often went hand in hand. If they were fragments of a biblical book or of a text otherwise known, the identification was easy, because the words could be looked up in a concordance to the Hebrew text of the OT. Similarly with texts known from Greek, Latin, or Ethiopic translations. But it was another matter when the fragments were part of texts previously unknown. There the identification of fragments depended on the color of the skin and ink, the forms of letters, the script used, the subject-matter of the text. Such texts tested the ingenuity of those who worked on them and consumed much time.

This process of identification and piecing together of the fragments began at the end of 1952, a short time after the fragments of Cave 4, discovered in September of that year, had been brought to the scrollery of the Palestine Archaeological Museum. The seven scholars eventually assembled to study and piece together these fragments labored at it in the scrollery until roughly 1960, when all that could be done on the jigsaw puzzle was "completed" and when the funds for their support came to an end. De Vaux reports that by August of 1955 the scholars had sorted out 330 texts; by the summer of 1956 they counted 381 texts, and by the end of June 1960 they counted 511 texts encased in 620 glass plates (DJD 6. 8). By the time DJD 7 was published in 1982, it included texts 4Q482 to 4Q520. Today we know that there are at least 584 fragmentary texts that have been identified. Thus the jigsaw puzzle was the first and major problem.

Between 1960 and 1975, those 584 texts of Cave 4 should have been published. That would have allowed 15 years for editorial work, a reasonable and not an impossible ideal. Actually, a tighter, but unrealistic, schedule of publication was decided on at a meeting of the editors at the Museum in the summer of 1958, which I attended: the manuscript of the volume on the minor caves was to be given to Clarendon Press by January 1959 (it appeared as DJD 3 in 1962). That of the biblical texts of the Pentateuch was due for June 1959 (it has not yet appeared). In January 1960 a manuscript containing the non-biblical texts of Hunzinger and Allegro was to be submitted (the volume with Allegro's texts appeared as DJD 5 in 1968). In June of 1960 the first volume of Milik's nonbiblical material was to be given to the publisher. In January 1961 the manuscript of the rest of the biblical texts was due for Clarendon Press. The texts of Strugnell were scheduled for June 1961, and those of Starcky for January 1962, with the rest of the Milik material ready for submission in June 1962. (A slightly different schedule is reported by M. Baigent and R. Leigh, *The Dead Sea Scrolls Deception* [London: Jonathan Cape, 1991] 39, but it is not clear where they obtained their information.)

To date only nine volumes in the DJD series of Clarendon Press have appeared, and volumes 2 and 8 have nothing to do with QS. Volume 2 was devoted to the texts from Wadi Murabba'at (1961), and volume 8 to the Greek Minor Prophets text of Naḥal Ḥever (1990).

The main reason for the delay of publishing the Cave 4 fragments has been the desire of the editors to whom the texts had been entrusted to write lengthy commentaries on the texts instead of publishing them quickly with photographs, a diplomatic transcription in modern Hebrew characters, a translation into some modern language, and brief notes on the reading of difficult letters. This desire to say the last word on a given text and the hidden concern to safeguard one's turf have created a monopoly and resulted in the incredible delay in publication, which is nothing less than an academic scandal.

For instance, J. T. Milik, who had published promptly Cave 1 fragments in 1955 (DJD 1) and Murabba'at texts in 1961 (DJD 2), eventually published in 1976 fragmentary copies of the original Aramaic text of *1 Enoch* (4QEn[a-g], 4QEnastr[a-d], and 4QEnGiants[a-d]), along with revisions of some related texts already published from Caves 1, 2, and 6, but now recognized as belonging to the Enochic corpus. His publication of the Cave 4 texts is accompanied with elaborate restorations of the text retroverted by him from Ethiopic into Aramaic and an extensive commentary, not to mention the diplomatic transcription of the Cave 4 texts in a latter part of the book (*The Books of Enoch: Aramaic Fragments of Qumrân Cave 4* [Oxford: Clarendon, 1976]). This book appeared 25 years after the discovery of the fragments. In it there is an elaborate introduction of 135 pp. in which Milik puts forth a thesis to explain the difference between the form of *1 Enoch* as previously known in its Ethiopic translation and the form now known from these Qumran texts. Since the Qumran astronomical section of the book of Enoch (4QEnastr) is longer than the Ethiopic form, and since the Qumran form of the book lacks the so-called Parables (chaps. 37–71) and has instead a section called "the Book of Giants" (previously known only in translation from extant Manichean literature), Milik considered the Parables to be a Christian substitution in the Ethiopic form of *1 Enoch* for the original Jewish form of Enoch, which contained the Giants section, but no Parables. This thesis, propounded with great erudition and elaborate discussion, has been espoused by no other scholar that I know of today. Yet it took Milik over fifteen years to produce that study. What he should have been content to do was publish the 4QEnoch texts with the photographs, his diplomatic transcription, English translation, and brief notes on readings. The time needed to produce the 1976 study held him up from publishing in brief form many of the other texts entrusted to him: the texts related to the *Testaments of the Twelve Patriarchs,* the Book of *Jubilees,* the Aramaic and Hebrew texts of Tobit, the Cave 4 fragments of the Manual of Discipline, of the Damascus Documents, the *Tĕhôrôt,* etc. Milik may have been the "fastest man with a fragment" and has published more than all the other team members, but it is now clear that too many important texts were entrusted to one person. (He has since passed some of these texts on to other persons; see § 94 below.)

Another factor in the delay has been the political situation in the Middle East. The Cave 4 texts were found in the Jordanian controlled West Bank in 1952, a few years after the first Arab-Israeli war of 1948–49. The political situation seethed until 29 October 1956, when Israel staged a preemptive strike on Egypt's Sinai Peninsula during the Suez Canal crisis. This state of affairs caused the disbanding of the team of scholars working in Jerusalem. After the UN ceasefire and the withdrawal of Israeli troops in November 1956, the conditions in East Jerusalem were very unsettled. The scholars returned to Jerusalem only in the spring of 1957. Because of fear that the Cave 4 fragments might be damaged, the plates of glass with the fragments between them had been boxed up and transported to the Ottoman Bank in Amman, Jordan, where they lay in the damp basement for several months. They were returned to the Jerusalem scrollery in the spring of 1957, and the scholars who then returned spent several weeks cleaning the mildew from the fragments in an attempt to preserve them. Some of the fragments had been put merely in brown manila envelopes, and they came back in the form of globs of glue, inseparable from the paper, and illegible. Thus a number of the fragments, especially biblical texts, were lost. By the summer of 1957 the work on the jigsaw puzzle and identification of texts had resumed.

The political situation was also responsible for another form of delay. The DJD series, which was first published in 1955, was at first called "Discoveries in the Judaean Desert." When volume 3, devoted to the fragments of the minor caves (2-3, 5-10), appeared in the series in 1962, it bore the series title "Discoveries in the Judaean Desert of Jordan." That title was also used for volumes 4 and 5, published in 1965 and 1968. When the Six-Day War took place in 1967 and Israel occupied East Jerusalem and the West Bank, Israeli authorities wanted to rename the series, "Discoveries in the Judaean Desert of Israel." That caused an uproar, and a manuscript of Cave 4 biblical texts, which had been prepared for publication by Patrick W. Skehan and was almost ready for the press, was held up by him, because he refused to have any mention of Israel on the titlepage of the book that would contain his work (*The New York Times,* 7 January 1973, p. 18). Skehan died on 9 September 1980, and his unpublished manuscript and texts have since been passed on to another scholar, Eugene C. Ulrich of Notre Dame University, who has finally put the first part of the manuscript in shape for publication. It is at present in the press and was announced to appear in December 1991; it is still awaited in May 1992.

Another factor in the delay of publication has been the doling out of these important fragmentary texts to graduate students for their doctoral dissertations at Harvard University by team members who are now professors there. Instead of publishing the fragments that were entrusted to them as established scholars, they have been spending their precious time directing such dissertations of students, to whom the texts had not been entrusted. The scandalous delay is thus compounded by an inequity. One has to be a graduate student of these professors at Harvard University in order to be privileged to publish such texts.

All these factors, scholarly monopoly and delay, Mideast political situation and its consequences, the doling out of texts to students, have created the problem recently alluded to in the news media.

86. What stirred up the recent interest in the QS?

First, the scandalous delay in publication of the majority of the Cave 4 texts had begun to annoy scholars all over the world. Many have complained about it. In 1977 Geza Vermes called it "the academic scandal *par excellence* of the twentieth century" (*The Dead Sea Scrolls: Qumran in Perspective,* 24). An international group of scholars, which met at the Dead Sea Scrolls Colloquium at Mogilany (near Cracow), Poland in 1989, published "The Mogilany Resolution 1989" (*Folia orientalia* 26 [1989] 229–30; also in *Qumran Chronicle* 1 [1990] 10–11). It called for the publication by the Clarendon Press of "plates of all as yet unpublished material as soon as possible as separate volumes and in advance of the accompanying definitive critical editions of that material"; it also called for the preparation of Qumran bibliographies, the publication of the Qumran Dictionary and Concordance of the Göttingen institute, and the quick publication in preliminary form of all Qumran texts in the *Revue de Qumran.* Though the thinking behind this resolution was something of a pipe-dream, it revealed the growing impatience of scholars everywhere with the delay in publication.

Second, in the U.S.A. much of the interest has been owing to the pressure put on scholars and institutions by one person, Hershel Shanks, the editor of the *Biblical Archaeology Review* and the *Bible Review* and head of the Biblical Archaeology Society of Washington, DC. In article after article since at least 1985 Shanks has prodded the dawdling scholars who are responsible for publication to release the materials. He and R. H. Eisenman, professor at the California State University, Long Beach, have been particularly responsible for prodding the Israel Antiquities Authority too to come to a decision to move in and pry loose from some of the editors texts that should have long since been published. At times, however, Shanks's rhetoric has verged on the excessive, e.g. when he speaks of "the cartel's earlier tooth-and-nail efforts to maintain the secrecy of the unpublished texts. These efforts were accompanied by a remarkable disdain for anyone who dared question the wisdom of the cartel" (*Facsimile Edition* [see § 95], xiii). Eisenman's questionable interpretations of the QS have also alienated many responsible persons from listening to his legitimate and justified pleas for the release of the Cave 4 materials. As a result, there has been a mixed-bag of blessings: with varied effects, some good, some not so good.

Third, the "bootlegging" of as yet unpublished texts by reconstructing them from a keyword-in-context concordance became front-page news in many American cities (see § 92 below). It has stirred up interest, but it has not been a help in the whole process.

Fourth, when it became known that photographs of the unpublished QS had been deposited in various institutions around the world, pressure was exerted by many people to have such photographs published independently of the definitive editions of the texts in the DJD series, witness the Mogilany Resolution mentioned above. For it was learned that there was a set of such photographs at Oxford, England, at the Ancient Biblical Manuscript Center in Claremont, CA, at the Huntington Library in San Marino, CA, and at the Hebrew Union College, Cincinnati, OH. When such news hit the headlines, all sorts of people began pressuring these institutions for the release of photographs. The director of the Huntington Library, William A. Moffett, finally decided that he would make copies of its photographs available to qualified scholars, judging that the library was not bound to any obligation of secrecy about them. This sparked at first a negative reaction in Israel, but afterwards the Israeli Antiquities Authority relented and made it known that they too would make photographs available to scholars who requested them (*New York Times,* 27 November 1991, A22).

87. Who assembled the team of scholars to work on Cave 4 fragments?

When the Cave 4 fragments were brought to the scrollery of the Palestine Archaeological Museum in East Jerusalem in 1952, they came under the authority of the Jordanian Department of Antiquities. At that time, G. Lankester Harding, an Englishman, was still the head of that department, even though the British Mandate of Transjordan had come to an end in 1948. Being an archaeologist and not a trained Semitic philologist, he sought the help and advice of the directors of various archaeological institutes then in East Jerusalem, the French Ecole Biblique, and the American, British, and German Schools. It was decided to assemble an international and intercredal team to work on the giant jigsaw puzzle that the fragments of Cave 4 created.

The veteran of the team was Jozef T. Milik, a Polish scholar then resident in Jerusalem, who had assisted de Vaux in excavating Caves 4 and 5 and Khirbet Qumran and had helped in the publication of the fragments of Cave 1 (DJD 1) and of those of Murabba'at (DJD 2). *Time* magazine labelled him "the Scrollery's fastest man with a fragment" (15 April 1957, p. 39). Frank M. Cross, Jr., then professor at McCormick Theological Seminary in Chicago, arrived in May of 1953 as the annual professor of the American School of Oriental Research in East Jerusalem with an assignment to work on the Cave 4 fragments. The deans of OT studies in England, G. R. Driver of Oxford and H. H. Rowley of Manchester, were asked to send a young recently graduated doctoral student to join the team. Rowley sent John Marco Allegro, who arrived at the end of 1953, and Driver sent John Strugnell of Jesus College, Oxford, who came in July 1954. The Frenchman Jean Starcky began work on Aramaic fragments in January 1954, and Patrick W. Skehan, professor at the Catholic University of America, Washington, DC, came in June 1954 as the annual professor of the American School in Jerusalem and continued as the director of the school in 1955–56; his task was to be a member of the team. Joachim Jeremias of Göttingen was also asked to send someone, and Claus Hunno Hunzinger arrived in October 1954 as a German member of the team. These were the original seven members of the international team, which was set up under the authority of G. Lankester Harding. R. de Vaux, the director of the Ecole Biblique and permanent resident in Jerusalem, was named the head of the team and the editor in chief of the DJD series, even though he was an archaeologist and not one of those to whom Cave 4 fragments were entrusted for publication.

88. Was any Qumran scroll published by someone who was not part of the international team?

The seven major scrolls of Qumran Cave 1 were published by American and Israeli scholars. None of them was a member of this team. Isaiah Scroll A (1QIsa^a), the Manual of Discipline (1QS), and the Pesher on Habakkuk (1QpHab) were published by Millar Burrows, of Yale University, in 1950–51; the Isaiah Scroll B (1QIsa^b), the Thanksgiving Psalms (1QH), and the War Scroll (1QM) were published by Eleazar Lipa Sukenik, of the Hebrew University of Jerusalem, Israel, in 1954; and the Genesis Apocryphon (1QapGen) was published by the Israeli scholars, Nahman Avigad and Yigael Yadin, in 1956. The texts from Cave 11 have also been published by others than the international team. The most important is the Temple Scroll (11QTemple^a), published by the Israeli scholar Yigael Yadin in 1977. Another Cave 11 text was the Psalms Scroll (11QPs^a), published in 1965 by James A. Sanders, then professor of OT at Union Theological Seminary in New York and annual professor at the American School of Oriental Research during 1961–62.

Another Cave 11 text was the Targum of Job (11QtgJob), of which the Dutch government through its Academy of Sciences secured the right of publication for two Dutch scholars, J. P. M. van der Ploeg and A. S. van der Woude, who published it in 1971.

Still another was the scroll of Leviticus (11QpaleoLev), which after the Six-Day War was still in the Museum safe. Now under Israeli occupation, the "new custodians officially assigned the Leviticus scroll to D. N. Freedman for study and publication"; he was then professor at the University of Michigan at Ann Arbor, MI, and published the text in 1985.

There have been also a number of smaller fragments from Cave 11 published by W. H. Brownlee, J. P. M. van der Ploeg, A. S. van der Woude, and C. Newsom, none of whom have been members of the international team assembled for the study of the Cave 4 fragments.

89. Why were there no Jewish scholars on the international team?

It has been said that R. de Vaux, being anti-Israel and antisemitic, failed to appoint any Jewish members to the team. "The only rule imposed on him — hardly necessary to articulate — was that the team include no Jews. It didn't." (H. Shanks, "The Dead Sea Scroll Monopoly," *The Washington Post,* 8 October 1991, p. A19). That, however, is a gratuitous allegation. Since it was only a few years after the first Arab-Israeli war of 1948–49, it was politically impossible that any Jew be named to the team, even though there were competent Jewish scholars a short distance away across the border and across the mined no-man's land between Jordanian controlled East Jerusalem and Israeli West Jerusalem. No Jew would have been permitted to enter East Jerusalem at that time. (As late as the spring of 1958, when I checked at the police-station in Jericho for permission to proceed to visit Khirbet Qumran, I was said by a Jordanian policeman, who thought that I did not understand any Arabic and who remarked to his colleague, to have *ism nuss-yahudi,* "a half-Jewish name"! So wary were they about Jewish presence in Jordan as late as 1958!) No, the exclusion of Jews from the international team was not because of anti-semitism; it was dictated by the political situation of the time. M. Baigent and R. Leigh (*The Dead Sea Scrolls Deception,* 31) claim that "the anti-Semitic de Vaux" used the political situation as a "handy pretext to exclude Israeli experts": "they could easily have been provided with photographs, or with some other access to the material. No such access was granted." But naive commentators such as Baigent and Leigh think that one can edit such difficult fragments only with the aid of photographs.

It has also been said that "the seven-man team de Vaux assembled consisted mostly of Catholic clerics" (H. Shanks, *The Washington Post,* 8 October 1991, p. A19). Again, that is an exaggeration. Of the seven original members of the team, three were Roman Catholic priests: the Pole J. T. Milik, a refugee who had fled Warsaw when the Communists took over and who studied in Rome at the Biblical Institute before coming to Jerusalem; the Frenchman J. Starcky, who had been a chaplain in the French army stationed in Syria during World War II; and the American P. W. Skehan, a priest of the Archdiocese of New York, professor at the Catholic University in Washington, DC.

The American Frank M. Cross, Jr. was a Presbyterian, as was the English layman John Strugnell (who has only within the last decade or so converted to Catholicism). The German Claus Hunno

Hunzinger was a Lutheran, and the Englishman John Marco Allegro was a dropout from a Methodist Seminary, who became an agnostic and author of several anti-Christian books (*The Sacred Mushroom and the Cross* [Garden City, NY: Doubleday, 1970] and *The Dead Sea Scrolls and the Christian Myth* [Buffalo, NY: Prometheus Books, 1984]). Hence the team was not originally "mostly of Catholic clerics."

Eventually, Hunzinger resigned from the team in 1958, and a French Catholic priest, Maurice Baillet, who had finished preparing for publication the fragments of the minor Caves 2–3 and 6–10 (DJD 3), was asked to take over the fragments that had been assigned to Hunzinger. He then became a member of the international team.

Shanks is right, however, when he says, "Strangely enough, in 1967, when Israel gained control of East Jerusalem (and the scrolls in the Palestine Archaeological Museum), it made no demands on the editing team — as, for instance, the addition of some Jews to the team. It required only that the work be speeded up so the world would be able to see the texts. This did not happen, and de Vaux died in 1971" (*The Washington Post*, 8 October 1991, p. A19).

90. Have the Cave 4 texts so far published been competently handled?

Most of the Cave 4 texts published either in the DJD series or in partial, preliminary editions have been competently handled. But there is one notorious exception. That is the volume published by John M. Allegro, *Qumrân Cave 4: I (4Q158–4Q186)* (DJD 5; Oxford: Clarendon, 1968). To give the devil his due, Allegro did publish definitively most of his lot of pesharim and biblical paraphrases in this book. It contains 29 texts, but it omitted one text that Allegro had previously published in preliminary form (4QPBless, in *JBL* 75 [1956] 174–76) and another that he subsequently published in *The Dead Sea Scrolls and the Christian Myth* (see § 89), 235–40 (4QTherapeia), a text that he misinterpreted and misnamed. He thought that it was a report of "medical" activity, but Israeli scholars have shown that it is merely a "writing exercise" (J. Naveh, *IEJ* 36 [1986] 52–55; J. C. Greenfield, ibid. 118–19).

In the DJD volume itself, some fragments have not been properly identified or joined; many readings are questionable, and the numbering of plates is confusing. The secondary literature on 15 texts that had been previously published in partial form was completely neglected (see my remedy of it, *CBQ* 31 [1969] 59–71). And of this volume, which numbers 111 pages (+31 plates), John Strugnell wrote a 113 page review, correcting many of the mistakes (*RevQ* 7 [1969–71] 163–276). Another writer has said of it, "In all, DJD V is the worst and the most untrustworthy Q-edition delivered to the reader since the beginning of the discovery" (K. Müller, *Einführung in die Methoden der biblischen Exegese* [ed. J. Schreiner; Würzburg: Echter Verlag, 1971] 310). In his review of Allegro's book, Strugnell quoted a medieval Latin distich: "'R' habet italicum liber hic, habet atque pelasgum, Necnon hebraeum, praetereaque nihil" (*RevQ* 7 [1969–71] 276), "This book has an Italian 'R' [pronounced *er*]; it also has a Greek one [pronounced *ro*], also a Hebrew one [pronounced *res*], and nothing else" [*Er-ro-res* and nothing else]!

91. How did it come about that there is a concordance of Cave 4 texts, when the texts themselves have not yet been published?

The concordance became a need as work on the jigsaw puzzle in the scrollery progressed. A concordance was not needed for the biblical texts, since one could easily consult the standard one, S. Mandelkern, *Veteris Testamenti concordantiae hebraicae atque chaldaicae* . . . (2 vols.; 2d ed.; Berlin: Margolin, 1925). But for the non-biblical texts of Cave 4 it was imperative, since there was really no other way of guaranteeing the proper joining of fragments of texts previously not known.

So in 1956 at an OT convention in Strasbourg, France, R. de Vaux made known to W. F. Albright, professor at the Johns Hopkins University, Baltimore, MD, the need to add a young scholar to the international team for the purpose of preparing such a concordance. I had just finished my doctoral work under Albright at that university and was en route to Rome for a year of postdoctoral study at the Biblical Institute, but had already applied for a fellowship for the following year (1957–58) at the American School of Oriental Research in Jerusalem. Albright introduced me to de Vaux in Strasbourg, and I became the person who would begin the work on the concordance in the scrollery during the year 1957–58.

I put on individual cards all the words of the Cave 4 fragments of the pesharim, the Manual of Discipline, the Damascus Document, Tobit, and many other Aramaic and Hebrew texts from the lots assigned to Milik and Starcky. I had devised a system whereby all the cards that belonged to a given text were numbered in sequence in the lower left-hand corner before they were sorted for alphabetization. That would enable us to reconstitute the cards in sequence and check them against the definitive reading of the texts, once the editors had finally published them, so that the concordance could also be published.

In the following year (1958–59) work on the concordance was continued by Raymond E. Brown, S.S. and in the year after that (1959–60) by Willard G. Oxtoby. Later on Javier Teixidor also contributed to the compiling of words for the concordance from non-biblical texts already published from other caves.

That concordance lay in cards in the scrollery from 1957, when it was begun, until the Six-Day War, when, I have been told by M. Baillet, it was dumped pell-mell into a closet in the scrollery. It must have been reconstituted some time after that, because in the late 80s the cards were photographed under the direction of J. Strugnell, of Harvard University, and Hartmut Stegemann, of Germany, and photographic reproductions in three volumes were to be made available only to the editors of the Cave 4 texts. I have seen only a volume of this form of the concordance, having been shown it by Milik when I visited him in Paris in 1990.

So it came about that a concordance became available for the study of Cave 4 nonbiblical texts, which were not yet even published in preliminary forms.

92. Who "bootlegged" Cave 4 texts by reconstructing them from the concordance?

"Bootleg" is the word that *The New York Times* (5 September 1991, p. A1) used of the tactic of reconstructing Cave 4 texts from the concordance that Brown, Oxtoby, Teixidor, and I had constructed. It was also described in the same article as "an end run around the scholarly blockade," perpetrated by a scholar at Hebrew Union College in Cincinnati, OH, and one of his graduate assistants. The scholar was Ben Zion Wacholder and the graduate student was Martin G. Abegg. *The Washington Post* (5 September 1991, p. A1) referred to them as "renegades." *The Washington Post* quotes Wacholder as saying, "Now I am an old man. . . . It is a painful thing to have so close something so rare. But I realized that if I waited, I would long be dead." So using a computer, the two of them reconstructed three sets of texts and published them in *A Preliminary Edition of the Unpublished Dead Sea Scrolls: The Hebrew and Aramaic Texts from Cave Four: Fascicle One* (Washington, DC: Biblical Archaeology Society, 1991). The texts so bootlegged are (a) 4QD[a-h], i.e. the eight Cave 4 fragmentary copies of the Damascus Document, (b) 4QMišm A-H, i.e. eight fragmentary copies of *Mišmĕrôt hakkôhănîm* (Priestly Courses), and (c) 4QS[e], i.e. a fragmentary copy five of the *Serek hayyaḥad,* or Manual of Discipline. Further volumes of this bootlegged version of Cave 4 texts are planned.

93. How can a concordance be used to reconstruct a text?

When the words of a given Cave 4 text were booked for the concordance, the root of the word or its dictionary form was entered on the card in the upper lefthand corner. Opposite that, in the righthand corner was recorded the name of the text, and the numbers of its fragment, column, and line. Then in the center of the card the key word, in the form in which it actually appears in the document, was entered with two or three words preceding and following it. The key word was underlined. This procedure eventually produces a keyword-in-context concordance. Sometimes a notation was added on the card to insure the proper understanding of it, especially if the same consonants could be read as a noun or a verb. It must be recalled that all the Hebrew and Aramaic texts are written only in consonants; there are no vowels or vocalic pointing of the text. As already explained, once the cards for a given text were complete, one for each word or prefixed preposition or conjunction, they were numbered in order in the lower lefthand corner for eventual reconstruction of the sequence of the cards in the order of the text itself. Only after this numbering were the cards alphabetized for the concordance proper, either for the Hebrew or the Aramaic concordance.

If one wants to reconstruct the text of a certain document from the concordance, one has only to begin with an underlined key word and then look up in the concordance the word that precedes or follows. That would give access to still other words that precede or follow. One could also check the order of words by referring to the number in the lower lefthand corner. In time, all the words on a given line would emerge from this sort of search. The only problem that would arise was when lines were fragmentary or lacunae existed in the text. Though a computer would not be really necessary, since the cards were numbered, it could be used possibly to speed up the search.

94. Can the Cave 4 texts so reconstructed be trusted?

That is not easy to answer. When we worked on the texts for the concordance in the scrollery, we had in front of us the fragments themselves under plates of glass, the photographs produced by the Museum photographer, the tentative transcription of the texts produced by the editor on whose texts we were working. We were thus able to control the tentative transcriptions, and at times I called to the attention of one editor or other a letter that had been misread. Such instances were corrected. But it is necessary to emphasize that the transcriptions, on which the concordance was based, were tentative, because there was always the possibility of improved readings, further joins to be made to the text from the many plates of "hopeless cases," the tiny fragments with a few letters on them that had not yet been joined with any certainty to the texts of the jigsaw puzzle thus far completed. Realizing that the transcriptions were provisional, I numbered the cards as I explained above, so that they could eventually be checked against the definitive readings in the published form.

The reconstructed texts in the bootlegged edition are thus not 100% perfect. But I have been told by the publisher H. Shanks that the German scholar Hartmut Stegemann has checked the text of 4QD against photos that he has of these texts and that these reconstructed texts are in general reliable, even though small fragments of ms. B have not been included, and sometimes the real text differs slightly from what Milik recorded about 30 years ago. See now "Computer-Generated Dead Sea Scrolls Texts 98% Accurate," *BARev* 18/1 (1992) 70.

In one case, Joseph Baumgarten, to whom the Cave 4 fragmentary texts of the Damascus Document have now been given over by Milik, has already published frg. 7 of 4QD^f (4Q268 7) in *JJS* 61 (1990) 157. So the interested reader can compare the "bootlegged" reconstructed text with Baumgarten's more definitive version.

95. Have the photographs of all the Cave 4 texts been published?

Under the editorship of Robert H. Eisenman and James M. Robinson, two volumes of photographic reproductions of Cave 4 texts have recently been published: *A Facsimile Edition of the Dead Sea Scrolls: Prepared with an Introduction and Index* (Washington, DC: Biblical Archaeology Society, 1991). In these volumes one finds photos not only of the Cave 4 texts, but of those of Wadi Murabba'at, Wadi Daliyeh, and Naḥal Ḥever. This publication makes available 1787 photos, but this may not be all of them, since the photos of Cave 4 have been said to number about 3000.

The photos made available in this publication do not come from any of the four institutions mentioned in § 86 above. Newspaper reports speak of an "anonymous source" (*The Washington Post,* 20 November 1991, p. A1). Rumor has it that they were part of the estate of the photographer of the Palestine Archaeological Museum, Najib Albina, who brought them to this country. After his death these photos came into the hands of a Long Beach, CA, lawyer, whom *The Washington Post* identifies as William J. Cox, and who is said to have contacted Eisenman. Funding for the publication of the volumes has come from the Irving I. Moskowitz Foundation of the Long Beach area.

96. Is this a wise or prudent course of action?

That remains to be seen. It is laudable in the sense that people now have access to the photographs of such precious texts, if they are able to figure out what photographs represent what, for the photographs are listed only according to the Palestine Archaeological Museum photographer's number.

The New York Times for 23 January 1992 (p. A7) reports that a judge of the District Court of Jerusalem, Israel has issued an injunction to restrain the further distribution of the Facsimile Edition in "any fashion, in Israel or elsewhere," because it contains the 121-line text of 4QMMT (see § 15 above), a text on which John Strugnell of Harvard University and Elisha Qimron of the University of the Negev, Beersheba, have been working. What will come of this? The publisher has been said to be willing to "abide by the order not to distribute the volumes, even outside of Israel" (*The Washington Post,* 23 January 1992, p. A11).

There is, of course, the danger that incompetent persons will try to read and interpret these texts and skew the whole enterprise (see the recent attempt mentioned in § 97). It is hardly likely, however, that responsible editors of scholarly periodicals will publish articles based on such photographs. They will undoubtedly insist on fresh photographs and proper facsimiles and will accept articles only from recognized scholars. In addition, the publication in time of the texts by the original editors and others recently coopted into the team will supersede such pioneer treatment. Moreover, there is no guarantee that the work of the team will always be what it should be. Recall the Allegro publication of DJD 4 (§ 90 above).

97. Have there been tendentious readings of the QS?

There have indeed. A recent example of such reading of a Cave 4 fragment has been given by Robert H. Eisenman, who having got access to some of the photos of the Huntington Library's collection, claimed that among them he found a small fragment that "refers to the execution of a Messianic leader" (*California State University, Long Beach, News Release,* 1 November 1991, p. 1; cf. *The New York Times,* 8 November 1991, p. A8): "This tiny scroll fragment puts to rest the idea presently being circulated by the Scroll editorial committee that this material has nothing to do with Christian origins in Palestine." Eisenman maintains that the five-line fragment about the putting to death of the leader of the community is "of the most far-reaching significance because it shows that whatever group was responsible for these writings was operating in the same general scriptural and Messianic framework of early Christianity." The fragmentary text to which Eisenman refers reads as follows:

0. [*'šr ktwb bspr*]
1. *yš'yhw hnby'* . . . [
2. [*y*]*pwl wyṣ' ḥwṭr mgz' yšy*[
3. *ṣmḥ dwyd yšpṭw 't* [
4. [ ]*whmytw nśy' h'dh ṣb*[
5. [ ]*m wbmḥwllwt wyṣw kwhn* [

0. [which is written in the book of]
1. Isaiah the prophet . . . [
2. [*will*] *fall. But there will go forth a branch from the stump of Jesse* (10:34–11:1),
3. the sprout of David. They will judge the (sign of the direct object) [
4. [ ] and the prince of the congregation put (*or:* will put) him to death *ṣb*[
5. [ ]*m* and with piercings. And the priest of [   ] shall command [

I have restored the introductory clause in line 0; something like that is needed to introduce the quotation from Isaiah, and such a clause is found in 4QFlor (4Q174) 1–2 i 15.

There is in this tiny fragment no explicit mention of a messiah. It cites Isa 11:1 about a branch from "the stump of Jesse," in apposition with which is added in line 3 "the sprout of David," a title already known from 4QFlor (4Q174) 1–2 i 11, where it is predicated of a Davidic king, to which 2 Sam 7:14 refers, and from 4QPBless 3, where it is used of an expected *mĕšîaḥ haṣṣedeq,* "Messiah of righteousness," to whom and to whose offspring is promised a "covenant of kingship" over God's people forever. These phrases are related to Jer 23:5 and 33:15. In other Qumran texts such phrases refer to the well-known messianic expectations of the community (see § 45). That there is anything Christian in such references is gratuitous eisegesis.

The verb that follows *dwyd* in line 3 is not easily read. It could be *yšptw,* as Eisenman has apparently read it; but it could also be simply *wyšpt,* "and he will judge." But Eisenman's translation, "and they shall be judged," is surely wrong, for this makes it a passive verb, which is then followed by the sign of the direct object (*'t*), an impossible Hebrew construction.

Line 4 is crucial. Eisenman reads the first three words as I have given them above, but he translates them, "and they put to death the leader of the community, the Bran[ch of David]." Eisenman reads the last two letters as *ṣm,* which he fills out as *ṣm[ḥ dwyd]*. This restoration might seem plausible, because the phrase is used at the beginning of line 3, but what he reads as *m* before the break is almost certainly *b*; the right side of a *m* would descend farther down than it does. Yet apart from that questionable restoration, there is a greater difficulty in his interpretation of the first three words. If they were to mean, "and they put to death the leader of the community," one would expect the sign of the direct object (*'t*) to precede *nśy' h'dh,* given the fact that *'t* occurs at the end of line 3. Eisenman reads the verb *whmytw* as the 3d pl. m. hiphil perfect of *mwt,* "die" (possibly with waw-conversive), but he fails to see that it could also be read as the 3d sg. m. hiphil perfect with a pronominal suffix, "and he killed him" (*or:* "and he will kill him"). Then the second and third words (*nśy' h'dh*) would then be the subject of the verb, in normal Hebrew word order: "The prince of the congregation will kill (*or:* has killed) him." This prince is mentioned elsewhere in the QS: in the broken text of 1QSb 5:20, where he is the object of a blessing; in the broken text of 4QpIsaᵃ 5–6:3; and in CD 7:20, where he is called *haššēbeṭ,* "the scepter," in an allusion to the oracle of Balaam in Num 24:17.

Eisenman reads the text as he has, because of his general thesis that the Qumran texts refer to the beginnings of Christianity. He identifies the Teacher of Righteousness in the QS with James, the brother of the Lord (Gal 1:19), the high priest Ananos, son of the Elder Ananos (= Annas of the gospel tradition) with the Wicked Priest, and the Apostle Paul with the Man of the Lie. I know of no other interpreter of the QS who agrees with him. He rides roughshod over the palaeographic dating of scrolls and fragments, the archaeological evidence that supports that dating, and the radiocarbon dating of them (see § 18).

If one were to grant Eisenman's understanding of this tiny text, one would have to cope with the conclusion easily drawn from it that the QS now offer fresh proof that Palestinian Jews did engage in capital punishment. That is a consequence that Eisenman would surely not countenance.

In any case, the incident shows how the reading and interpretation of a Qumran text can be manipulated by somebody who has prejudged the matter in support of a pet thesis.

98. Have there been other tendentious readings of the QS?

Yes, there have been. In fact, this mode of interpreting the DSS has been going on ever since they were first published. Years ago, the French scholar André Dupont-Sommer read a paper on the Pesher on Habbakuk from Cave 1 before the French Academy on 26 May 1950 (see *Le Monde,* 28–29 May 1950, p. 43), which he claimed spoke of a Teacher of Righteousness, who was an "exact prototype of Jesus, particularly as a martyred prophet, revered by followers as the suffering Servant of the Lord in Deutero-Isaiah" (thus summarized by Edmund Wilson in his notorious book *The Scrolls from the Dead Sea* [New York: Oxford University Press, 1955] 55). Dupont-Sommer was subsequently quoted in an article in the Parisian newspaper, *Le Figaro Littéraire* (24 February 1951) p. 3, entitled, "A-t-il existé, soixante ans avant le Christ, un Maître de Justice qui prêcha la doctrine de Jésus et fut crucifié comme lui?" (Did there exist, sixty years before Christ, a Teacher of Righteousness who preached the doctrine of Jesus and was crucified as he was?). This was claimed to be an exposé of what the Dead Sea Scrolls really reveal.

The article was actually a review of Dupont-Sommer's book, *Aperçus préliminaires sur les manuscrits de la Mer Morte* (Paris: Adrien Maisonneuve, 1951; translated as *The Dead Sea Scrolls: A Preliminary Survey* [New York: Macmillan, 1952]). The reviewer claimed that the QS revealed two startling things: The Jewish sect of the New Covenant was Essene, and thus in the very bosom of Judaism preparation was made for Christianity; and between 67 and 63 B.C. there was executed the first Christ, quite like the second one, who was known as the Teacher of Righteousness. Dupont-Sommer is quoted as exclaiming, "All these similarities constitute an ensemble that is almost mind-boggling." In his book, Dupont-Sommer wrote:

> Everything in the Jewish New Covenant heralds and prepares the way for the Christian New Covenant. The Galilean Master, as He is presented to us in the writings of the New Testament, appears in many respects as an astonishing reincarnation of the Master of Justice {i.e. the Teacher of Righteousness}. Like the latter He preached penitence, poverty, humility, love of one's neighbor, chastity. Like him, He prescribed the observance of the Law of Moses, the whole Law, but the Law finished and perfected, thanks to His own revelations. Like him He was the Elect and the Messiah of God, the Messiah redeemer of the world. Like him He was the object of the hostility of the priests, the party of the Sadducees. Like him He was condemned and put to death. Like him he pronounced judgement on Jerusalem, which was taken and destroyed by the Romans for having put Him to death. Like him, at the end of time, He will be the supreme judge. Like him He founded a Church whose adherents fervently awaited His glorious return. In the Christian Church, just as in the Essene Church, the essential rite is the sacred meal, whose ministers are the priests. Here and there at the head of each community there is the overseer, the 'bishop'. And the ideal of both Churches is essentially that of unity, communion in love — even going so far as the sharing of common property (*Dead Sea Scrolls,* 99).

"Similarities" there may be, but Dupont-Sommer's case was highly overdrawn, as he himself subsequently realized, and, scholar that he was, he became in later publications about the QS much more guarded in his claims. "Under attack" from "the Catholic establishment," Dupont-Sommer is said by Baigent and Leigh to have "sought shelter behind more circumspect phraseology" (*The Dead Sea Scrolls Deception,* 44), a tendentious way of putting it. Those claims of Dupont-Sommer were made in the 50s. Now that the dust has died down and everyone has forgotten about those claims, anyone who reads the

Pesher on Habakkuk today realizes that similarities between the Teacher of Righteousness and Jesus there may be, but also that it scarcely supports the overdrawn caricature that Dupont-Sommer had concocted.

Another tendentious reading of the QS came from John Marco Allegro, one of the original international team. He is said to have been "an agnostic," "the only philologist in the group" with already "five publications to his credit in academic journals," thus "the only one to have established a reputation for himself before working on the scrolls. All the others were unknown at the time" (Baigent and Leigh, *The Dead Sea Scrolls Deception*, 29; similarly 45). But apart from Allegro's being an agnostic, all the rest of these claims are manifest nonsense; Cross, Milik, Skehan, and Starcky were already established scholars. Allegro may well have published some articles in academic journals, but Baigent and Leigh say nothing about the quality of them. Moreover, Allegro was the only member of the team to bring himself to utter incredible nonsense about them, alleging that important and controversial material in the scrolls was being withheld by the rest of his colleagues.

The matter came to a head when Allegro delivered three broadcasts on BBC radio in northern England on 16, 23, 30 January 1956. The second talk sparked a notice in the *New York Times*, "Christlike Story of Scrolls Cited" (24 January 1956, p. 33), and the third talk a similar story headlined, "Christian Bases Seen in Scrolls" (5 February 1956, p. 2). The last mentioned quoted Allegro as saying:

> The origins of some Christian rituals and doctrines can be seen in the documents of an extremist Jewish sect that existed for more than 100 years before the birth of Jesus Christ. . . . the historical basis of the Lord's Supper and part at least of the Lord's prayer and the New Testament teaching of Jesus were attributable to the Qumranians, who called themselves the Sons of Zadok. . . . The "Teacher of Righteous" [sic], the leader of the monastic community in the first century before Christ, was persecuted and probably crucified by Gentiles at the instigation of a wicked priest of the Jews.

Similarly, *Time* magazine (6 February 1956, p. 88) summed up the talks under the headline, "Crucifixion before Christ" and quoted Allegro as maintaining that the priest-king Alexander Janneus

> descended on Qumran and arrested its leader, the myster-
> ious "Teacher of Righteousness," whom he turned over to
> his mercenaries to be crucified. . . . A Qumrân manuscript
> speaks in shocked tones of the enormity of this crime. . . .
> When the Jewish king had left, [the community] took
> down the broken body of their Master to stand guard over
> it until Judgment Day. For they believed that the terrible
> events of their time were surely heralding the visitation of
> God Himself, when the Kingdom of Heaven [would] come
> in. . . . They believed their Master would rise again and
> lead his faithful flock (the people of the new testament,
> as they called themselves) to a new and purified Jeru-
> salem. . . . What is clear is that there was a well-defined
> Essenic pattern into which Jesus of Nazareth fits. What
> theologians make of that is really outside my province. I
> just give my findings.

But other members of the international team working in the Jeru-salem scrollery, who had become fed up with Allegro's charges and allegations, eventually sent a letter to the editor of *The Times* of London (16 March 1956, p. 11):

> Sir. — It has come to our attention that considerable con-
> troversy is being caused by certain broadcast statements
> of Mr. John Allegro, of the University of Manchester, con-
> cerning the Dead Sea Scrolls. We refer particularly to such
> statements as imply that in these scrolls a close connexion
> is to be found between a supposed crucifixion of the
> 'teacher of righteousness' of the Essene sect and the Cruci-
> fixion and Resurrection of Jesus Christ. The announced
> opinions of Mr. Allegro might seem to have special weight,
> since he is one of the group of scholars engaged in editing
> as yet unpublished writings from Qumran.

In view of the broad repercussions of his statements, and the fact that the materials on which they are based are not yet available to the public, we, his colleagues, feel obliged to make the following statement. There are no unpublished texts at the disposal of Mr. Allegro other than those of which the originals are at present in the Palestine Archaeological Museum where we are working. Upon the appearance in the Press of citations from Mr. Allegro's broadcasts we have reviewed all the pertinent materials, published and unpublished. We are unable to see in the texts the 'findings' of Mr. Allegro.

We find no crucifixion of the 'teacher,' no deposition from the cross, and no 'broken body of their Master' to be stood guard over until Judgment Day. Therefore there is no 'well-defined Essenic pattern into which Jesus of Nazareth fits,' as Mr. Allegro is alleged in one report to have said. It is our conviction that either he has misread the texts or he has built up a chain of conjectures which the materials do not support.

The letter was signed by de Vaux, Milik, Skehan, Starcky, and Strugnell. Allegro answered the letter in a reply, which toned down a few statements and appeared in *The Times* on 20 March 1956, p. 13. (For a whitewashing of Allegro and his subsequent moves, see Baigent and Leigh, *The Dead Sea Scrolls Deception,* 50–60.)

In the same year Allegro published his popular book, *The Dead Sea Scrolls* (Harmondsworth: Penguin, 1956), of which *Time* said in a review (1 October 1956, p. 44): it "prudently plays down this wild surmise," that the NT's "Jesus Christ may have been modeled on the scrolls' 'Teacher of Righteousness,' who, said Allegro on the basis of guesswork, was also crucified."

In all of this tendentious writing, one detects the thought that, if things turn up in the QS that are similar to Christian teaching or to Jesus of Nazareth, then it calls in question something that is either valued by Christians or regarded by them as unique. What is mystifying in such thinking is that such mavericks believe that Christians are unwilling to admit that Christianity emerged from a Jewish matrix. Suppose the Qumran community did celebrate a sacred meal, over which a priest presided, and at it consumed bread and wine. Does that somehow undermine Christian faith in the eucharist or belief in the real presence of Christ's body and blood in that sacrament? More problematic still is the notion, Why should anyone want to exaggerate the similarities that might become evident? Such tendentious reading of the QS is simply *scrollduggery*.

99. Is there any truth to the claim that Allegro made that his colleagues on the team were suppressing texts?

The Sunday Express of London (12 January 1958) reported that Allegro charged that his colleagues were delaying the publication of some of Cave 4 material. "There has been some quite inexplicable delay in the publication of some of the findings in the Dead Sea Scrolls. I am not suggesting there is anything sinister in the delay but it is a fact that some of my colleagues are apparently reluctant to make some of the findings public." "No material is made available to the other editors until Father de Vaux or his deputy, Father J. T. Milik, has seen it first. I am not suggesting that they have withheld any of the material. But then, with the present set-up, I have no means of knowing whether they have or not."

Of course, there has been delay in publishing the Cave 4 materials, a delay that can only be called scandalous, and that has been rightly criticized by many others besides Allegro. But Allegro's accusation in 1958 was condemnation by insinuation, and it has to be recognized for what it is, a libellous accusation. How can anyone defend himself against such an allegation? Personally, I never heard of any such supervision of texts by de Vaux or Milik. That accusation was made by Allegro during the year that I was working in the scrollery, and it was clear that he was making it because he was trying to get back at his colleagues for exposing his statements on BBC for what they were, utter nonsense.

Yet Allegro was making such charges in 1958, at a time when the jigsaw puzzle was still being put together. It was hardly the time when much of the material could have been published. Allegro's colleagues did at times during those years between 1952 and 1958 publish texts in partial or preliminary form, just as he had. But those charges were made by Allegro in 1958, *ten years* before his own volume (DJD 5) would appear (1968). At that time he was just as delinquent in publishing as the others. He had, indeed, published a dozen of the texts in partial or preliminary form, but these were put out in a very confusing and incompetent fashion, about which scholars loudly complained. Such charges about his colleagues withholding documents because they realized that they might "upset a great many basic teachings of the Christian church" continued to be made by him as late as 1966 ("The Untold Story of the Dead Sea Scrolls," *Harper's Magazine* [August 1966] 46–54), at a time when he still had not published his own volume of texts.

In that *Sunday Express* article Allegro is also quoted as saying, "The Dead Sea area is proving so rich in archaeological discoveries that a Jewish Christian Library may soon be uncovered, giving views on Jesus by his contemporaries outside the Bible. This will obviously be a matter of vast importance." Unfortunately, thirty-three years have passed since Allegro made that prediction, and there has not yet been such a discovery of a "Jewish Christian Library." There is no reason to think that such a discovery is impossible. But again, so what? Suppose we were to find some writings that describe Jesus, his way of life, or his teachings. It would remain to be seen what effects such writings would have. The niggling fears that Allegro sought to stir up did not eventuate, and if the library were to be discovered with such a description of Jesus, interest not fear would be the reaction of most Christians.

100. Has there been a conspiracy to hold up the publication of the scrolls?

This too has often been alleged. What has given rise to the suspicion that there may be a conspiracy at work is the delay in publication on the part of the international team. They have been delinquent and have been sitting on texts entrusted to them for at least 30 years. This naturally makes people think that these scholars want to keep a secret and are reluctant to let the populace at large know what the texts contain. It raises the suspicion that perhaps such texts, coming from a time so close to the beginnings of Christianity and to the development of what came to be known as rabbinical Judaism, might reveal something detrimental to or subversive of orthodox Christianity or normative Judaism.

This was, in part, the accusation of Allegro cited above. But Edmund Wilson too insinuated as much when he noted that Jewish scholars shied away from the DSS "for fear of their destroying the authority of the Masoretic text of the Bible" and that Christian scholars working on the scrolls "fear 'that the uniqueness of Christ is at stake' as well as a reciprocal resistance to admitting that the morality and mysticism of the Gospels may perfectly well be explained as the creation of several generations of Jews working by and for themselves, in their own religious tradition, and that one need not assume the miracle of a special magnanimous act of God to allow the salvation of the human race" (*The Scrolls from the Dead Sea* [New York: Oxford University Press, 1955] 82, 98). Wilson also claimed that "New Testament scholars, it seems, have almost without exception boycotted the whole subject of the scrolls. The situation in this field is peculiar. It is precisely the more 'liberal' scholars in Britain and the United States who have been most reluctant to deal with the scrolls, for the reason that these liberals tend to assume that the doctrines known as Christian were not really formulated till several generations after Jesus' death" (ibid., 99). Such Jewish and Christian attitudes as Wilson cites have helped build up the impression that there is a conspiracy afoot to suppress the QS.

What Wilson did not realize was that most of the NT scholars, whom he was criticizing at that time, had been well trained in Hellenism, according to the Bultmannian tradition, and that most of them could not read or interpret the unpointed Hebrew and Aramaic texts that were then coming to light and that were having such an impact on the background of NT writings. It took at least a decade or more before that problem was remedied, and NT scholars came to cope with the Semitic background of the NT.

More recently, those accusations of Allegro and Wilson have been repeated by Michael Baigent and Richard Leigh in *The Dead Sea Scrolls Deception,* already referred to above. They not only repeat the idea that there has been an attempt to suppress the scrolls, but attribute it all to "the 'Ecole Biblique gang'" (quoting an expression used in one of Allegro's letters). The conspiracy had been masterminded by

Roland de Vaux, former director of the Ecole, who, they claim, was under orders of the Biblical Commission of the Roman Catholic Church, and especially of the Vatican's Sacred Congregation for the Doctrine of the Faith. Baigent and Leigh's book is a mixed bag of good information, drawn from all sorts of documents heretofore inaccessible (the papers of the late John Allegro) and from recent interviews with leading DSS scholars, and of many, many errors, misinterpretations, and gratuitous allegations. The whole idea of a Vatican conspiracy to suppress the scrolls that it portrays is ludicrous nonsense. The only involvement that the Vatican ever had with the DSS has already been described in § 10 above. That involvement was not an effort to suppress the scrolls, but to acquire them from the Bedouins at a time when foreign funds were needed. The Vatican sought to acquire some of the Cave 4 fragments for its Library, a perfectly understandable move on its part, given the quality of its library and museum.

101. But do the QS contain anything that would tend to undermine Christian faith?

So far there has been nothing of this sort. Nothing that has been brought to light in the QS contradicts anything that Christians hold dear. Nothing militates against "the uniqueness of Jesus," if that is a concern of the Christian — or, better put, of a mature Christian with a non-fundamentalist background. That the Teacher of Righteousness of the Qumran community may have taught something similar to what Jesus taught is not really troubling to any mature Christian.

Wilson once wrote, "These new documents have thus loomed as a menace to a variety of rooted assumptions, from matters of tradition and dogma to hypotheses that are exploits of scholarship" (*Scrolls from the Dead Sea,* 100). Again, "it would seem an immense advantage for cultural and social intercourse — that is, for civilization — that the rise of Christianity should, at last, be generally understood as simply an episode of human history rather than propagated as dogma and divine revelation. The study of the Dead Sea scrolls — with the direction it is now taking — cannot fail, one would think, to conduce to this" (ibid., 108).

One understands what Wilson was trying to say, but, as F. M. Cross pointed out years ago, to anyone trained in Christian theology —

not to mention the English language — that first sentence in the second quotation of Wilson is unintelligible. "The terms 'rise of Christianity' and 'dogma' do not belong to the same universe of discourse so that no theologian, or philosopher for that matter, would dream of propagating one as the other; and no one denies, least of all the Christian, that the rise of Christianity is 'simply an episode of human history'". . . . Wilson is "merely expressing a confusion common to the era of the fundamentalist-modernist fights of a generation ago." Christians who share his confusion "may be badly shaken up as the implications of the scrolls are spelled out," but "those acquainted with contemporary theology or with critical biblical scholarship are well aware that the events conceived in Christian . . . dogma as 'acts of God' are continuous with, and indistinguishable from other events of history so long as they are viewed by the historian as historian. Indeed, the Christian doctrine of revelation means just this, that God chooses to give meaning to history, not to suspend it" (*The New York Times Book Review,* 16 October 1955, p. 31).

The answer to the question was once well formulated in *Time* magazine: "The only Christians whose faith the scrolls can jolt are those who have failed to see the paradox that the churches have always taught: that Jesus Christ was a man as well as God — a man of a particular time and place, speaking a specific language, revealing his way in terms of a specific cultural and religious tradition. For Christians who want to know more of that matrix in which their faith was born, the People of the Scrolls are reaching a hand across the centuries" (15 April 1957, p. 43).

SELECT BIBLIOGRAPHY

Allegro, John, *The Dead Sea Scrolls: A Reappraisal* (2d ed.; London: Penguin Books, 1964). This book has much useful information about the discovery and contents of the QS, but it has to be read with discernment because of the author's tendentious interpretation of many items in the texts.

Charlesworth, James H. (ed.), *John and the Dead Sea Scrolls* (new ed.; New York: Crossroad, 1990). A slightly revised reprinting of *John and Qumran* (London: Chapman, 1972). It contains good articles, now somewhat dated, by R. E. Brown, J. L. Price, A. R. C. Leaney, A. Jaubert, J. H. Charlesworth, G. Quispel, M.-E. Boismard, and W. H. Brownlee.

——. "Sense or Sensationalism? The Dead Sea Scrolls Controversy." *Christian Century* 109/4 (29 January 1992) 92–98.

Cross, F. M., Jr. *The Ancient Library of Qumran & Modern Biblical Studies: Revised Edition* (Garden City, NY: Doubleday, 1961; repr. Grand Rapids, MI: Baker, 1980). One of the early reliable accounts of the discovery of the DSS and their impact. Unfortunately, it is more than a bit out of date.

De Vaux, Roland, *Archaeology and the Dead Sea Scrolls* (The Schweich Lectures of the British Academy 1959; London: Oxford University Press, 1973 [see § 2].

Dupont-Sommer, A. *The Essene Writings from Qumran* (Oxford: Basil Blackwell, 1961; repr. Magnolia/Gloucester, MA: Peter Smith, 1971). This book has a good introduction and a generally reliable translation of most of the important QS; it marks plainly the columns and lines, so that one can easily find a passage. Some of the more recently published texts are not found here.

Dupont-Somer, A. and M. Philonenko (eds.), *La Bible: Ecrits inter-testamentaires* (Bibliothèque de la Pléiade; Paris: Gallimard, 1987). A good French translation of 1QS, 11QTemple, CD, 1QM, 1QH, 11QPsᵃ, 1QpHab, 4QpNah, 4QpPs37, 1QapGen, 4QFlor, 4QTestim, 11QMelch, 4QŠirŠabb, 4QWiles, 1QMyst and many other non-Qumran intertestamental writings.

Fitzmyer, Joseph A. *The Dead Sea Scrolls: Major Publications and Tools for Study, Revised Edition* (SBL Resources for Biblical Study 20; Atlanta, GA: Scholars, 1990). This book lists all the texts from the eleven caves of Qumran and from the other sites (Masada, Murabbaʿat, Ḥever, Ṣeʾelim, Mishmar, Mird, and Cairo) that have been published; it is also a bibliographic guide to select the topics associated with the DSS.

Fujita, N. S. *A Crack in the Jar: What Ancient Jewish Documents Tell Us about the New Testament* (New York/Mahwah, NJ: Paulist, 1986). A passable, fairly recent account of the DSS, which tells more about them than their impact on the New Testament. The account is unfortunately garbled by the introduction of extraneous texts from Wadi ed-Daliyeh and the Samaritans.

Gaster, T. H. *The Dead Sea Scriptures: In English Translation with Introduction and Notes* (3d ed.; Garden City, NY: Doubleday, 1976). The translation of the texts is quite free; no indication is given of columns or lines.

Knibb, M. A. *The Qumran Community* (Cambridge, UK/London/ New York: Cambridge University, 1987). This book contains a fresh English translation of CD, 1QS, 1QSᵃ, 1QH, 1QapGen, 4QprNab, 4QpNah, 1QpHab, 4QpPs, 4QFlor, 4QTestim.

Laperrousaz, E.-M. *Qoumrân: L'Etablissement essénien des bords de la Mer Morte: Histoire et archéologie du site* (Paris: Picard, 1976). A more or less independent study of the archaeology of Khirbet Qumran.

Lohse, Eduard, *Die Texte aus Qumran: Hebräisch und deutsch* (2d ed.; Munich: Kösel; Darmstadt: Wissenschaftliche Buchgesell-schaft, 1971). A very useful vocalized edition of the Hebrew texts, with a good German translation: of 1QS, 1QSᵃ, 1QSᵇ, CD, 1QH, 1QM, 1QpHab, 4QPBless, 4QTestim, 4QFlor, 4QpNah, 4QpPsᵃ (in part). Unfortunately, it contains none of the most recently published texts. There is nothing like it in English.

Maier, Johann, *The Temple Scroll: An Introduction, Translation & Commentary* (JSOTSup 34; Sheffield, UK: JSOT Press, 1985). An English translation by R. T. White of *Die Tempelrolle vom Toten Meer* (Munich/Basel: Reinhardt, 1978).

Milik, J. T. *Ten Years of Discovery in the Wilderness of Judaea* (SBT 26; London: SCM; Naperville, IL: Allenson, 1959). One of the early reliable accounts of the discovery of the DSS and their impact. Unfortunately, it is more than a bit out of date.

Murphy-O'Connor, Jerome and James H. Charlesworth (eds.), *Paul and the Dead Sea Scrolls* (New York: Crossroad, 1990). A slightly revised reprinting of *Paul and Qumran: Studies in New Testament Exegesis* (ed. J. Murphy-O'Connor; London: Chapman, 1968). It contains good articles, now somewhat dated, by P. Benoit, J. A. Fitzmyer, J. Gnilka, M. Delcor, J. Murphy-O'Connor, K. G. Kuhn, J. Coppens, F. Mussner, and W. Grundmann.

Stendahl, K. (with J. H. Charlesworth), *The Scrolls and the New Testament* (New York: Crossroad, 1992). A reprint of the Harper and Bros. 1957 collection of essays, authored by K. Stendahl, O. Cullmann, W. H. Brownlee, K. G. Kuhn, E. Vogt, K. Schubert, S. E. Johnson, B. Reicke, W. D. Davies, R. E. Brown, J. A. Fitzmyer, and N. N. Glazer.

Vermes, G. *The Dead Sea Scrolls in English: Third Edition* (London: Penguin Group, 1987). This book contains a short introduction and a generally reliable translation of the majority of the now available QS, even including a good number of those more recently published. However, only the columns are numbered, but not the lines, so that it is not easy to find a passage in this translation.

——. *The Dead Sea Scrolls: Qumran in Perspective* (London: Collins, 1977; repr. Philadelphia, PA: Fortress, 1981).

Wacholder, Ben Zion, *The Dawn of Qumran: The Sectarian Torah and the Teacher of Righteousness* (Cincinnati, OH: Hebrew Union College, 1983). See § 46 above.

Yadin, Y. *The Message of the Scrolls* (ed. J. H. Charlesworth; New York: Crossroad, 1992). Charlesworth contributes a preface to this reprint of Yadin's popular story of the scrolls, first published by Grosset & Dunlap in 1962.

INDEXES

1. Biblical and DSS

2. Topical Index

Aaron, 28, 43, 53–54, 64, 73–74, 81–82, 97, 120, 129–32

Abbreviations of the DSS, xv–xviii

Abraham, Abram, 21, 34–35, 75, 94, 131–32

Aemilius Scaurus, 19

Albina, Najib, 157

Alexander Janneus, 19, 59–61, 164

Alexander the Great, 93

All Souls Unitarian Church, 10

American School of Oriental Research, 4, 8, 38, 149–50, 153

Anan ben David, 29

Ananos, son of Ananos the Elder, 160

Ancient Biblical Manuscript Center, Claremont, CA, 148

Antigonus of Socho, 56

Antiochus IV Epiphanes, 93, 96–97

Antony of Egypt, 141

Apocalyptic literature, 42–44

Apostrophe to Zion, 38

Arab-Jewish War, First, 5–6, 8, 151

Arabic, 27

Aramaic, 14–15, 19, 21–24, 26–27, 34, 37, 39–41, 44–46, 61, 96, 104, 112, 114–16, 120, 145, 149, 154, 156

Archaeology, 2–5, 7, 11, 16, 18, 22–23, 66, 101, 110, 149, 160, 171–72

Athanasius Yeshue Samuel, Mar (Metropolitan), 8

Atonement, Day of, 39, 58, 75–76, 86, 88, 91

Babylon, 30, 41, 96

Balaam, Oracle of, 54, 57, 63, 160

Bar Cochba, 26, 40

Baraita, 46

Beatitudes, 23, 117–19, 137

Belial, 30, 43, 50, 70–72, 129, 139

Biblical Archaeology Society, 147

Biblical Commission, 169

Biblical Institute, Rome, 151

Bibliothèque Nationale, Paris, 6–7

Bitenosh, 21

Bohan, Stone of, 2

190

192   101 Questions on the Dead Sea Scrolls

3. Modern Authors

198